CASTLE WAITING
VOLUME I

THE LUCKY ROAD

LINDA MEDLEY

LETTERING &
PRODUCTION BY
TODD KLEIN

Castle Waiting Volume 1: The Lucky Road

FIRST PRINTING 2000
SECOND PRINTING 2002, FIRST OLIO EDITION

Published by Olio Press
P.O. Box 1953
Portland, OR
97207

First Edition

ISBN 0-9651852-3-0

10 9 8 7 6 5 4 3 2 1

Printed in Canada

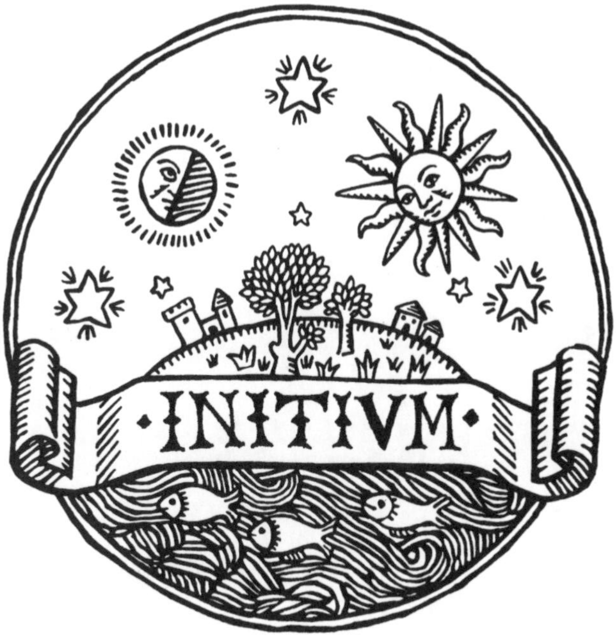
·INITIVM·

The rule of the road is a paradox quite,
Though custom has prov'd it so long;
If you go to the left, you go right,
If you go to the right, you go wrong.

–Mother Goose

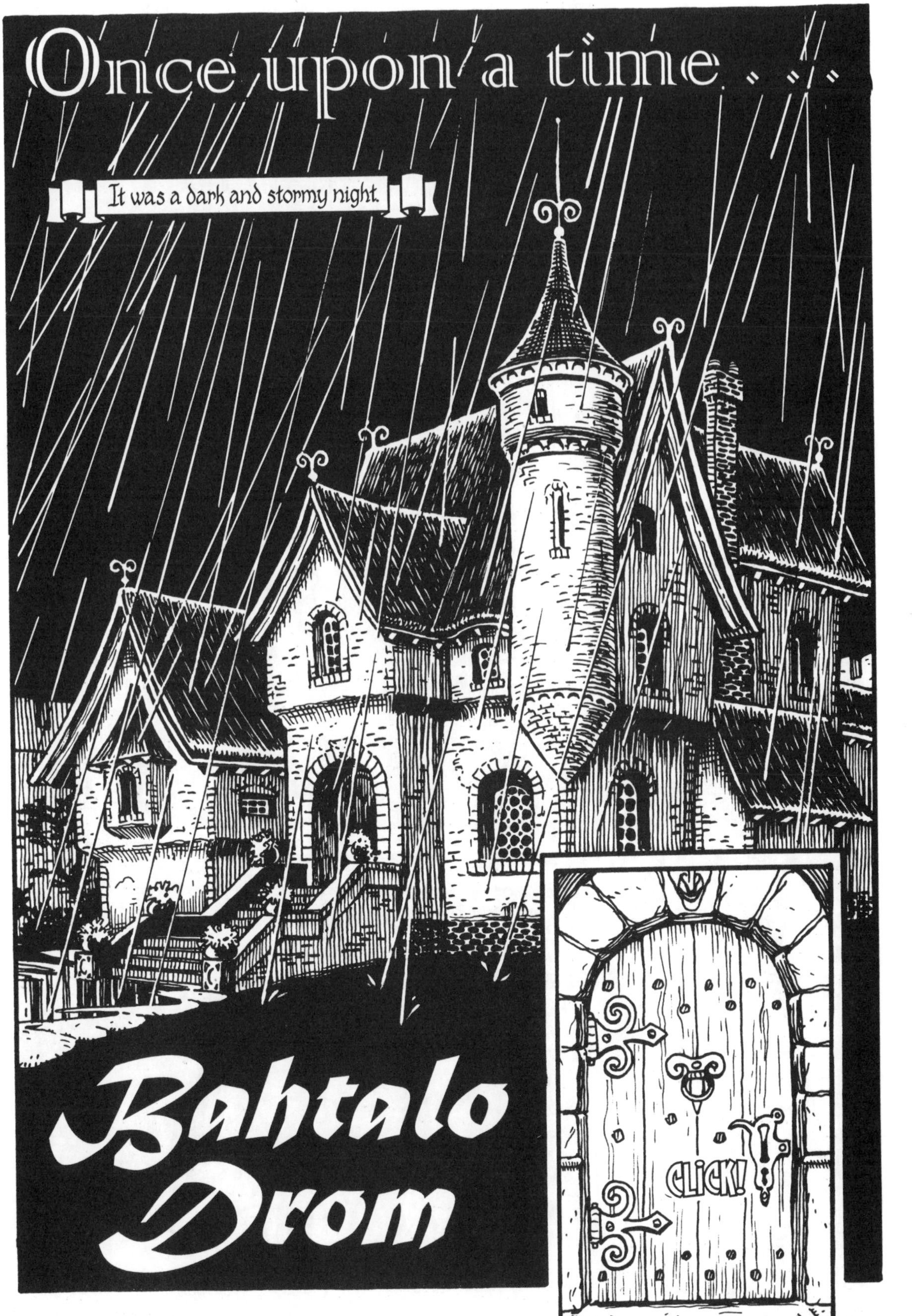
Once upon a time . . .
It was a dark and stormy night.
Bahtalo Drom
CLICK!

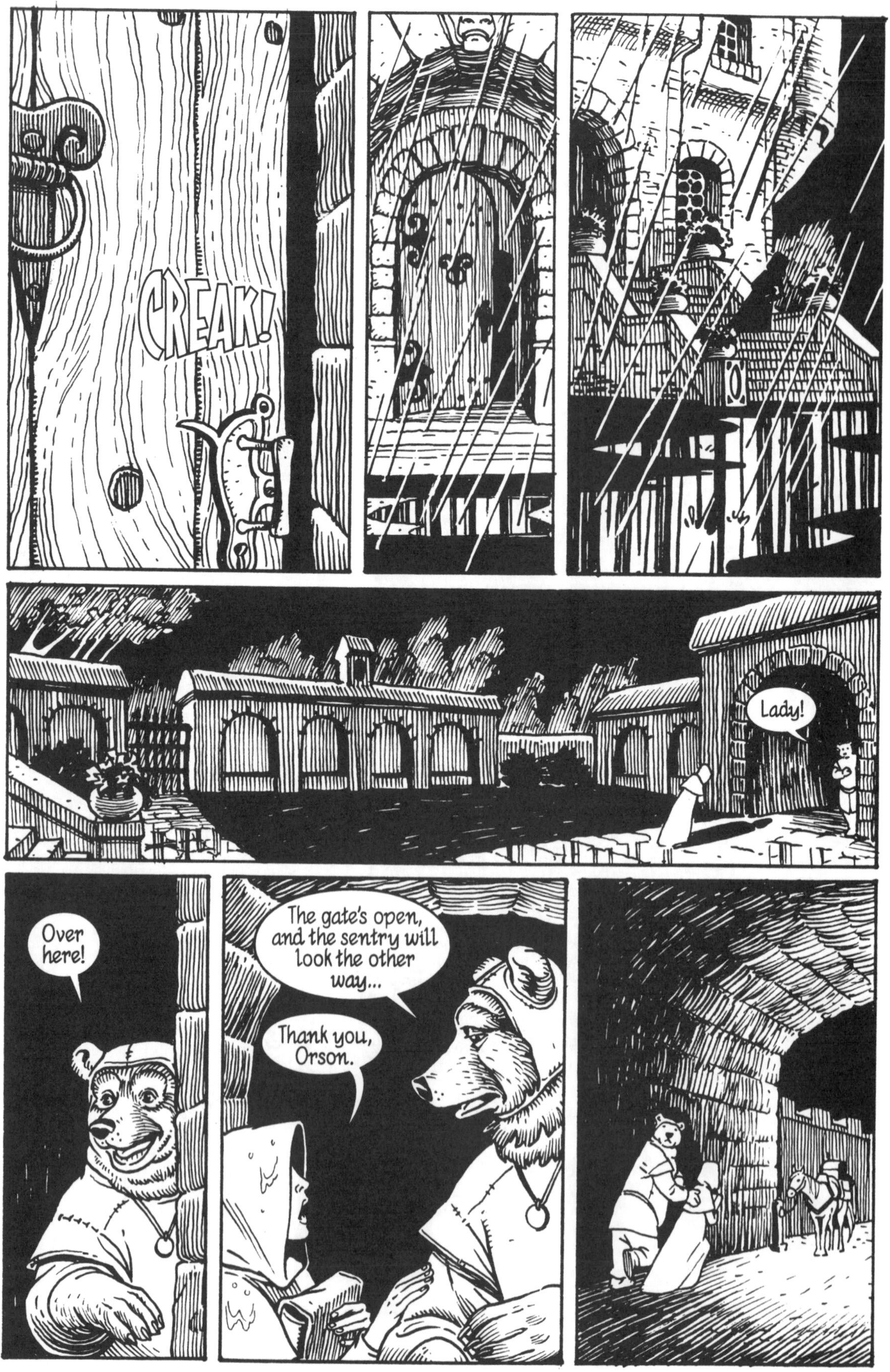
CREAK!
Lady!
Over here!
The gate's open, and the sentry will look the other way...
Thank you, Orson.

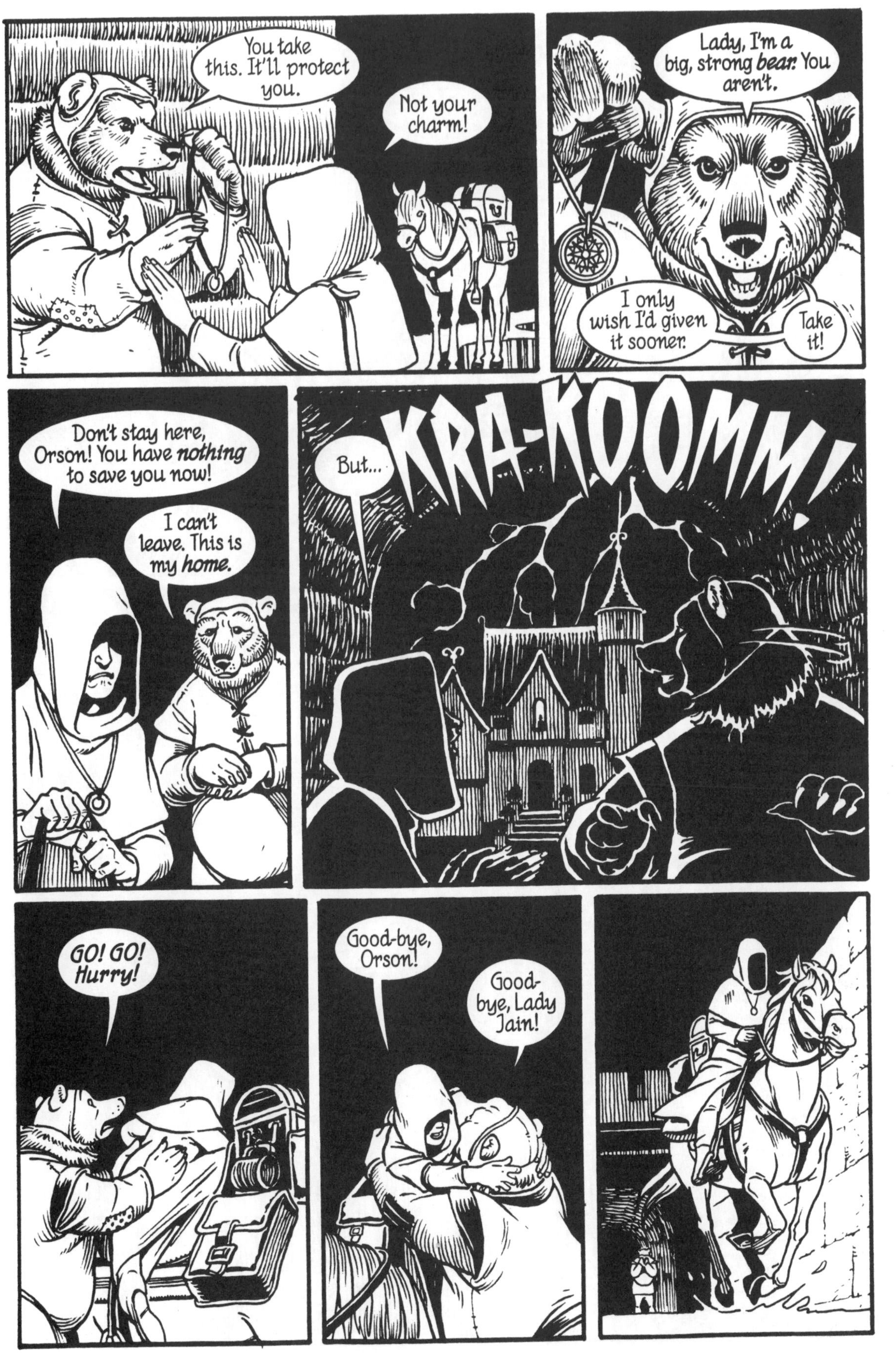
You take this. It'll protect you.
Not your charm!
Lady, I'm a big, strong bear! You aren't.
I only wish I'd given it sooner.
Take it!
Don't stay here, Orson! You have nothing to save you now!
I can't leave. This is my home.
But...
KRA-KOOMM!
GO! GO! Hurry!
Good-bye, Orson!
Good-bye, Lady Jain!

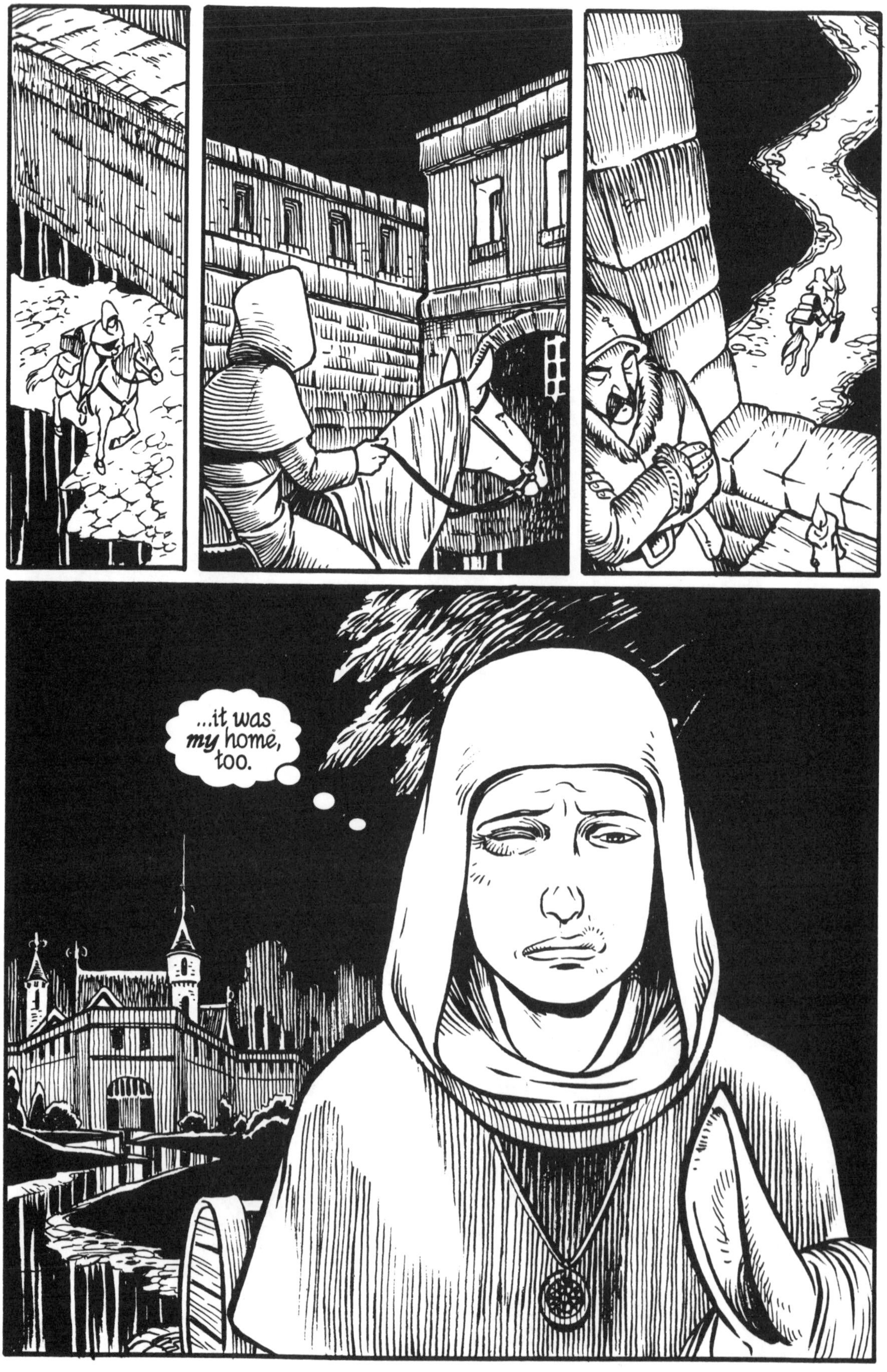
...it was my home, too.

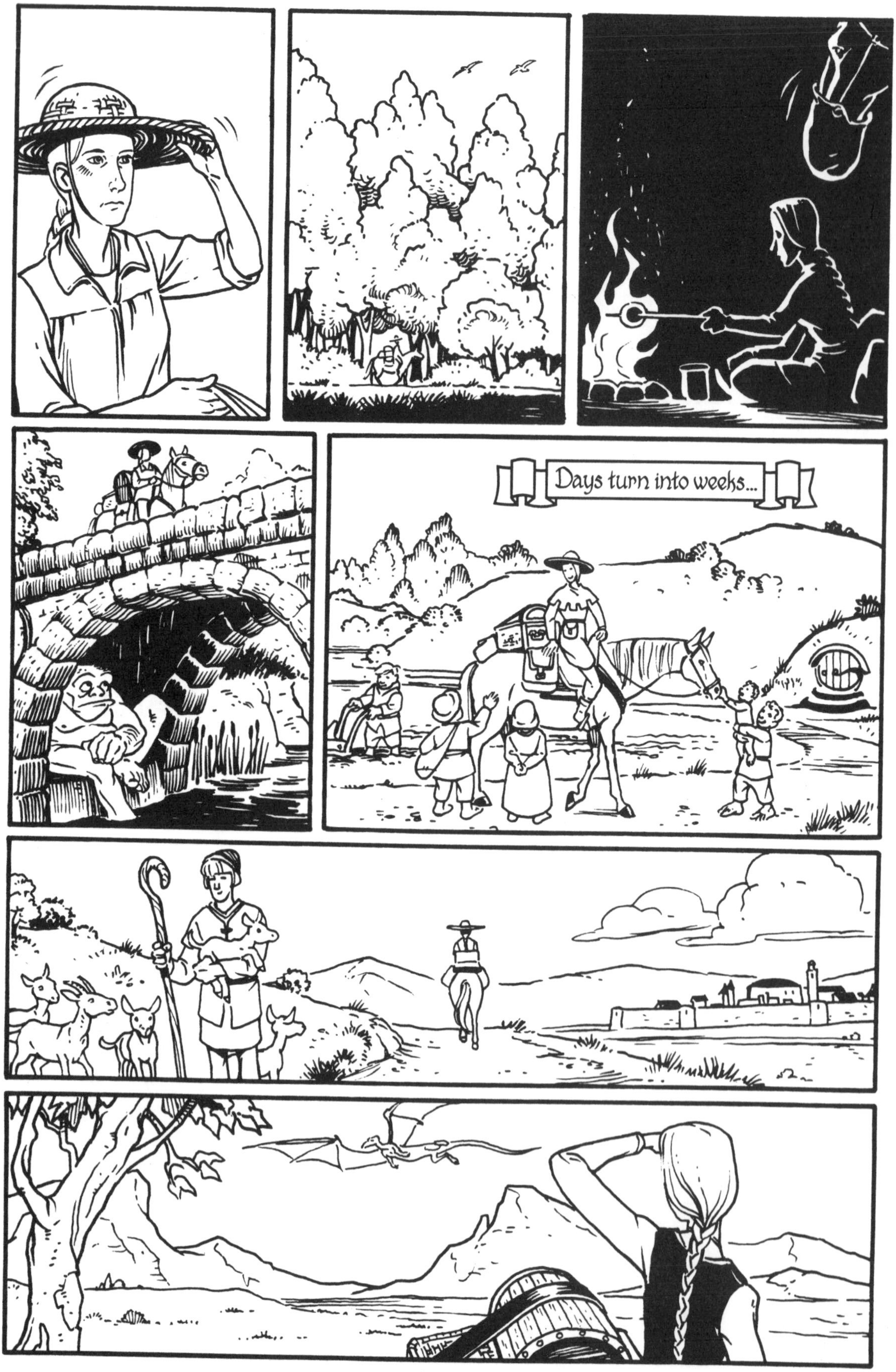
Days turn into weeks...

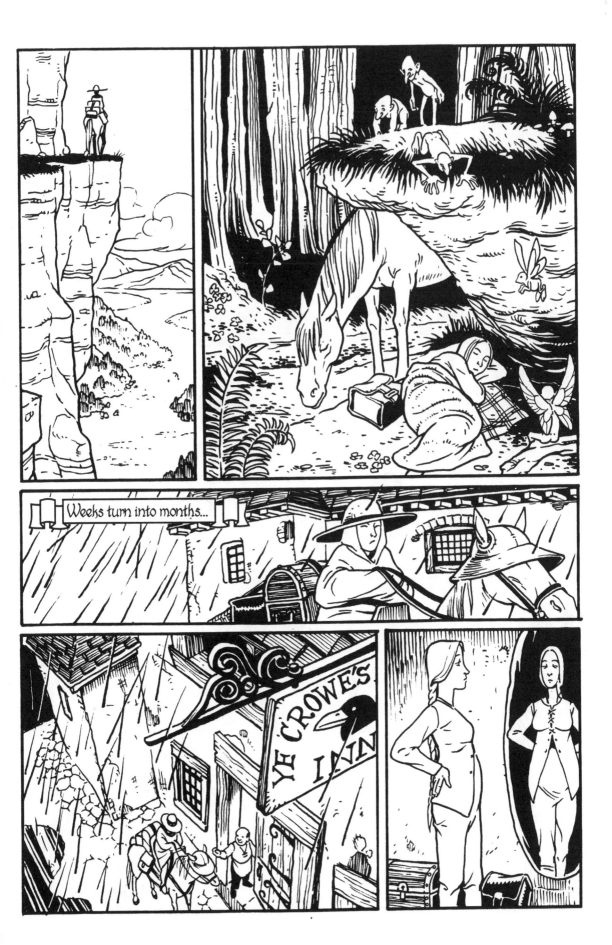

Weeks turn into months...

YE CROWE'S INN

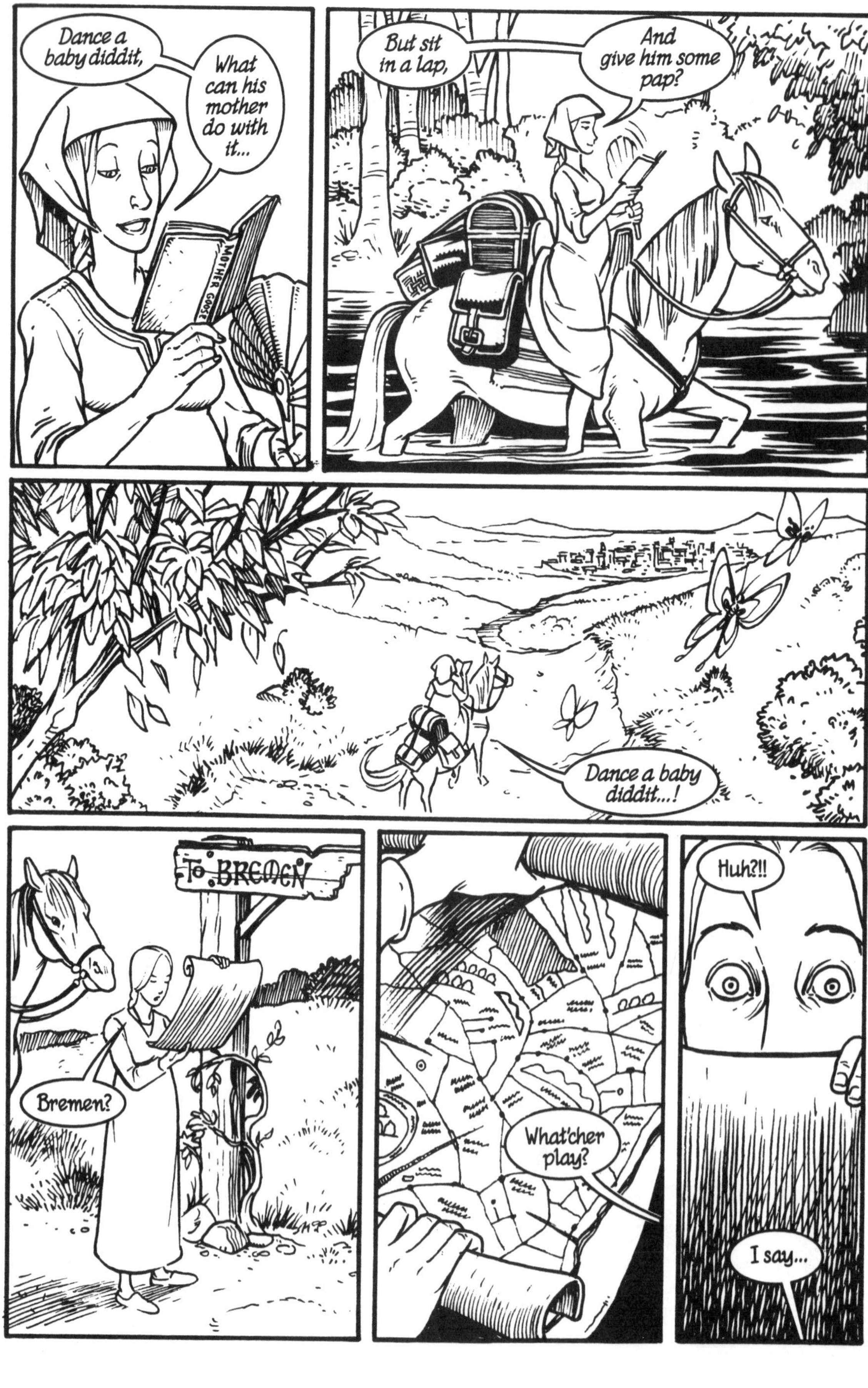
Dance a baby diddit,
What can his mother do with it...
MOTHER GOOSE
But sit in a lap,
And give him some pap?
Dance a baby diddit...!
TO BREMEN
Bremen?
What'cher play?
Huh?!!
I say...

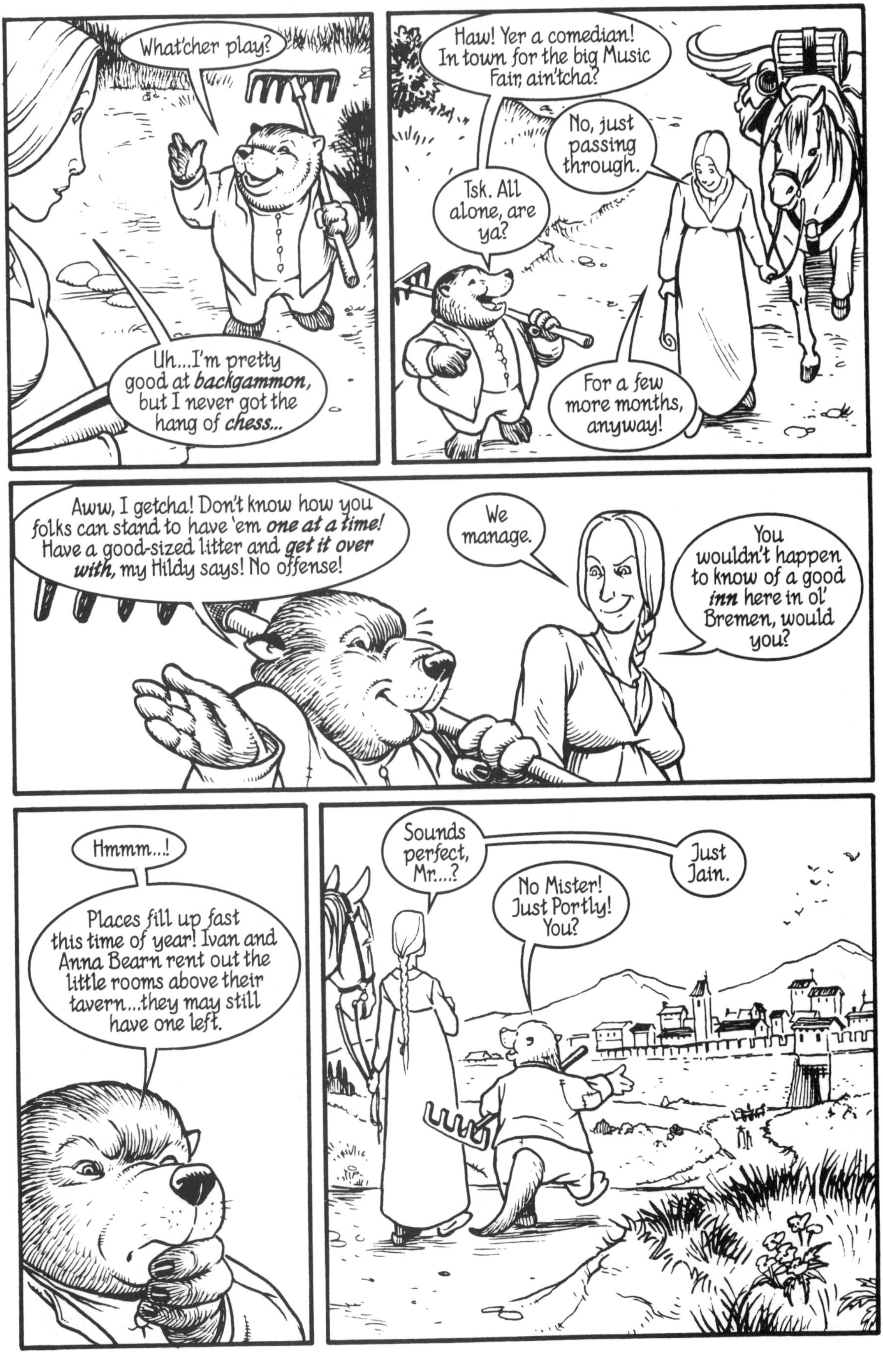
What'cher play?
Uh...I'm pretty good at **backgammon**, but I never got the hang of **chess**...
Haw! Yer a comedian! In town for the big Music Fair, ain'tcha?
No, just passing through.
Tsk. All alone, are ya?
For a few more months, anyway!
Aww, I getcha! Don't know how you folks can stand to have 'em **one at a time!** Have a good-sized litter and **get it over with,** my Hildy says! No offense!
We manage.
You wouldn't happen to know of a good **inn** here in ol' Bremen, would you?
Hmmm...!
Places fill up fast this time of year! Ivan and Anna Bearn rent out the little rooms above their tavern...they may still have one left.
Sounds perfect, Mr....?
Just Jain.
No Mister! Just Portly! You?

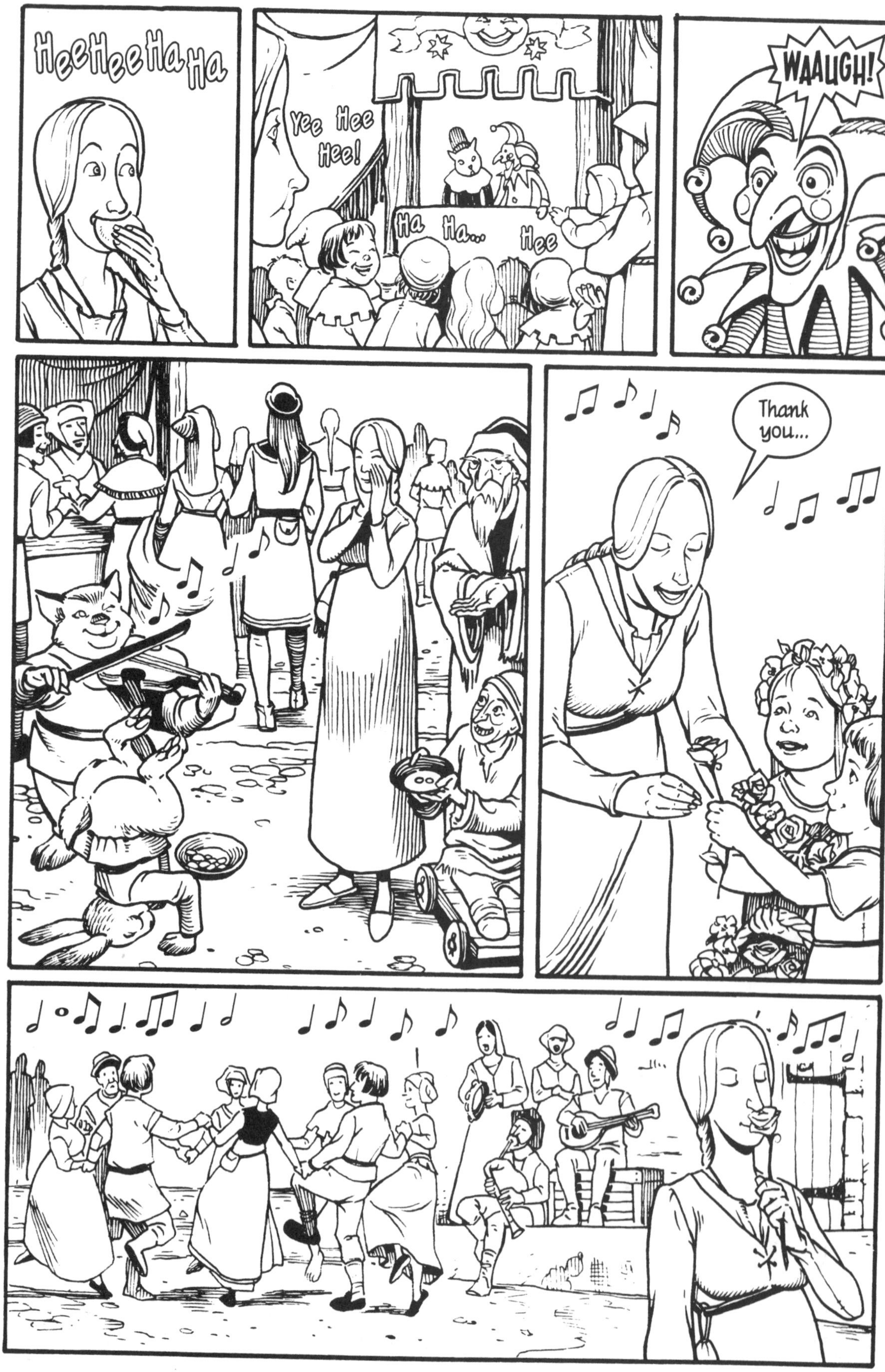
HeeHeeHaHa
Yee Hee Hee!
Ha Ha... Hee
WAAUGH!
Thank you...

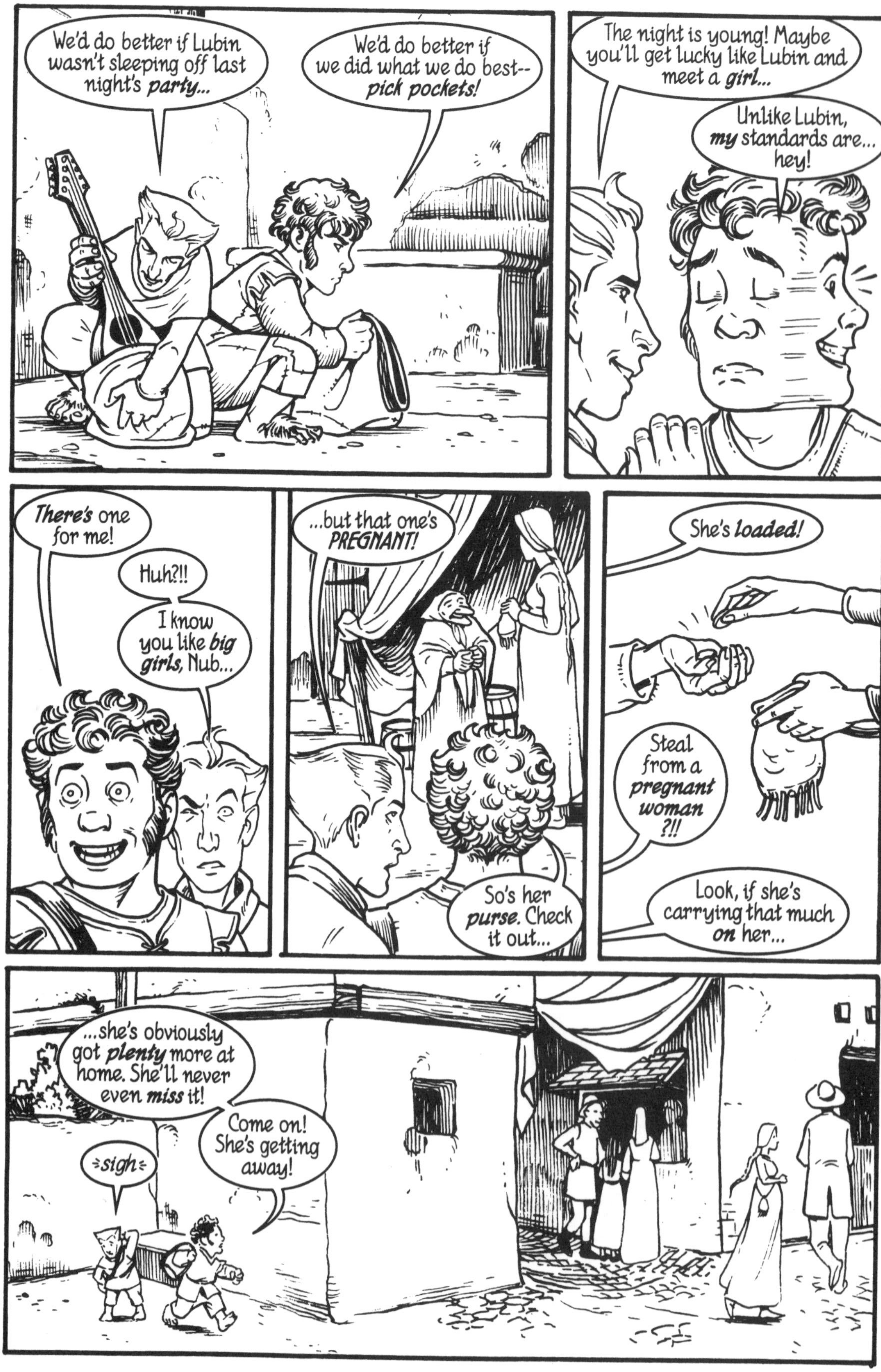
We'd do better if Lubin wasn't sleeping off last night's party...
We'd do better if we did what we do best-- pick pockets!
The night is young! Maybe you'll get lucky like Lubin and meet a girl...
Unlike Lubin, my standards are... hey!
There's one for me!
Huh?!!
I know you like big girls, Nub...
...but that one's PREGNANT!
So's her purse. Check it out...
She's loaded!
Steal from a pregnant woman ?!!
Look, if she's carrying that much on her...
...she's obviously got plenty more at home. She'll never even miss it!
sigh
Come on! She's getting away!

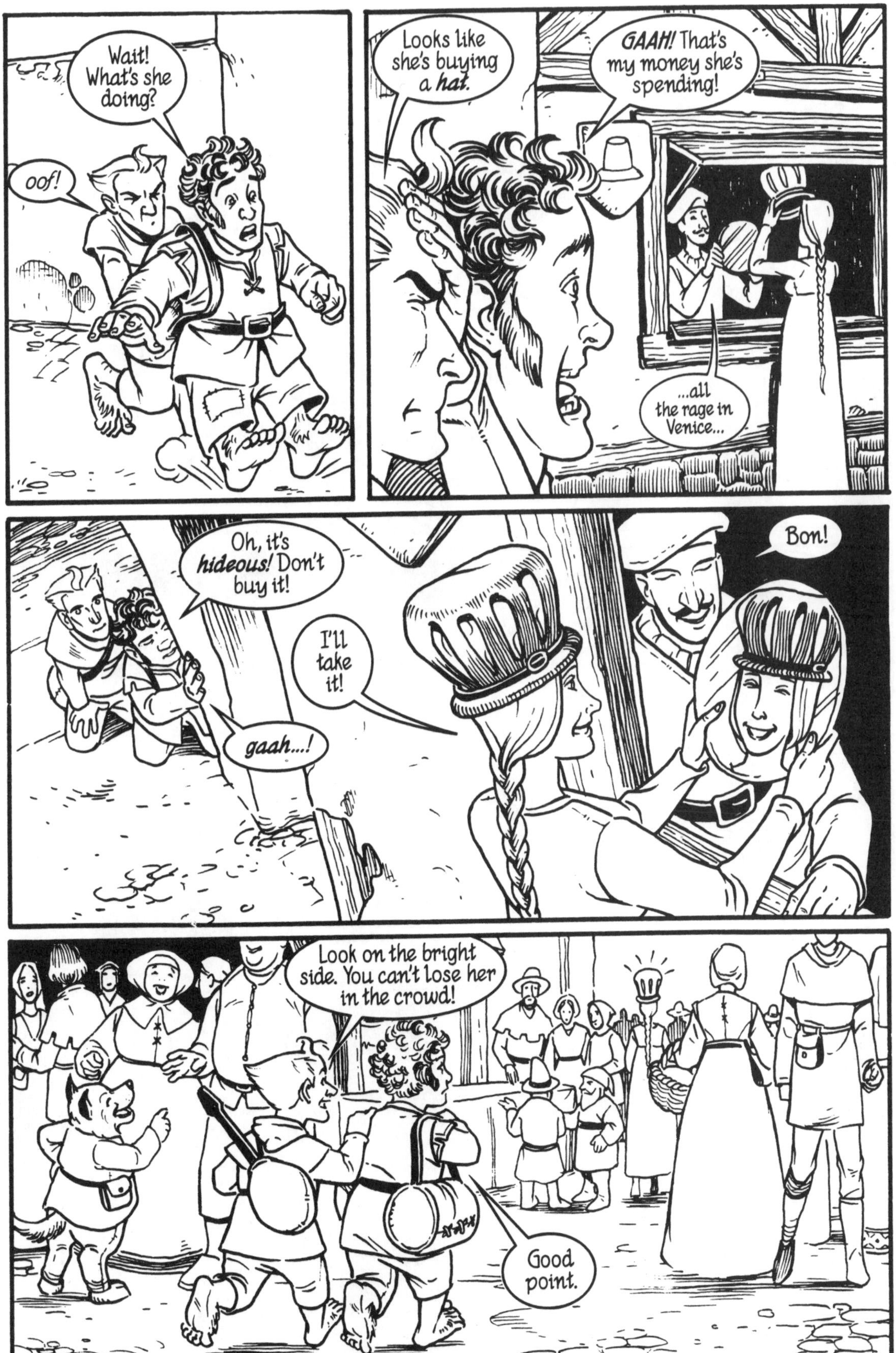
Wait! What's she doing?
oof!
Looks like she's buying a ***hat***.
GAAH! That's my money she's spending!
...all the rage in Venice...
Oh, it's ***hideous!*** Don't buy it!
I'll take it!
gaah...!
Bon!
Look on the bright side. You can't lose her in the crowd!
Good point.

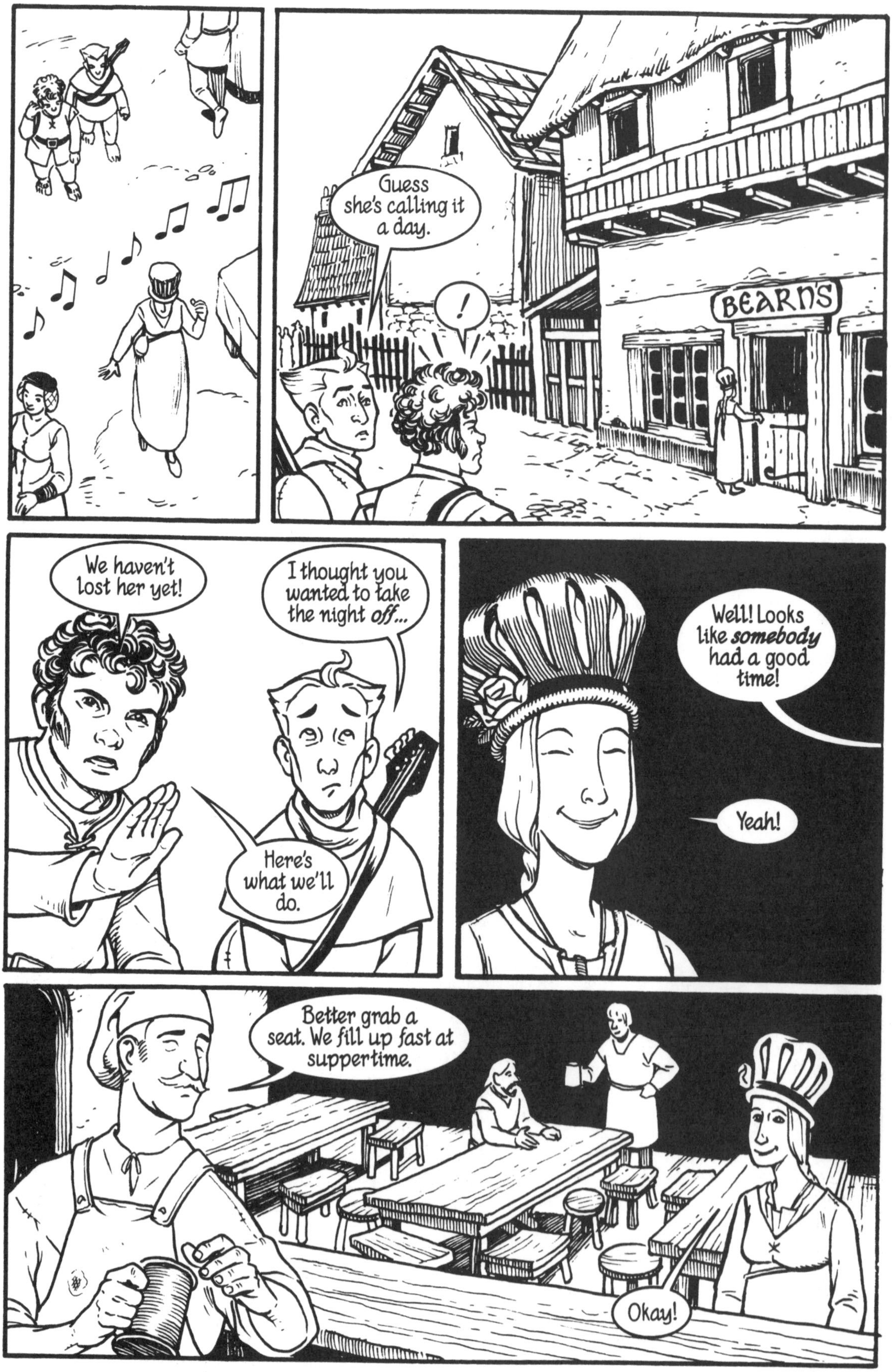
Guess she's calling it a day.
!
BEARN'S
We haven't lost her yet!
I thought you wanted to take the night *off*...
Here's what we'll do.
Well! Looks like ***somebody*** had a good time!
Yeah!
Better grab a seat. We fill up fast at suppertime.
Okay!

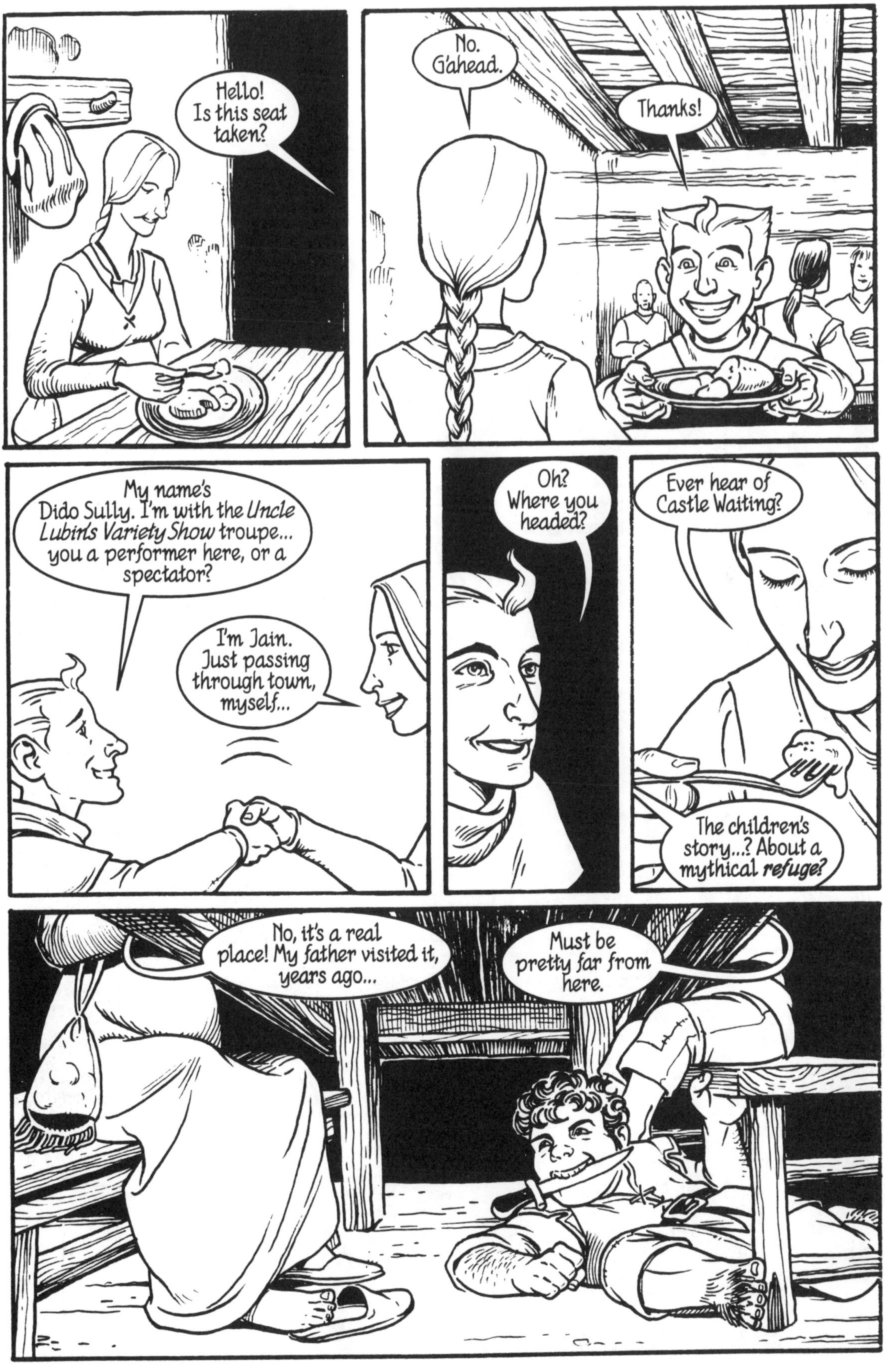
Hello! Is this seat taken?
No. G'ahead.
Thanks!
My name's Dido Sully. I'm with the *Uncle Lubin's Variety Show* troupe... you a performer here, or a spectator?
I'm Jain. Just passing through town, myself...
Oh? Where you headed?
Ever hear of Castle Waiting?
The children's story...? About a mythical ***refuge?***
No, it's a real place! My father visited it, years ago...
Must be pretty far from here.

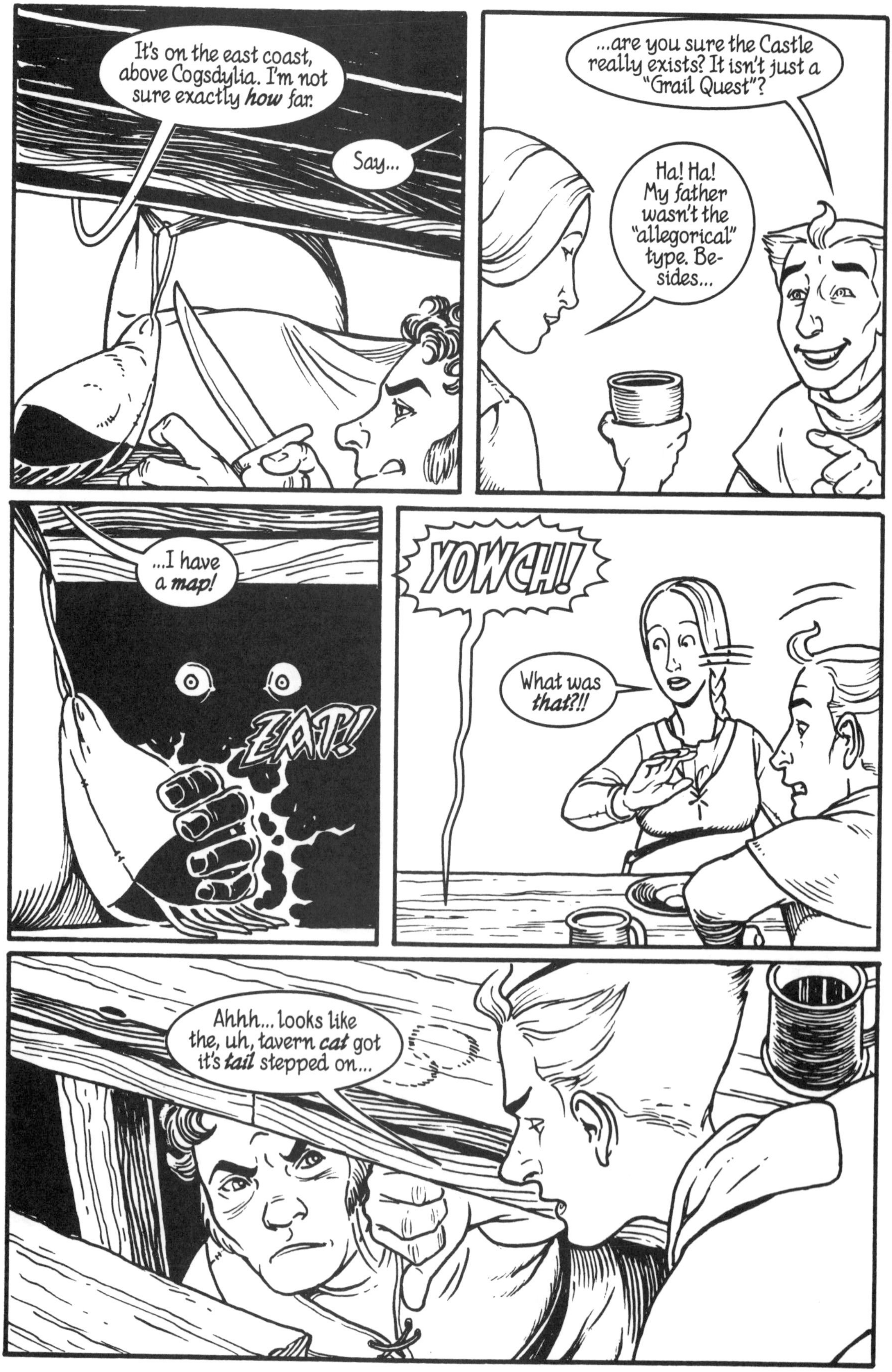
It's on the east coast, above Cogsdylia. I'm not sure exactly *how* far.
Say...
...are you sure the Castle really exists? It isn't just a "Grail Quest"?
Ha! Ha! My father wasn't the "allegorical" type. Be-sides...
...I have a *map!*
ZAT!
YOWCH!
What was *that?!!*
Ahhh... looks like the, uh, tavern *cat* got it's *tail* stepped on...

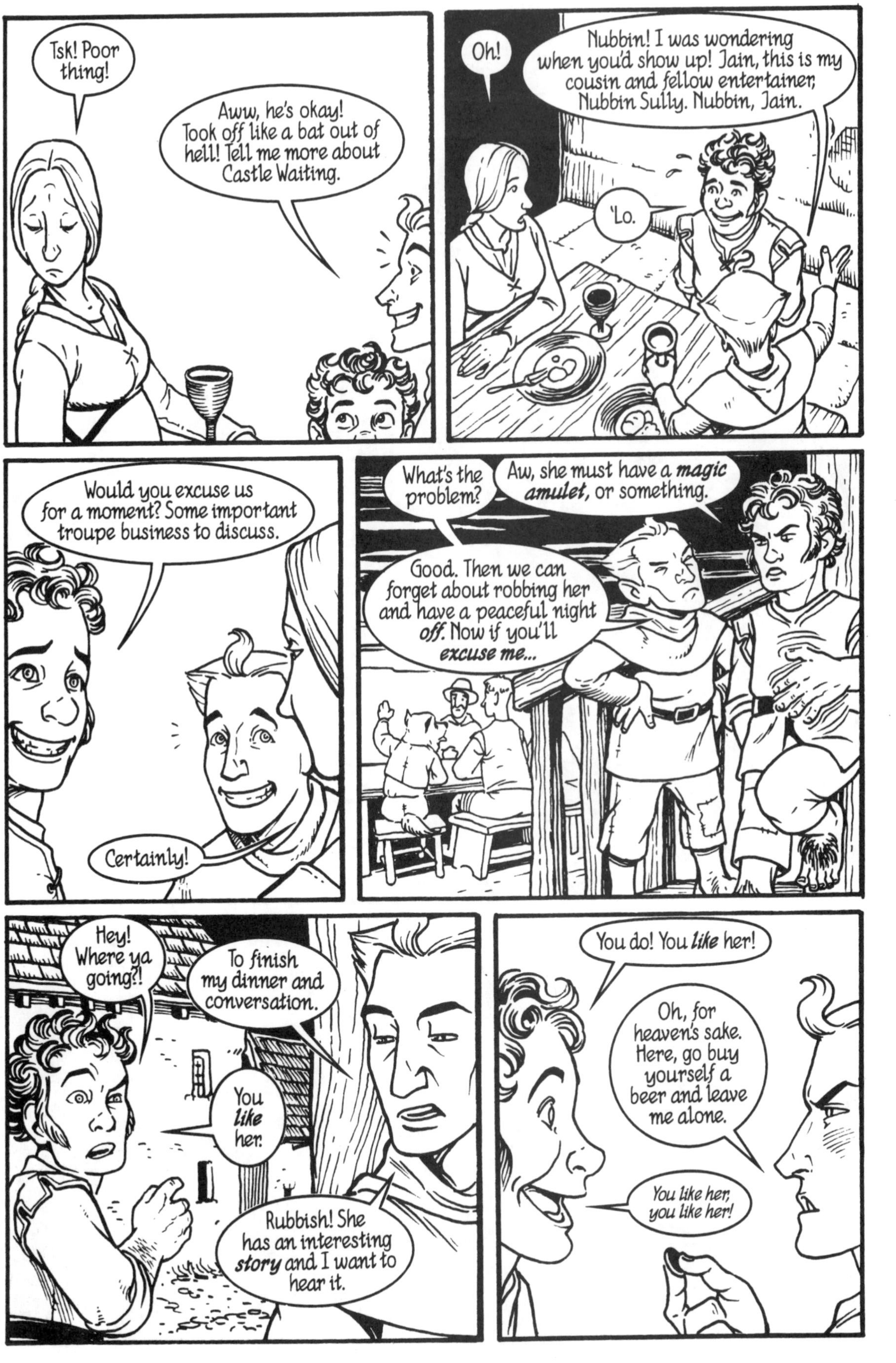
Tsk! Poor thing!
Aww, he's okay! Took off like a bat out of hell! Tell me more about Castle Waiting.
Oh!
Nubbin! I was wondering when you'd show up! Jain, this is my cousin and fellow entertainer, Nubbin Sully. Nubbin, Jain.
'Lo.
Would you excuse us for a moment? Some important troupe business to discuss.
Certainly!
What's the problem?
Aw, she must have a **magic amulet**, or something.
Good. Then we can forget about robbing her and have a peaceful night **off**. Now if you'll **excuse me...**
Hey! Where ya going?!
To finish my dinner and conversation.
You **like** her.
Rubbish! She has an interesting **story** and I want to hear it.
You do! You **like** her!
Oh, for heaven's sake. Here, go buy yourself a beer and leave me alone.
You like her, you like her!

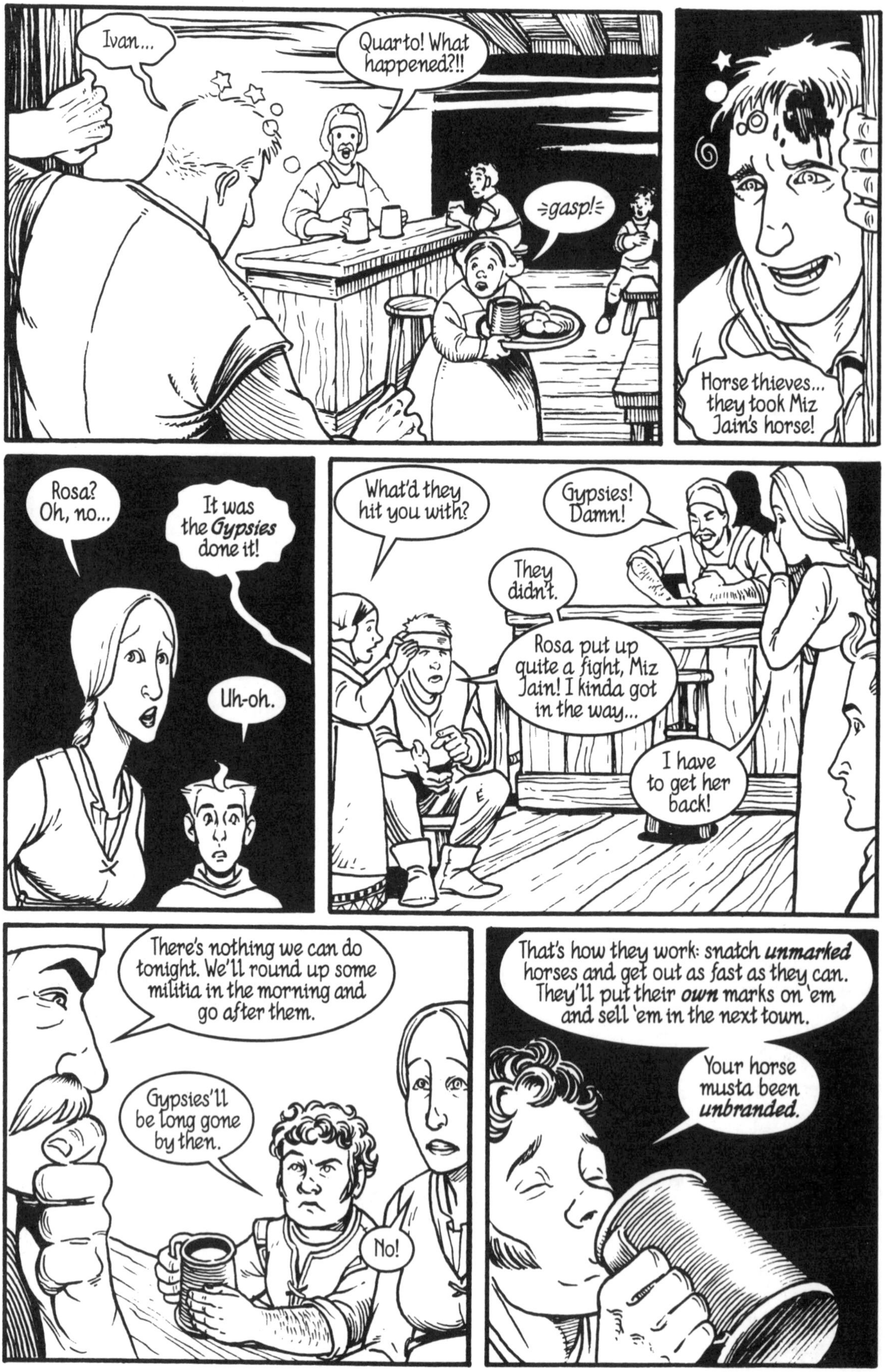
Ivan...
Quarto! What happened?!!
gasp!
Horse thieves... they took Miz Jain's horse!
Rosa? Oh, no...
It was the *Gypsies* done it!
Uh-oh.
What'd they hit you with?
Gypsies! Damn!
They didn't.
Rosa put up quite a fight, Miz Jain! I kinda got in the way...
I have to get her back!
There's nothing we can do tonight. We'll round up some militia in the morning and go after them.
Gypsies'll be long gone by then.
No!
That's how they work: snatch *unmarked* horses and get out as fast as they can. They'll put their *own* marks on 'em and sell 'em in the next town.
Your horse musta been *unbranded*.

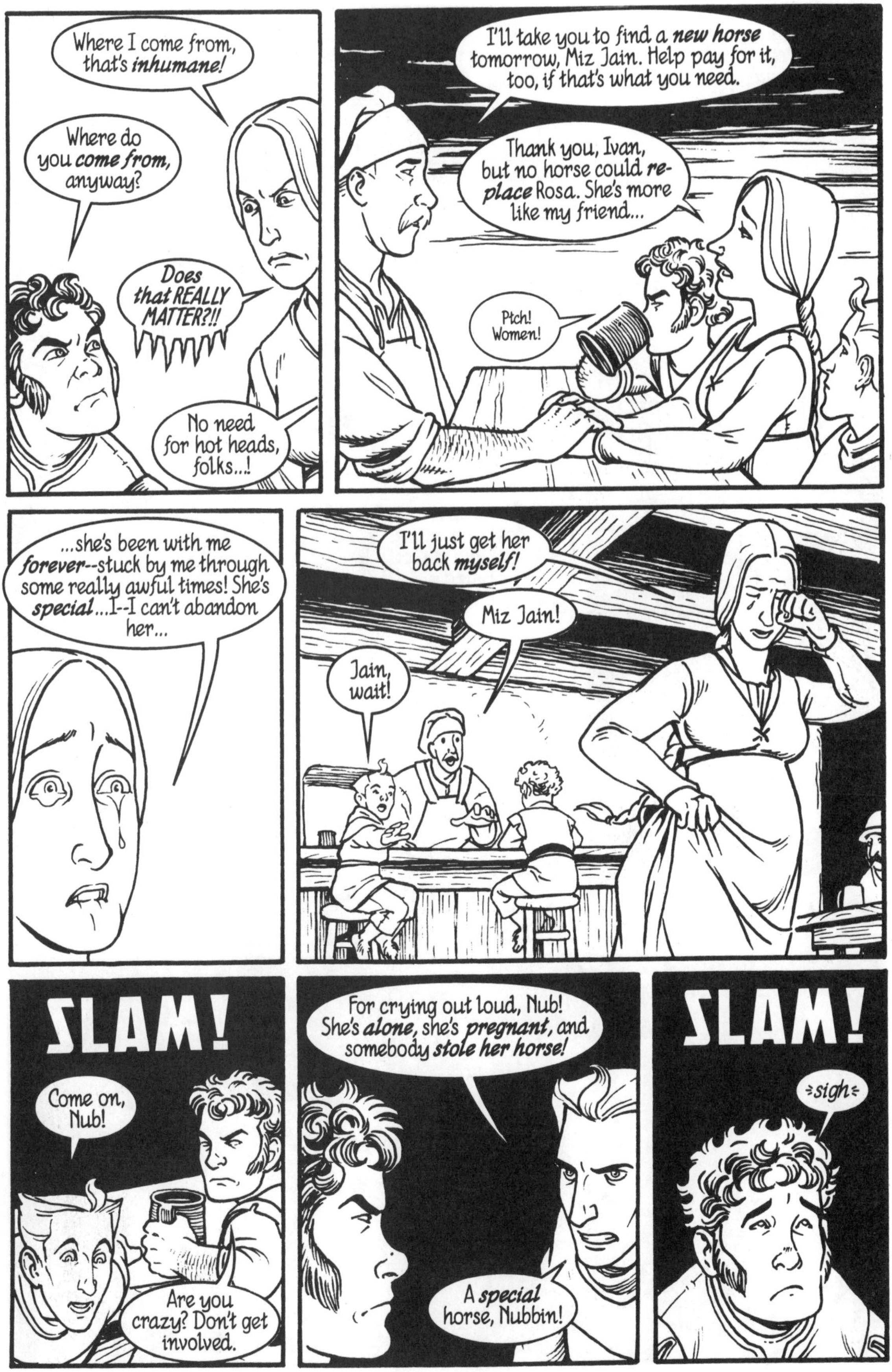
Where I come from, that's *inhumane!*
Where do you *come from,* anyway?
Does that REALLY MATTER?!!
No need for hot heads, folks...!
I'll take you to find a ***new horse*** tomorrow, Miz Jain. Help pay for it, too, if that's what you need.
Thank you, Ivan, but no horse could ***re-place*** Rosa. She's more like my friend...
Ptch! Women!
...she's been with me ***forever***--stuck by me through some really awful times! She's ***special***...I--I can't abandon her...
I'll just get her back ***myself!***
Miz Jain!
Jain, wait!
SLAM!
Come on, Nub!
Are you crazy? Don't get involved.
For crying out loud, Nub! She's ***alone***, she's ***pregnant***, and somebody ***stole her horse!***
A ***special*** horse, Nubbin!
SLAM!
sigh

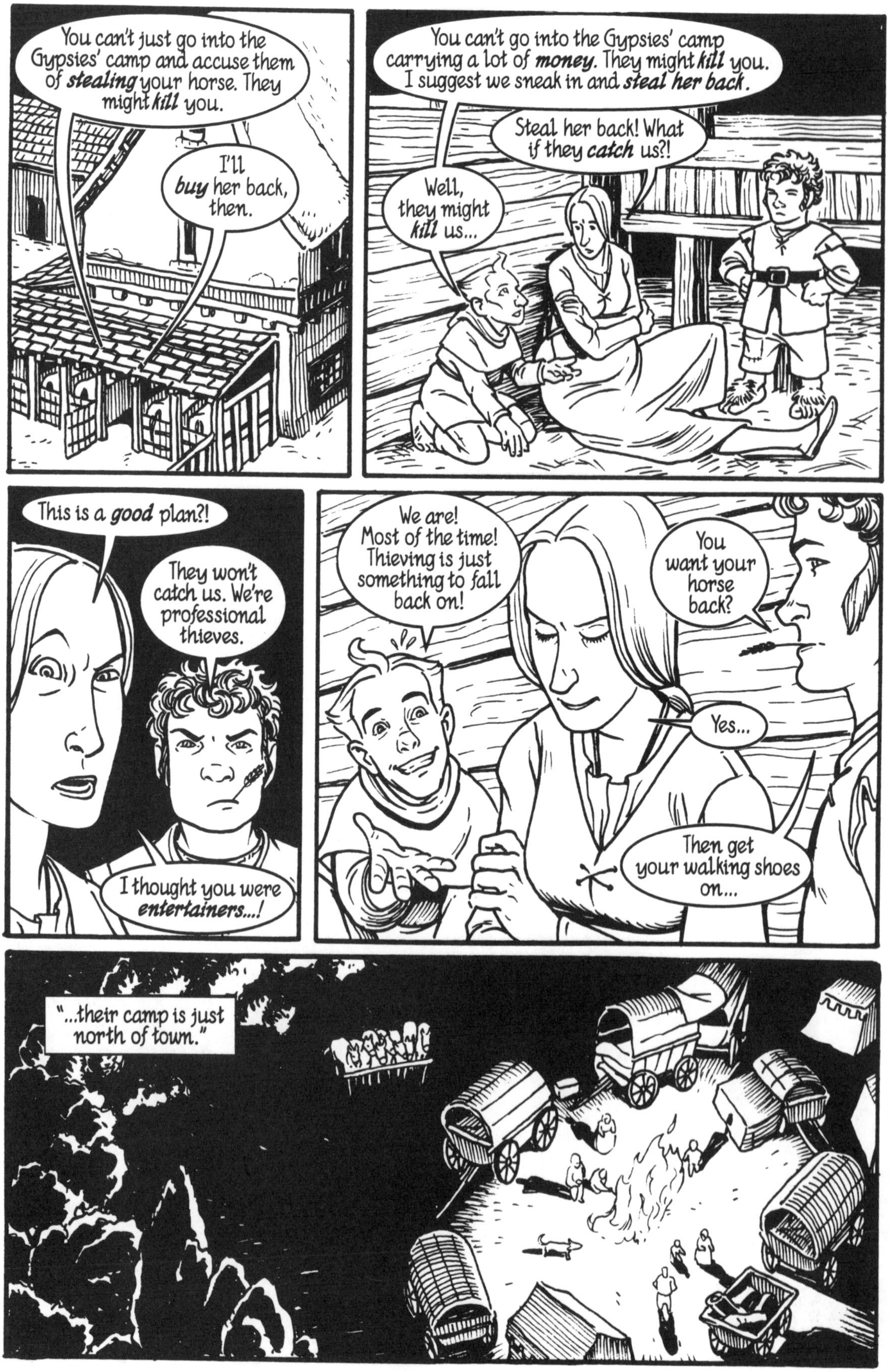

You can't just go into the Gypsies' camp and accuse them of *stealing* your horse. They might *kill* you.
I'll *buy* her back, then.
You can't go into the Gypsies' camp carrying a lot of *money*. They might *kill* you. I suggest we sneak in and *steal her back*.
Steal her back! What if they *catch* us?!
Well, they might *kill* us...
This is a *good* plan?!
They won't catch us. We're professional thieves.
I thought you were *entertainers*...!
We are! Most of the time! Thieving is just something to fall back on!
You want your horse back?
Yes...
Then get your walking shoes on...
"...their camp is just north of town."

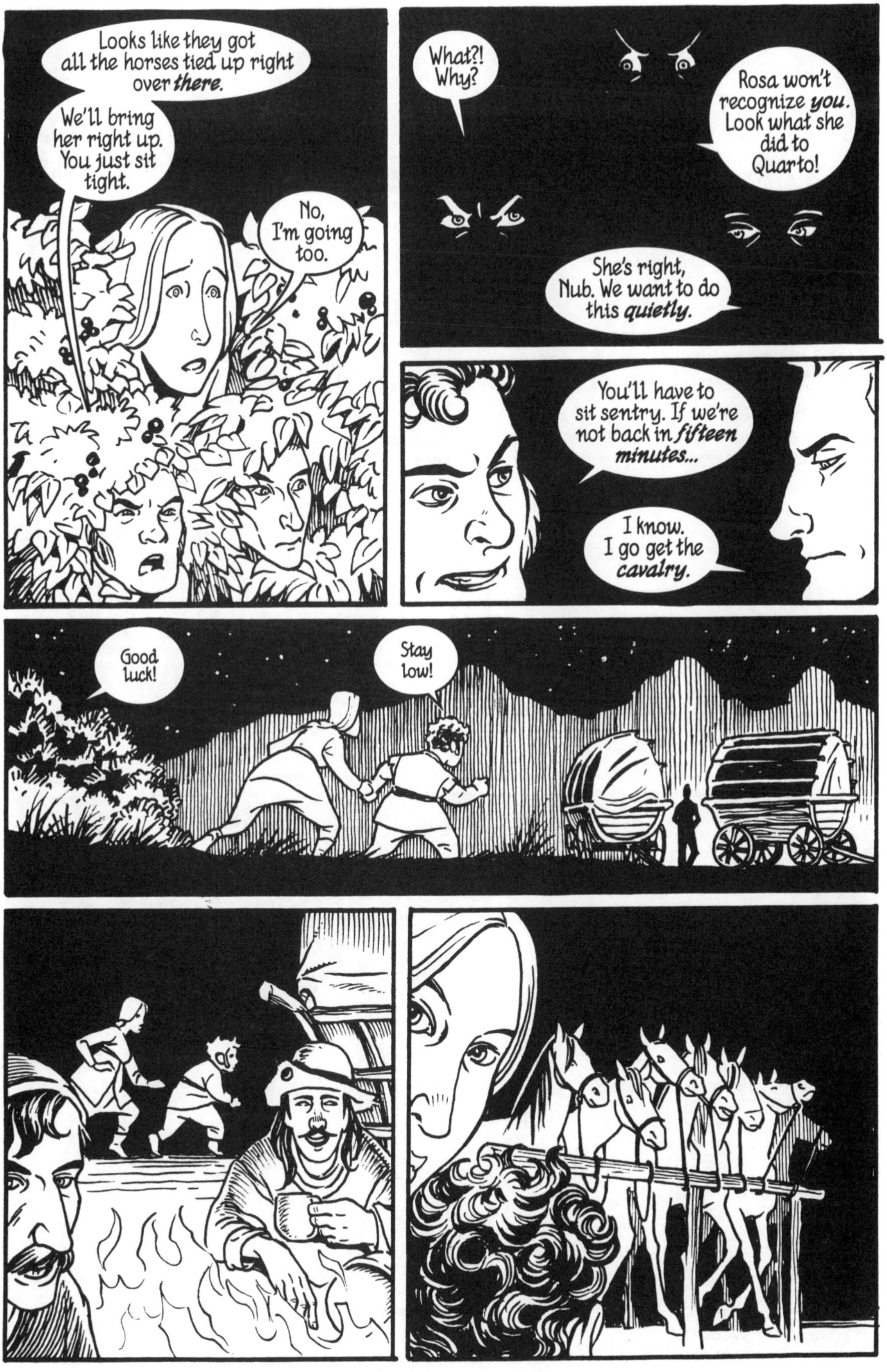
Looks like they got all the horses tied up right over *there*.
We'll bring her right up. You just sit tight.
No, I'm going too.
What?! Why?
Rosa won't recognize *you*. Look what she did to Quarto!
She's right, Nub. We want to do this *quietly*.
You'll have to sit sentry. If we're not back in *fifteen minutes*...
I know. I go get the *cavalry*.
Good luck!
Stay low!

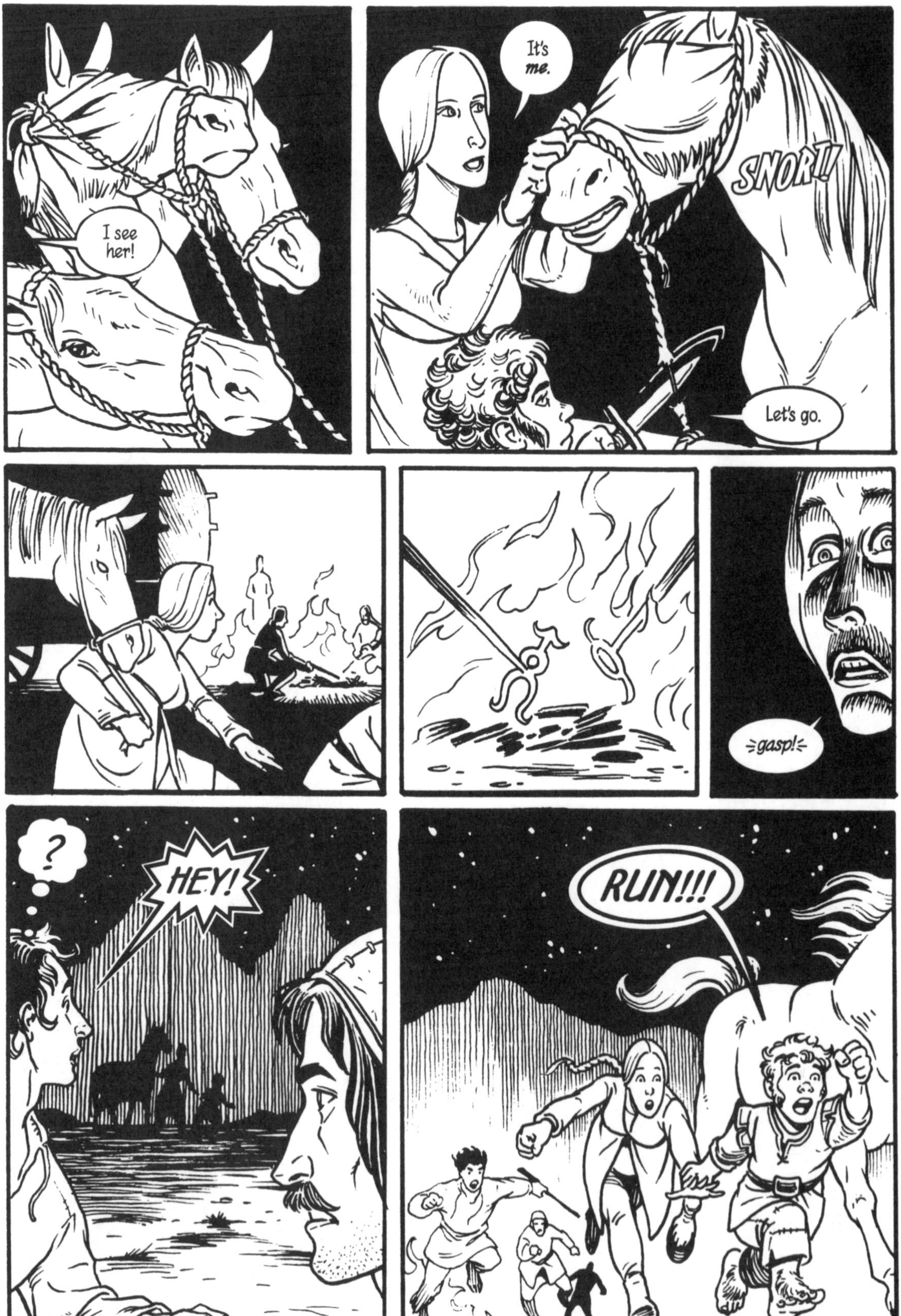
I see her!
It's me.
SNORT!
Let's go.
gasp!
?
HEY!
RUN!!!

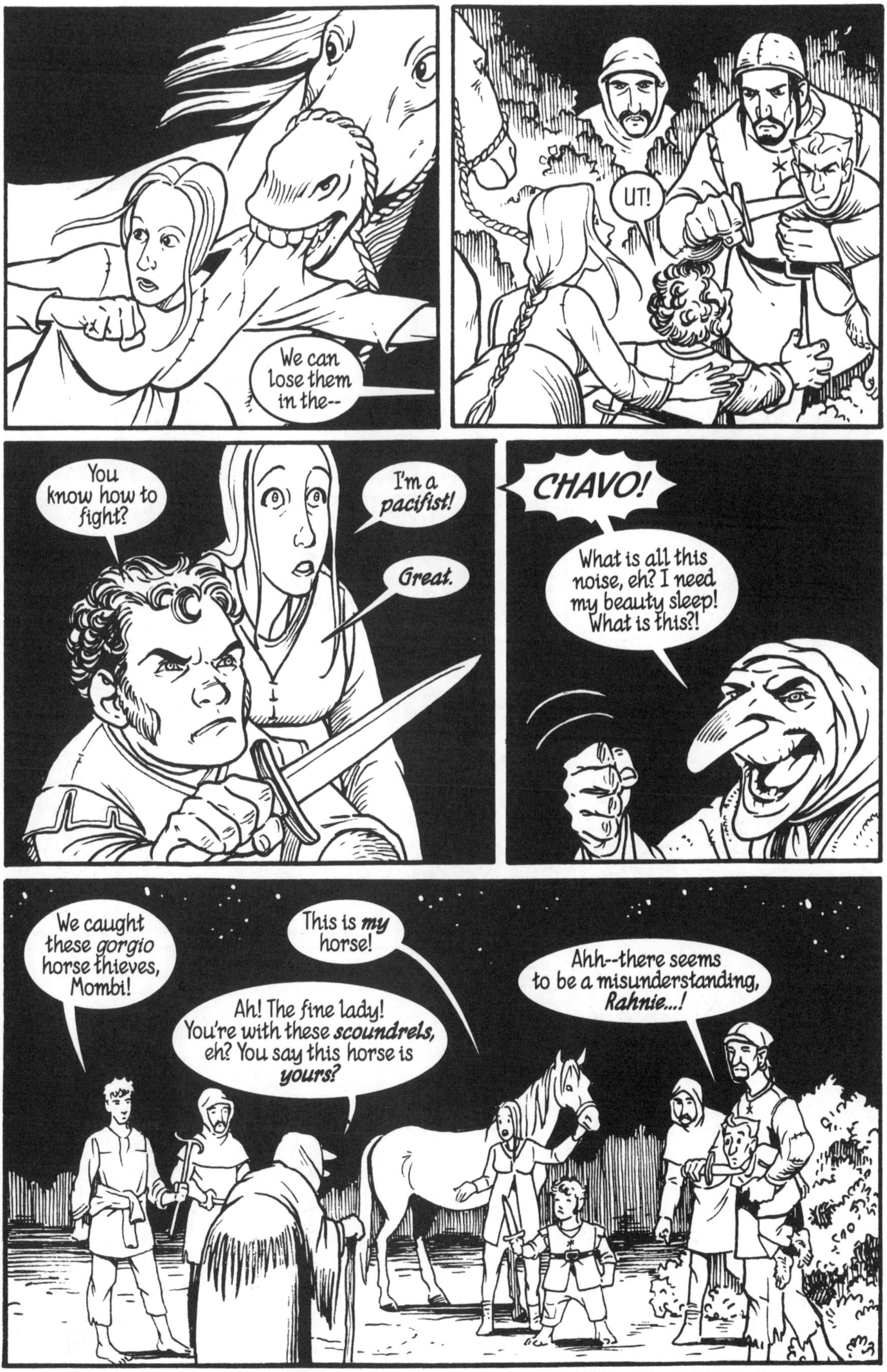
We can lose them in the--
UT!
You know how to fight?
I'm a *pacifist!*
Great.
CHAVO!
What is all this noise, eh? I need my beauty sleep! What is this?!
We caught these *gorgio* horse thieves, Mombi!
This is *my* horse!
Ah! The fine lady! You're with these *scoundrels,* eh? You say this horse is *yours?*
Ahh--there seems to be a misunderstanding, *Rahnie...!*

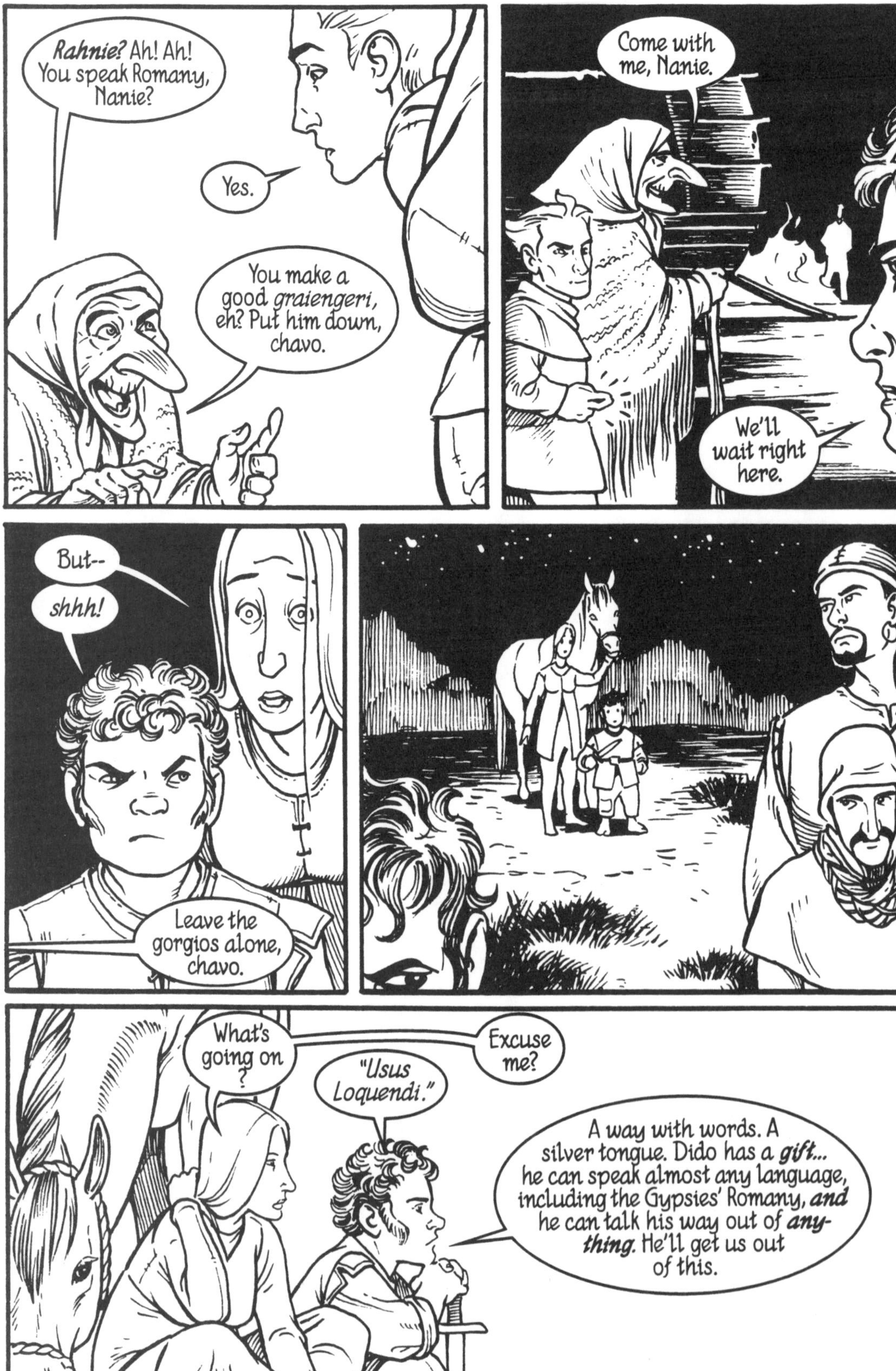
Rahnie? Ah! Ah! You speak Romany, Nanie?
Yes.
You make a good *graiengeri,* eh? Put him down, chavo.
Come with me, Nanie.
We'll wait right here.
But--
shhh!
Leave the gorgios alone, chavo.
What's going on ?
Excuse me?
"*Usus Loquendi.*"
A way with words. A silver tongue. Dido has a ***gift...*** he can speak almost any language, including the Gypsies' Romany, ***and*** he can talk his way out of ***any-thing***. He'll get us out of this.

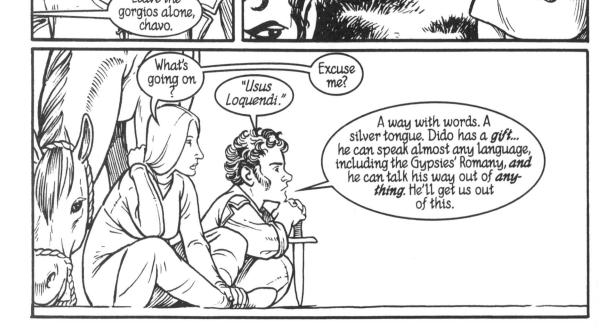

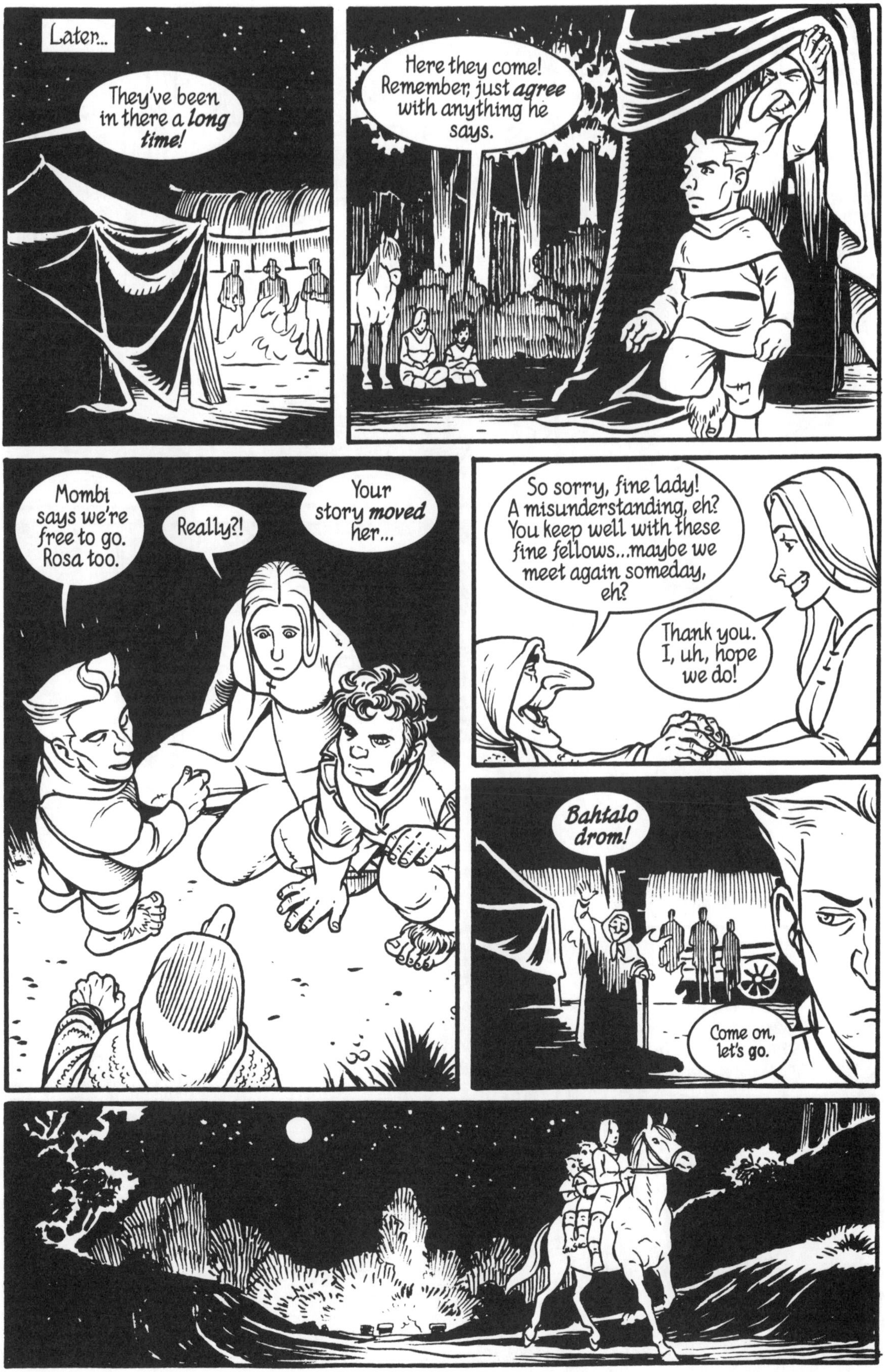
Later...
They've been in there a *long time!*
Here they come! Remember, just *agree* with anything he says.
Mombi says we're free to go. Rosa too.
Really?!
Your story *moved* her...
So sorry, fine lady! A misunderstanding, eh? You keep well with these fine fellows...maybe we meet again someday, eh?
Thank you. I, uh, hope we do!
Bahtalo drom!
Come on, let's go.

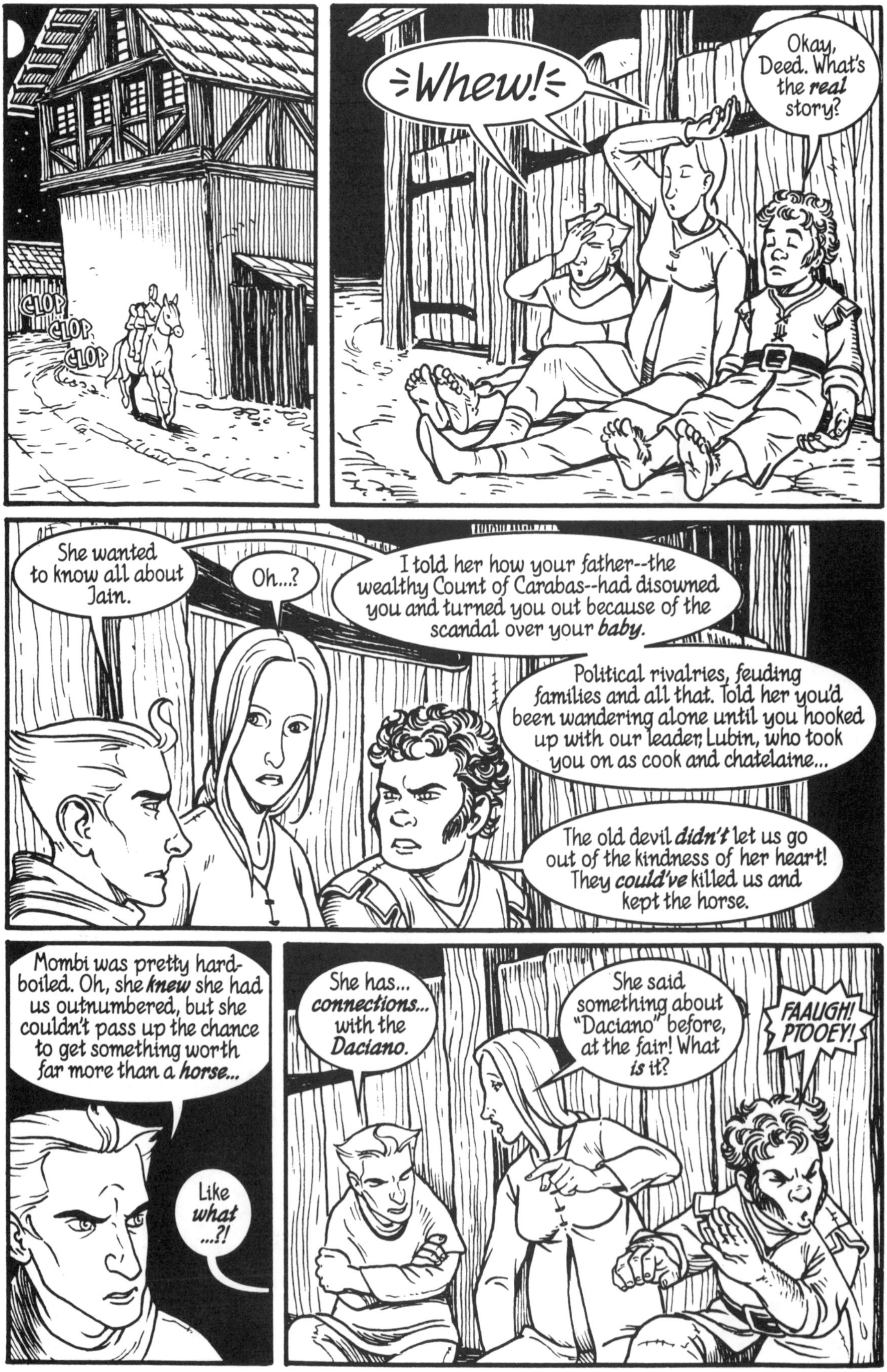
CLOP
CLOP
CLOP
Whew!
Okay, Deed. What's the *real* story?
She wanted to know all about Jain.
Oh...?
I told her how your father--the wealthy Count of Carabas--had disowned you and turned you out because of the scandal over your *baby*.
Political rivalries, feuding families and all that. Told her you'd been wandering alone until you hooked up with our leader, Lubin, who took you on as cook and chatelaine...
The old devil *didn't* let us go out of the kindness of her heart! They *could've* killed us and kept the horse.
Mombi was pretty hard-boiled. Oh, she *knew* she had us outnumbered, but she couldn't pass up the chance to get something worth far more than a *horse*...
Like *what* ...?!
She has... *connections*... with the *Daciano*.
She said something about "Daciano" before, at the fair! What *is* it?
FAAUGH! PTOOEY!

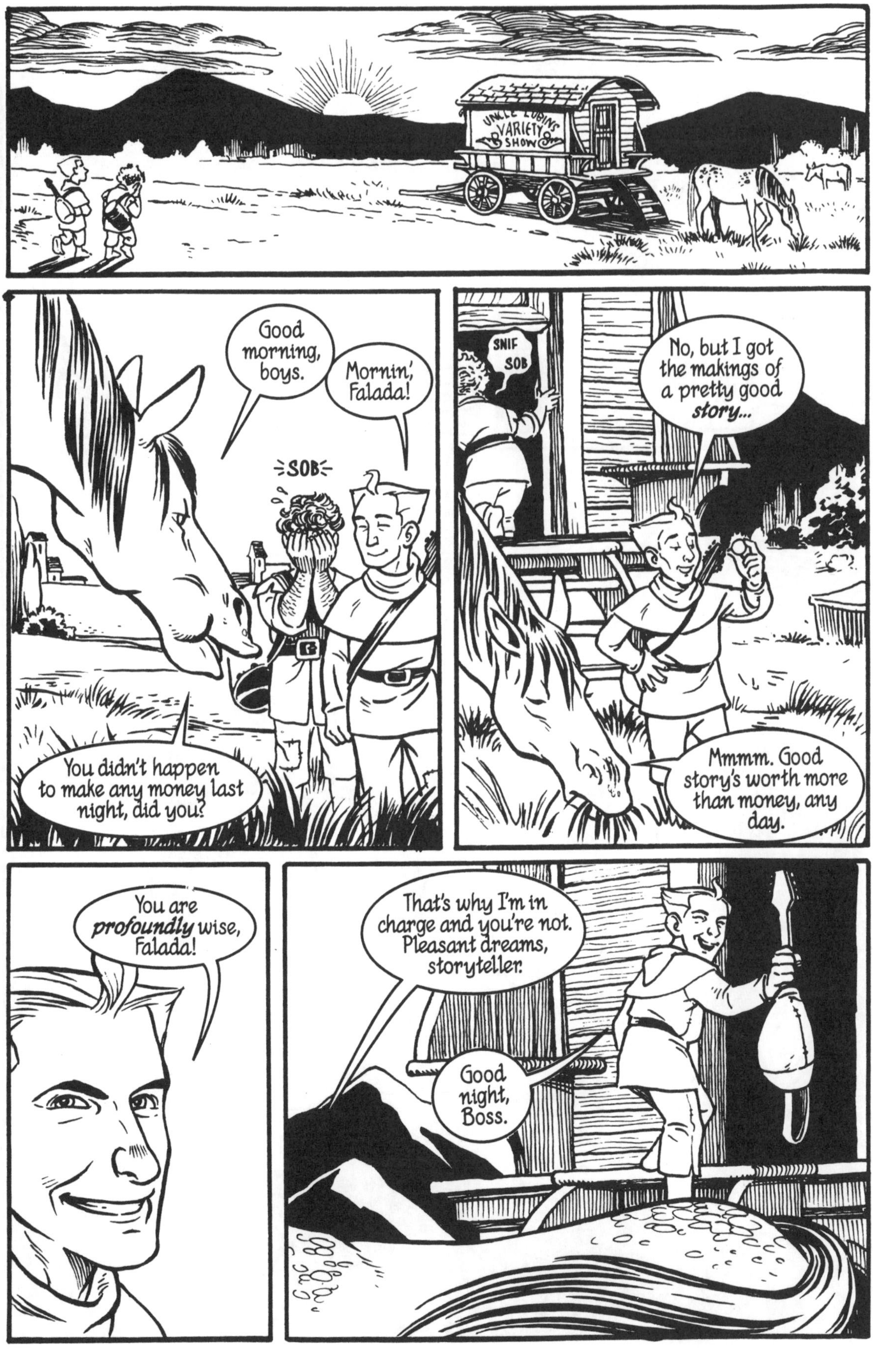
UNCLE LUBIN'S VARIETY SHOW
Good morning, boys.
Mornin', Falada!
SOB
You didn't happen to make any money last night, did you?
SNIF
SOB
No, but I got the makings of a pretty good *story...*
Mmmm. Good story's worth more than money, any day.
You are *profoundly* wise, Falada!
That's why I'm in charge and you're not. Pleasant dreams, storyteller.
Good night, Boss.

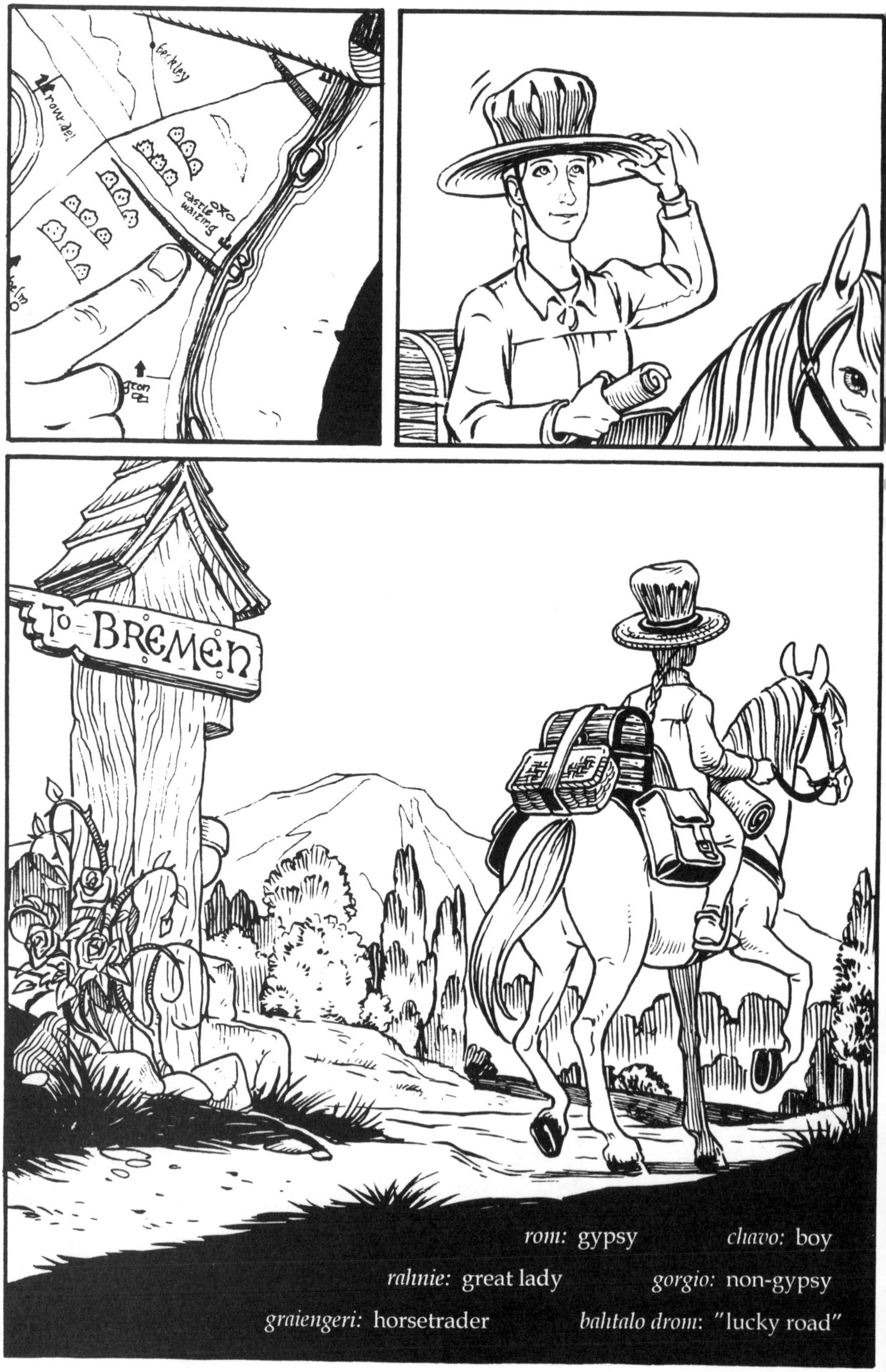
beckley
castle waizing
To BREMEN
rom: gypsy
chavo: boy
rahnie: great lady
gorgio: non-gypsy
graiengeri: horsetrader
bahtalo drom: "lucky road"

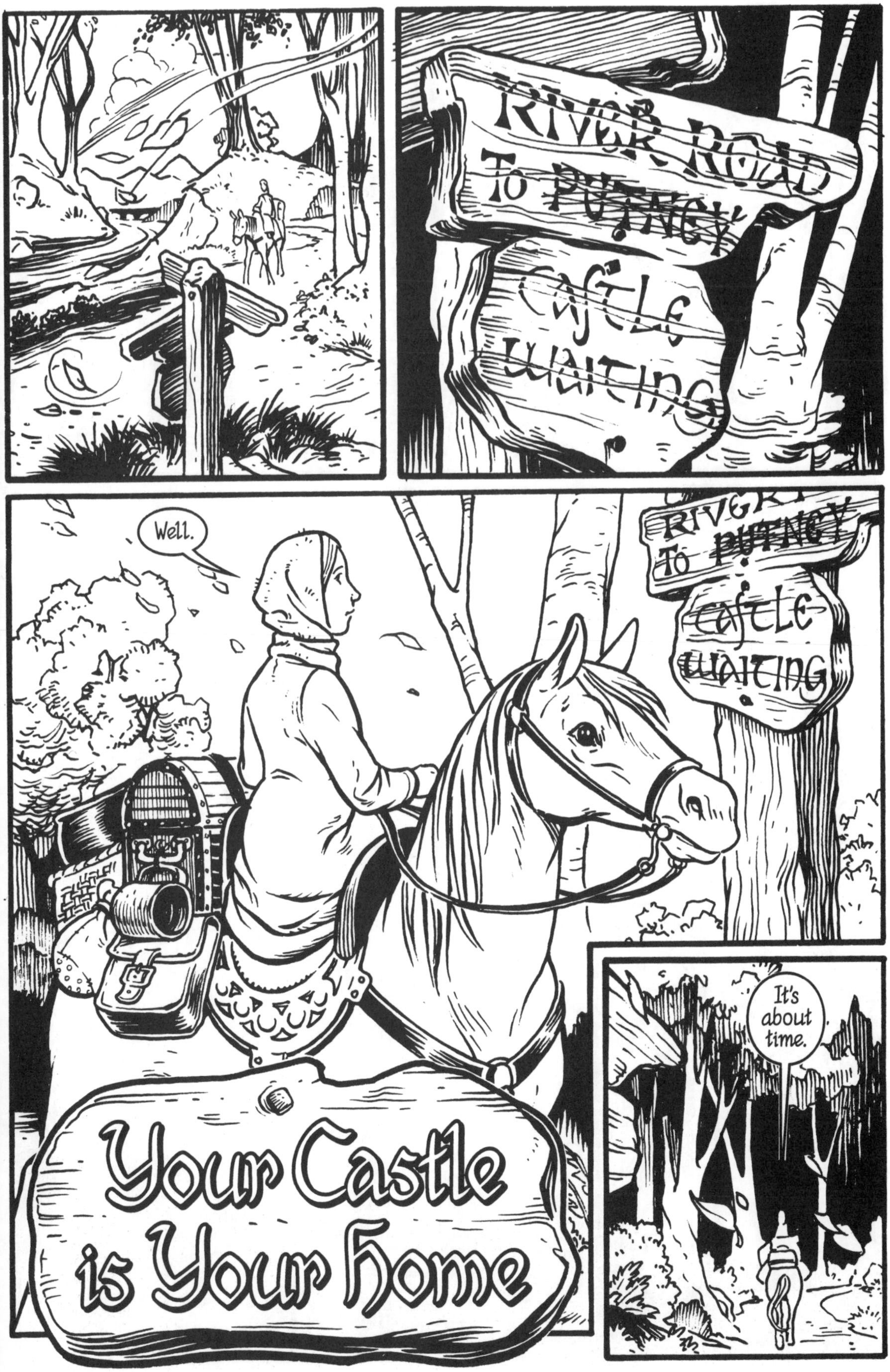

RIVER ROAD
TO PUTNEY
CASTLE
WAITING
Well.
Your Castle is Your Home
It's about time.

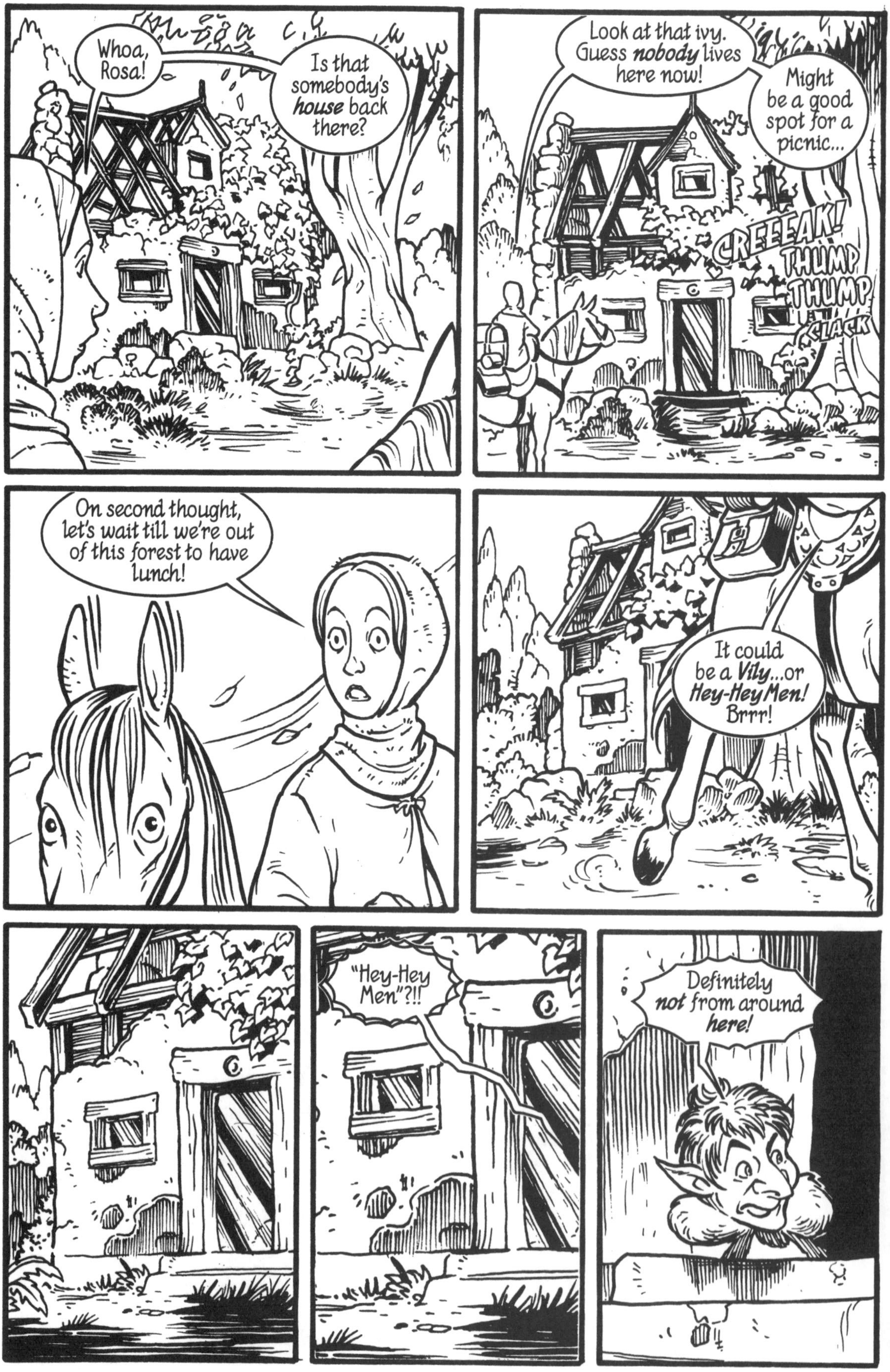
Whoa, Rosa!
Is that somebody's **house** back there?
Look at that ivy. Guess **nobody** lives here now!
Might be a good spot for a picnic...
CREEEAK!
THUMP
THUMP
SLACK
On second thought, let's wait till we're out of this forest to have lunch!
It could be a ***Vily***...or ***Hey-Hey Men!*** Brrr!
"Hey-Hey Men"?!!
Definitely ***not*** from around ***here!***

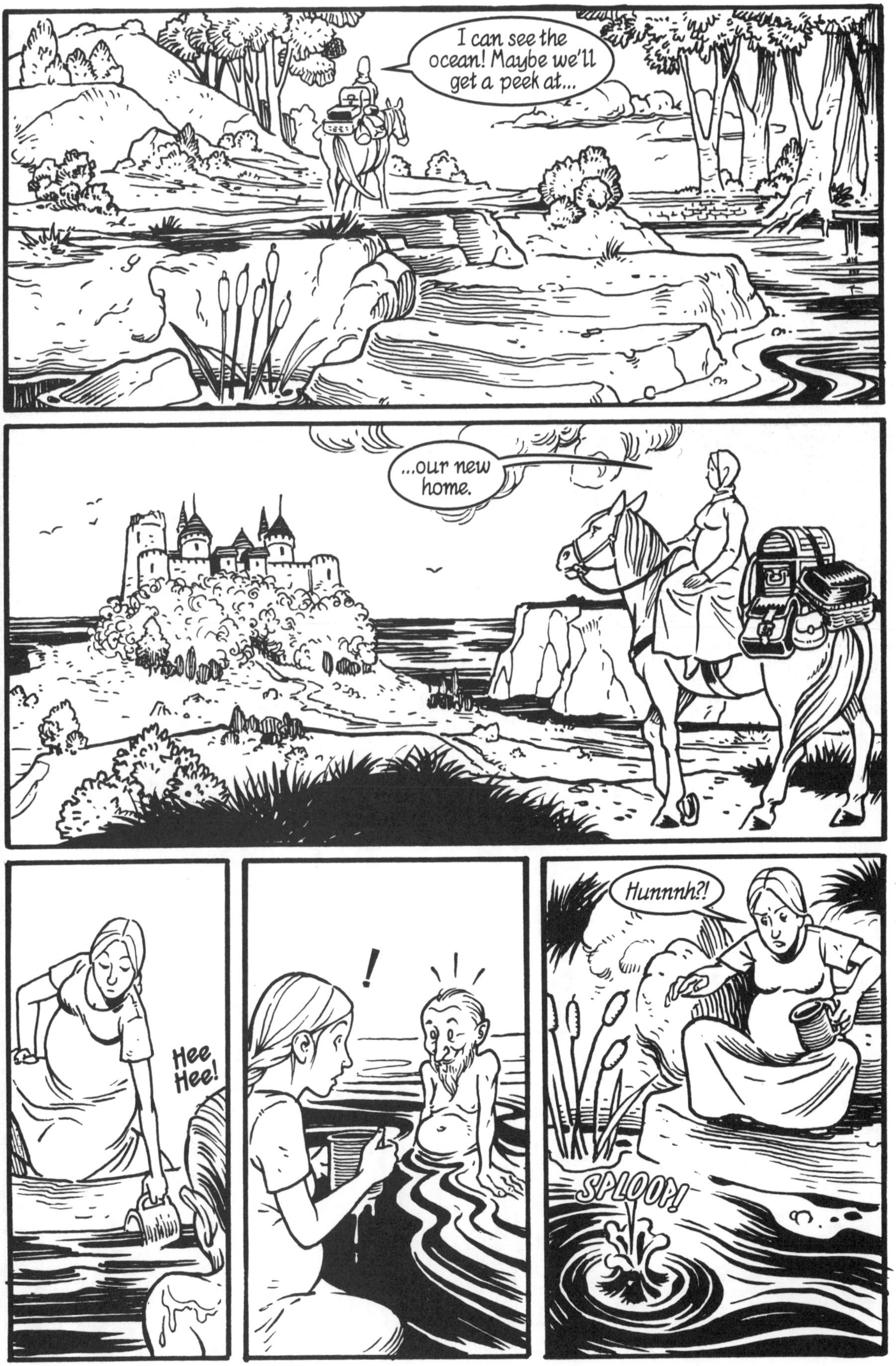
I can see the ocean! Maybe we'll get a peek at...
...our new home.
Hee Hee!
!
Hunnnh?!
SPLOOP!

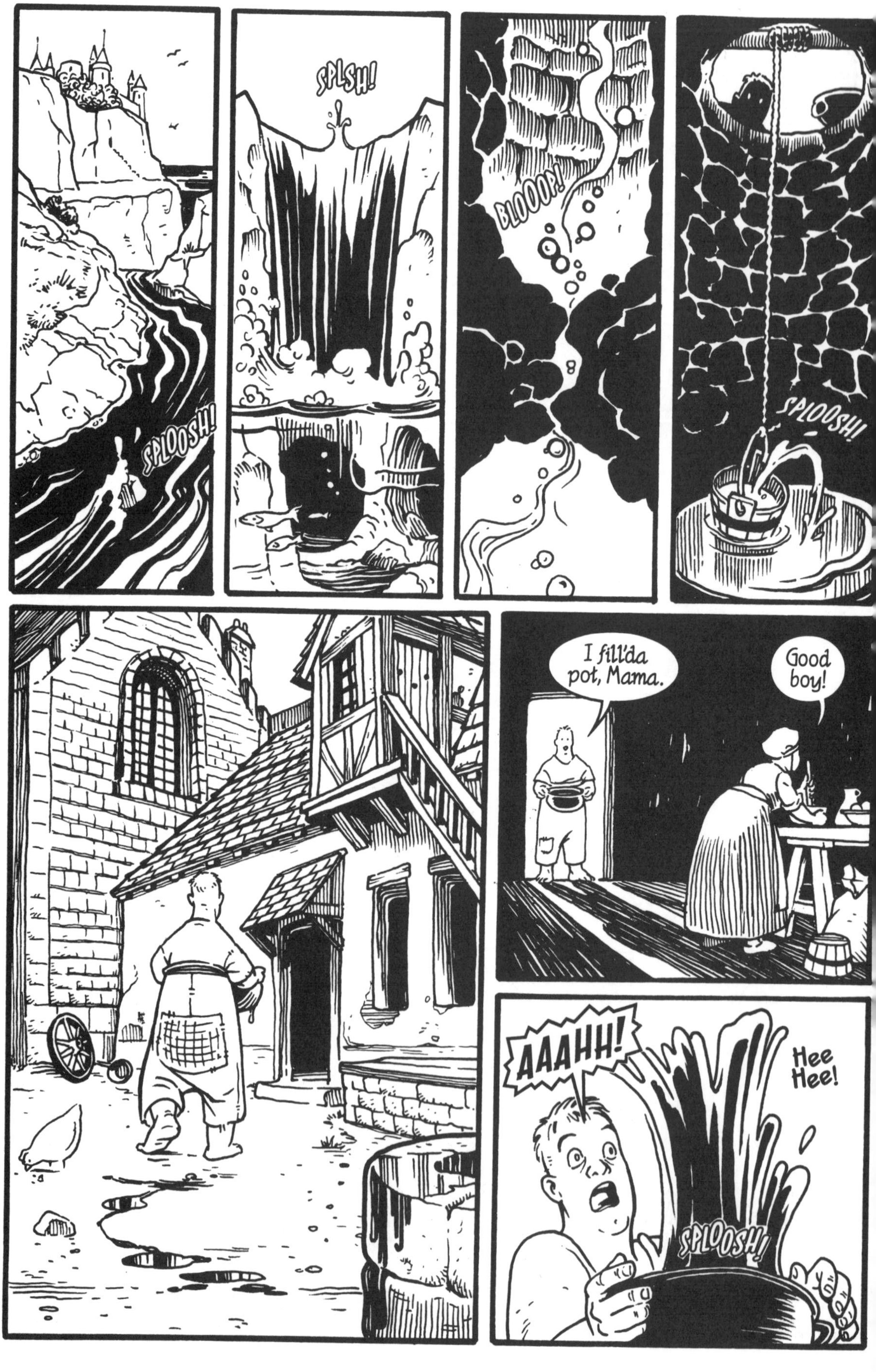
SPLOOSH!
SPLSH!
BLOOOP!
SPLOOSH!
I fill'da pot, Mama.
Good boy!
AAAHH!
Hee Hee!
SPLOOSH!

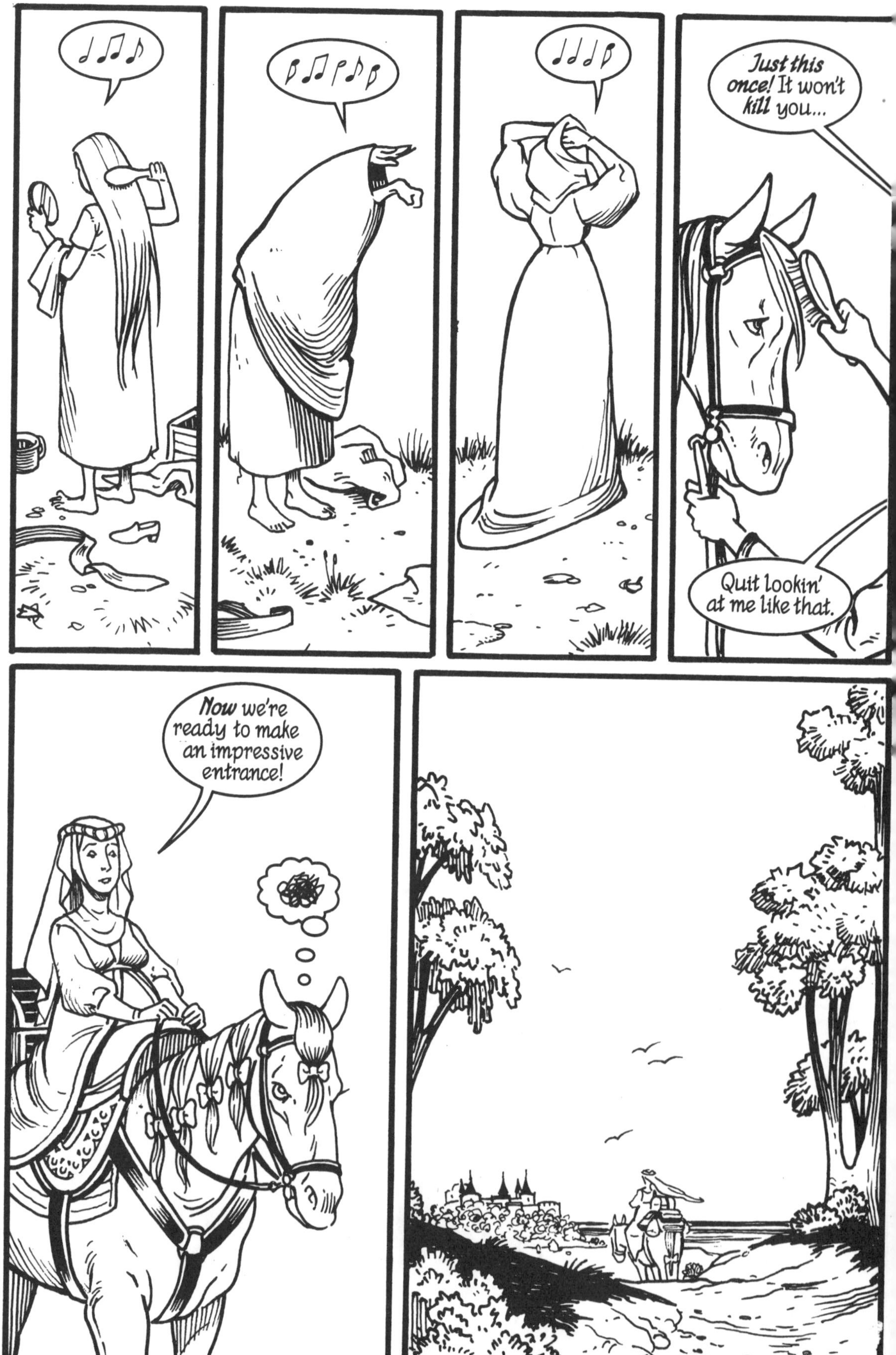
Just this once! It won't kill you...
Quit lookin' at me like that.
Now we're ready to make an impressive entrance!

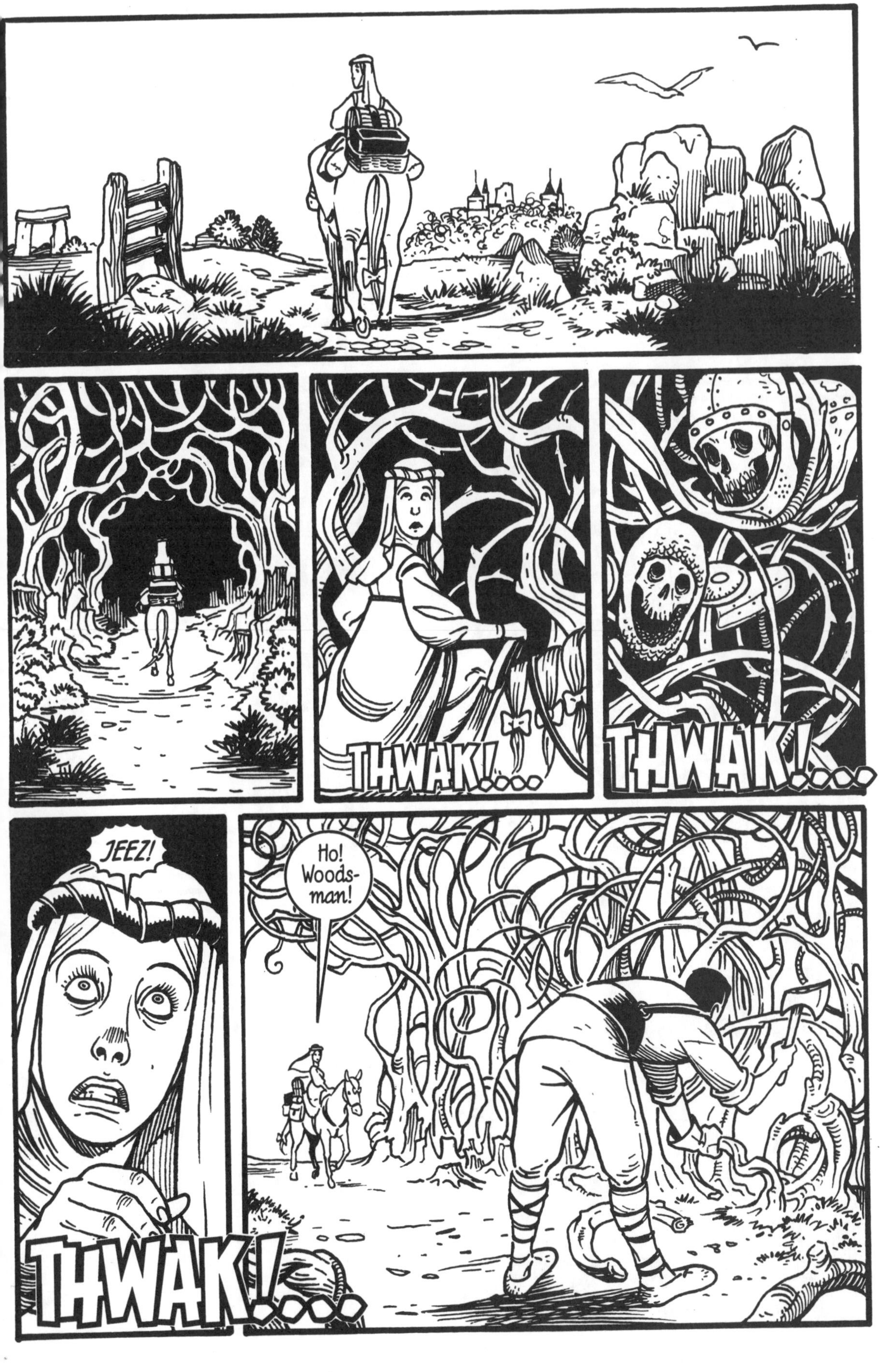
THWAK!....
THWAK!....
JEEZ!
THWAK!....
Ho! Woods-man!

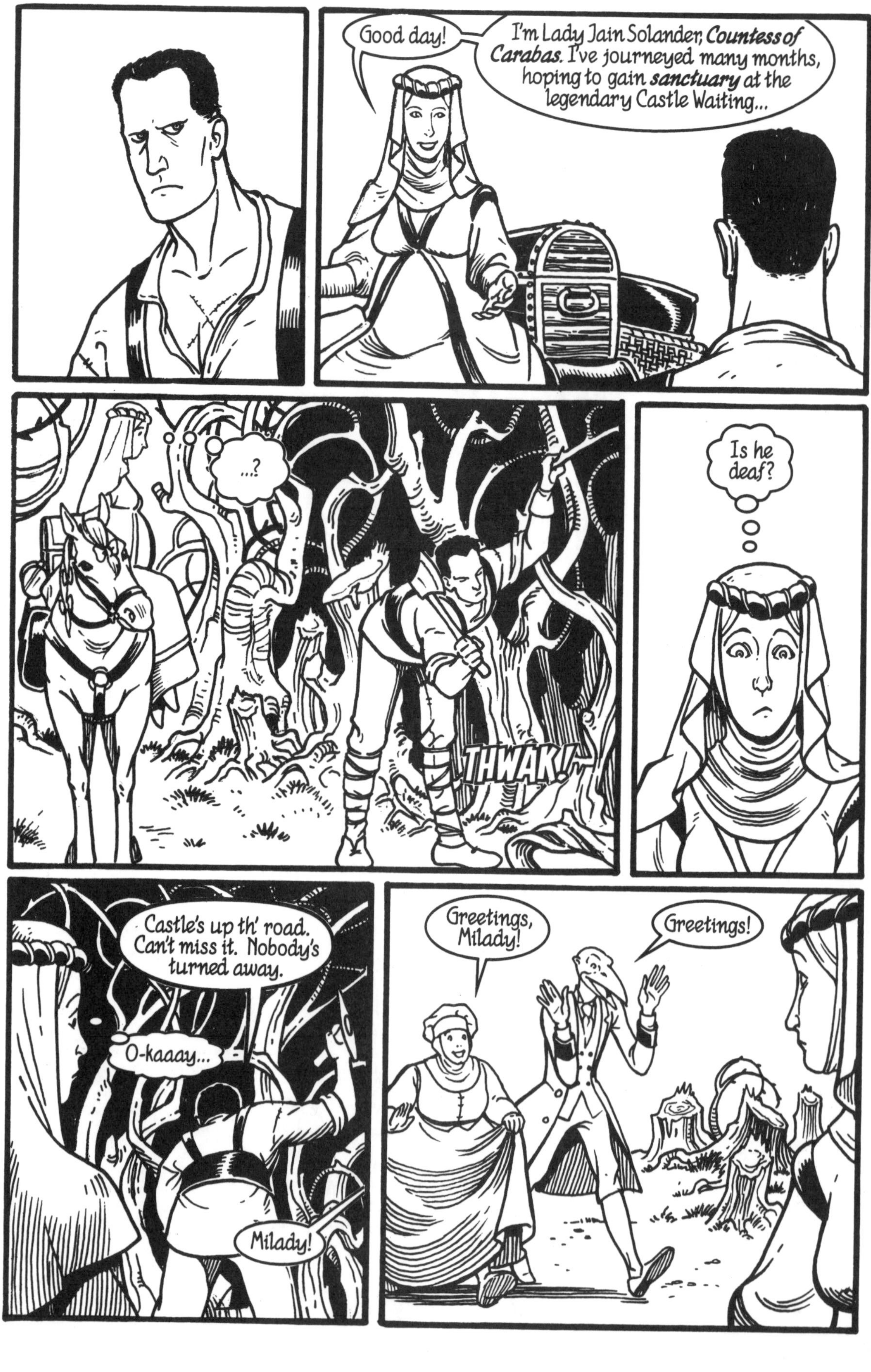
Good day!
I'm Lady Jain Solander, *Countess of Carabas.* I've journeyed many months, hoping to gain *sanctuary* at the legendary Castle Waiting...
...?
THWAK!
Is he deaf?
Castle's up th' road. Can't miss it. Nobody's turned away.
O-kaaay...
Milady!
Greetings, Milady!
Greetings!

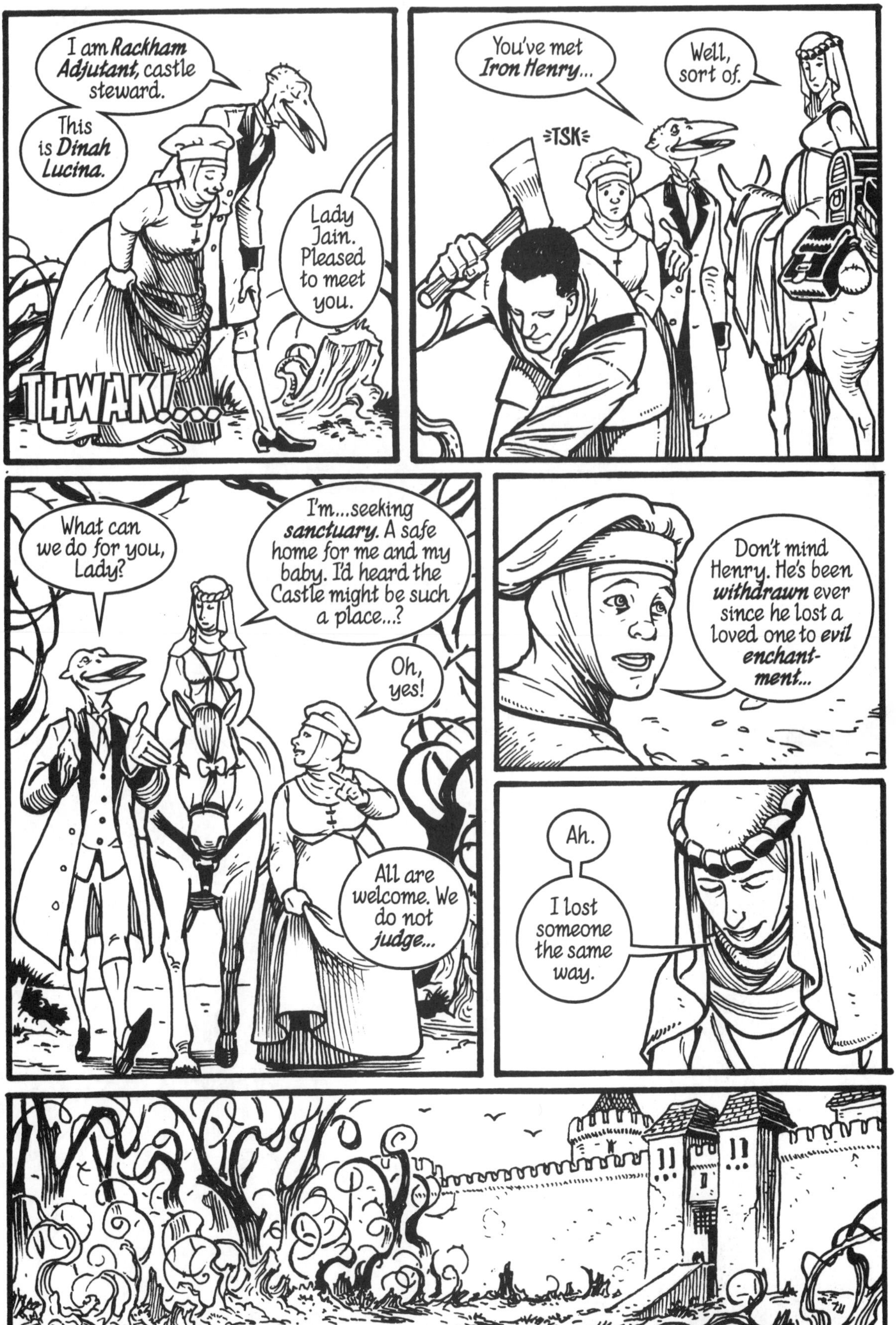

I am *Rackham Adjutant,* castle steward.
This is *Dinah Lucina.*
Lady Jain. Pleased to meet you.
THWAK!...
You've met *Iron Henry*...
Well, sort of.
TSK
What can we do for you, Lady?
I'm...seeking *sanctuary.* A safe home for me and my baby. I'd heard the Castle might be such a place...?
Oh, yes!
All are welcome. We do not *judge...*
Don't mind Henry. He's been *withdrawn* ever since he lost a loved one to *evil enchantment...*
Ah.
I lost someone the same way.

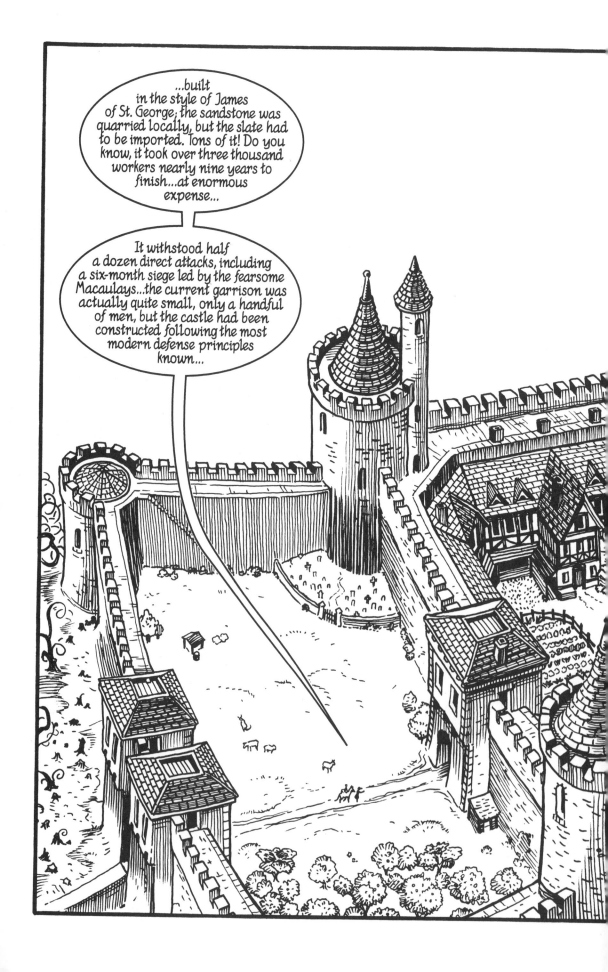

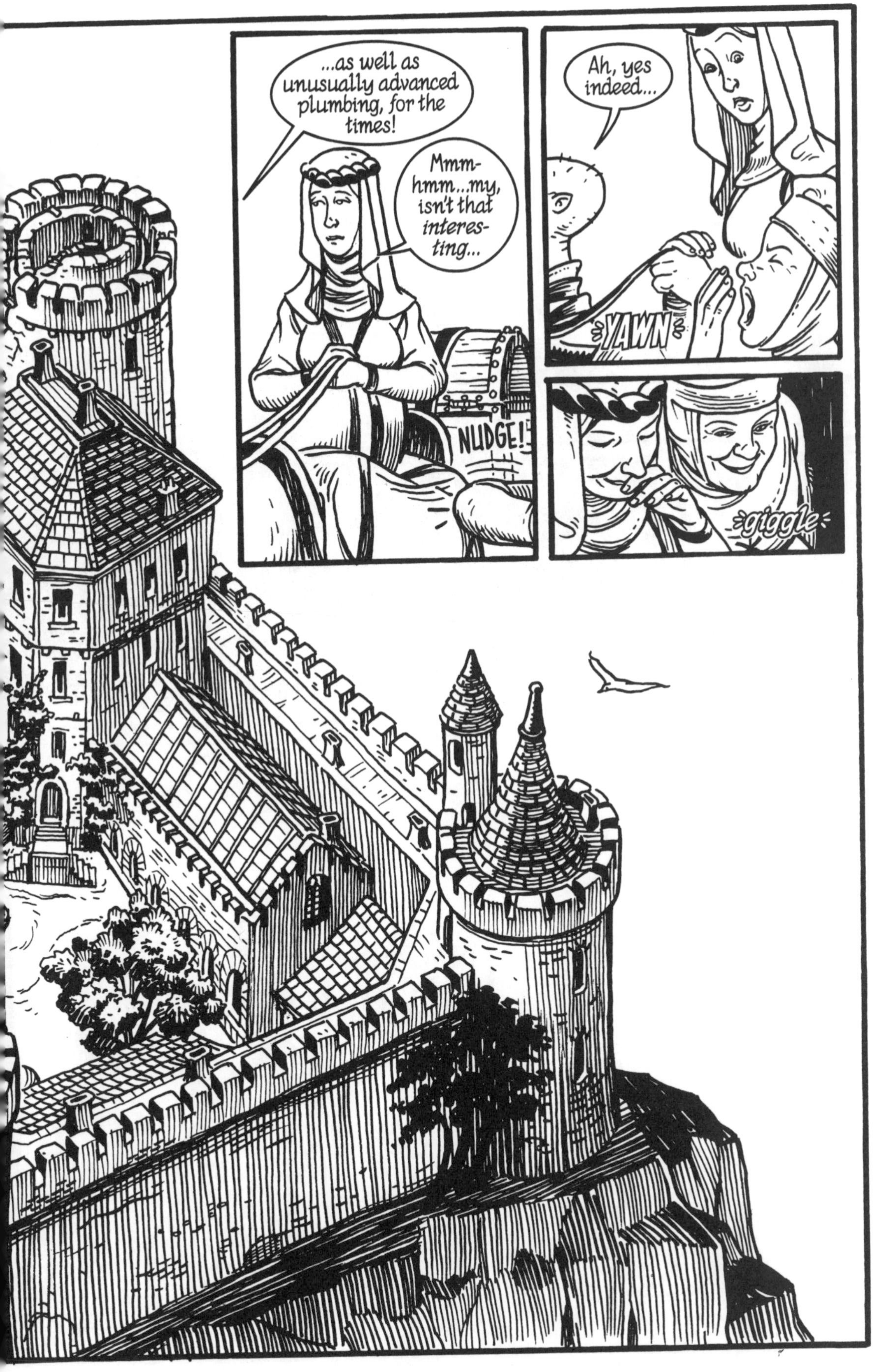
...as well as unusually advanced plumbing, for the times!
Mmm-hmm...my, isn't that interes-ting...
NUDGE!
Ah, yes indeed...
YAWN
giggle

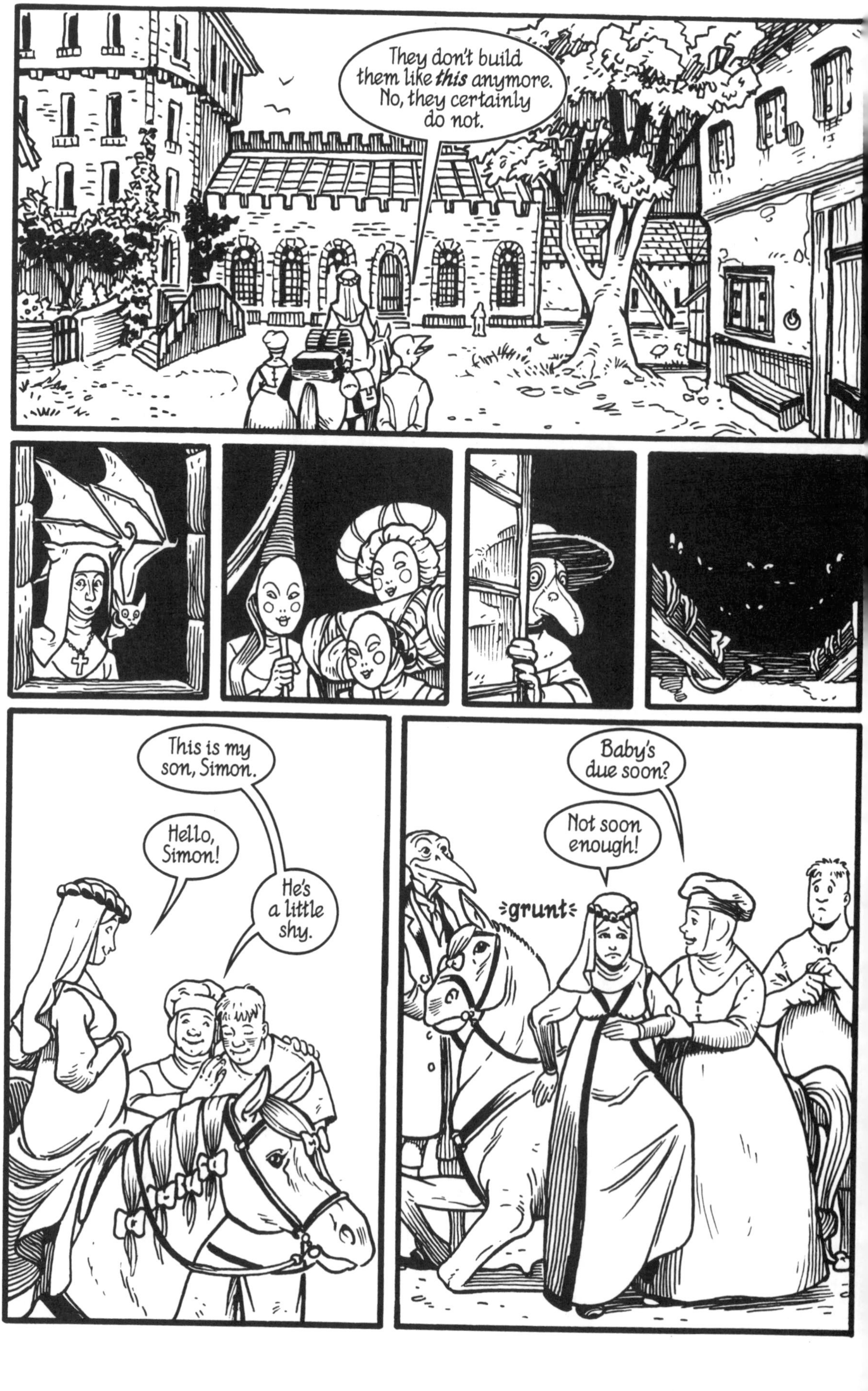
They don't build them like *this* anymore. No, they certainly do not.
This is my son, Simon.
Hello, Simon!
He's a little shy.
Baby's due soon?
Not soon enough!
grunt

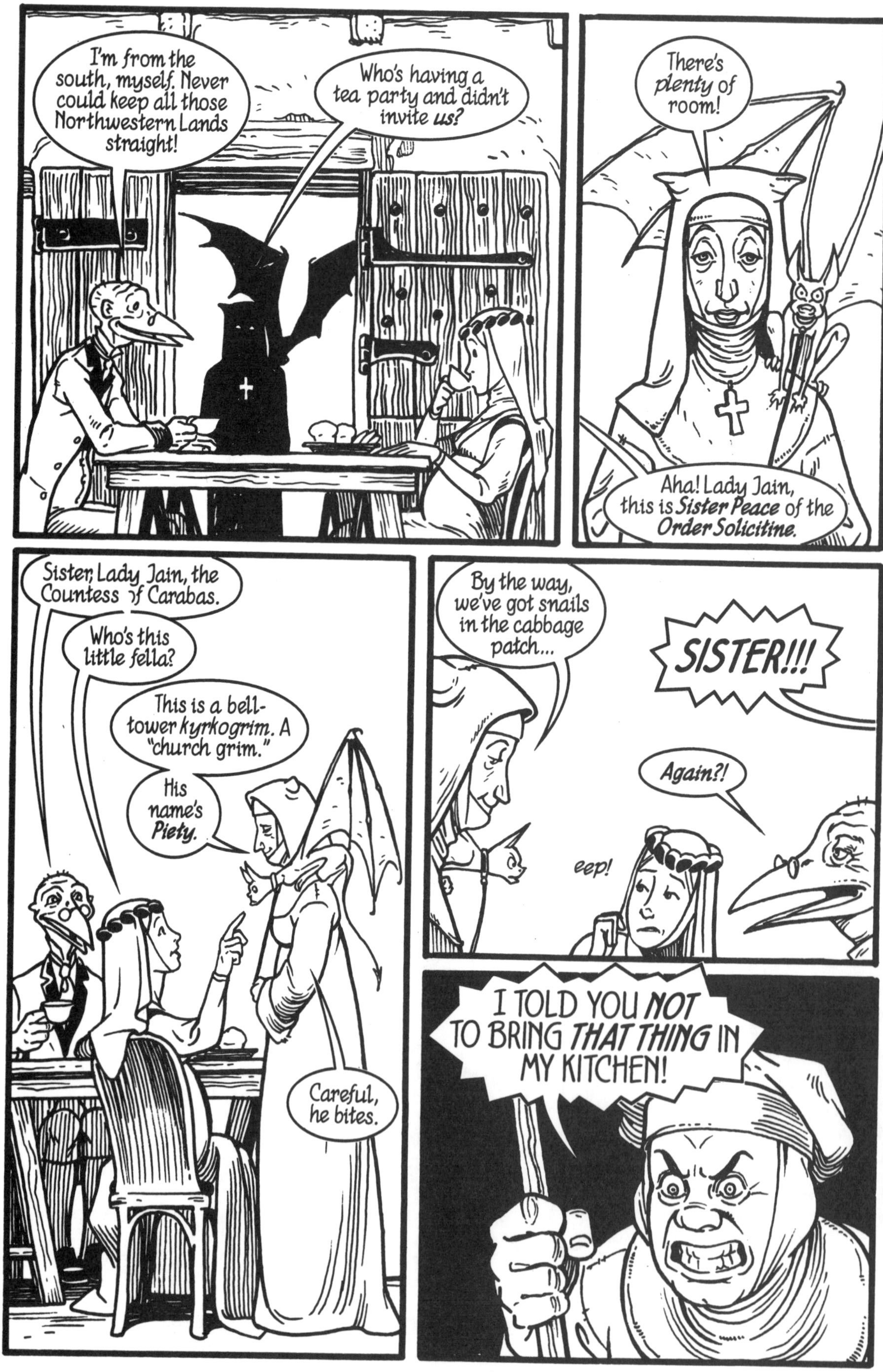
I'm from the south, myself. Never could keep all those Northwestern Lands straight!
Who's having a tea party and didn't invite *us?*
There's *plenty* of room!
Aha! Lady Jain, this is **Sister Peace** of the **Order Solicitine.**
Sister, Lady Jain, the Countess of Carabas.
Who's this little fella?
This is a bell-tower *kyrkogrim*. A "church grim."
His name's *Piety.*
Careful, he bites.
By the way, we've got snails in the cabbage patch...
SISTER!!!
Again?!
eep!
I TOLD YOU *NOT* TO BRING *THAT THING* IN MY KITCHEN!

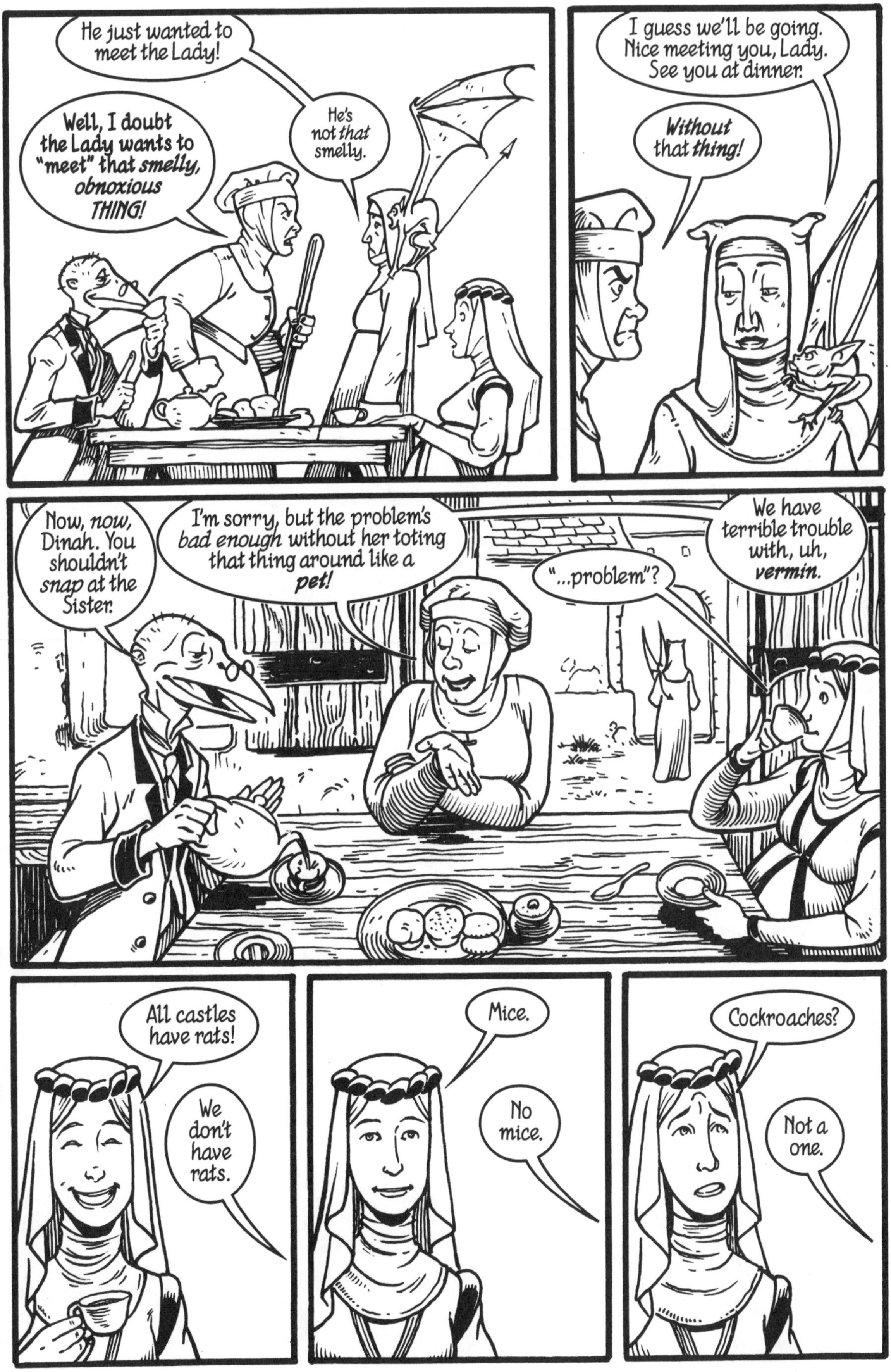
He just wanted to meet the Lady!
Well, I doubt the Lady wants to "meet" that *smelly, obnoxious THING!*
He's not *that* smelly.
I guess we'll be going. Nice meeting you, Lady. See you at dinner.
Without that *thing!*
Now, *now,* Dinah. You shouldn't *snap* at the Sister.
I'm sorry, but the problem's *bad enough* without her toting that thing around like a *pet!*
"...problem"?
We have terrible trouble with, uh, ***vermin.***
All castles have rats!
We don't have rats.
Mice.
No mice.
Cockroaches?
Not a one.

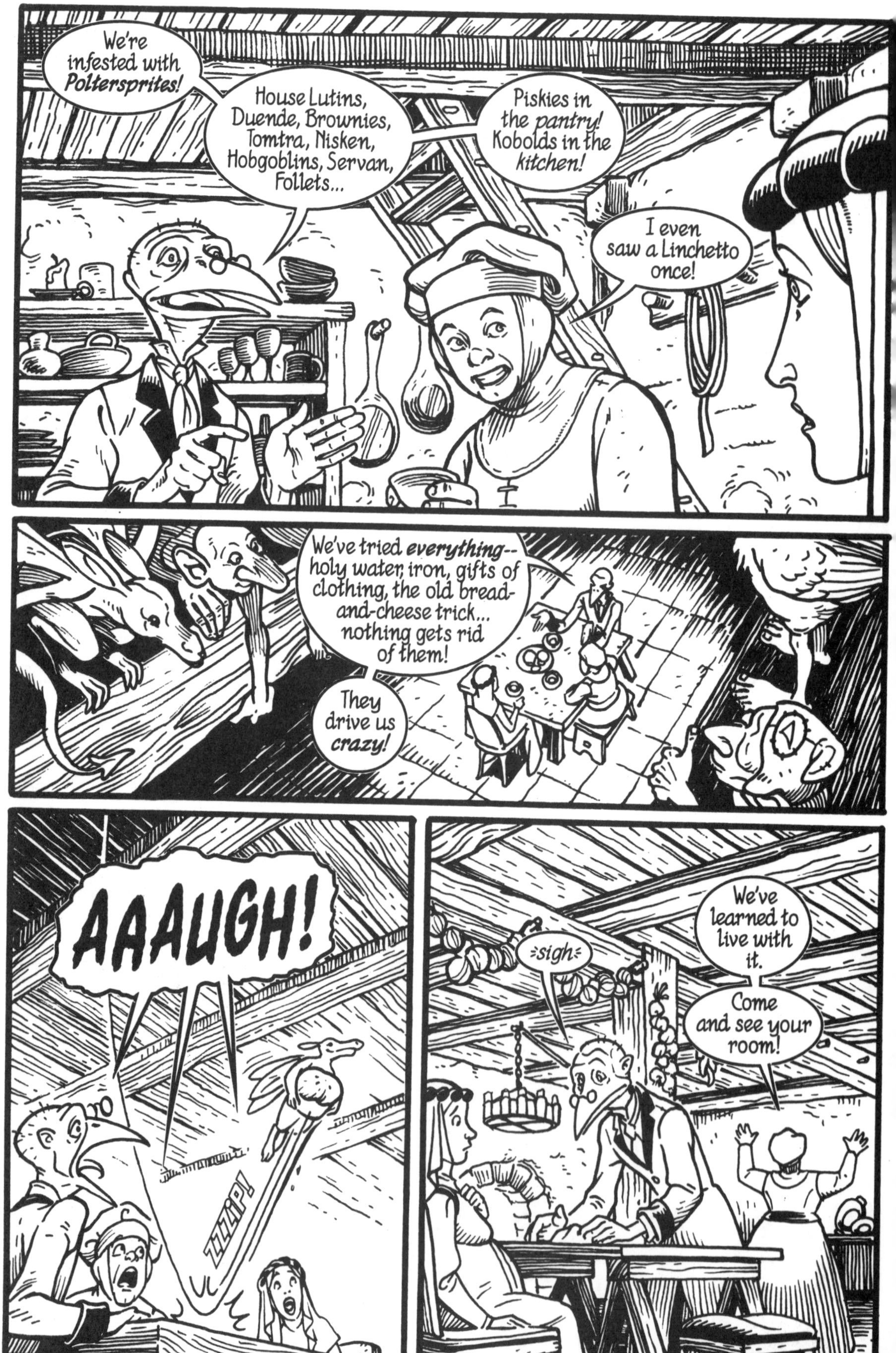
We're infested with Poltersprites!
House Lutins, Duende, Brownies, Tomtra, Nisken, Hobgoblins, Servan, Follets...
Piskies in the pantry! Kobolds in the kitchen!
I even saw a Linchetto once!
We've tried everything--holy water, iron, gifts of clothing, the old bread-and-cheese trick... nothing gets rid of them!
They drive us crazy!
AAAUGH!
ZZZIP!
sigh
We've learned to live with it.
Come and see your room!

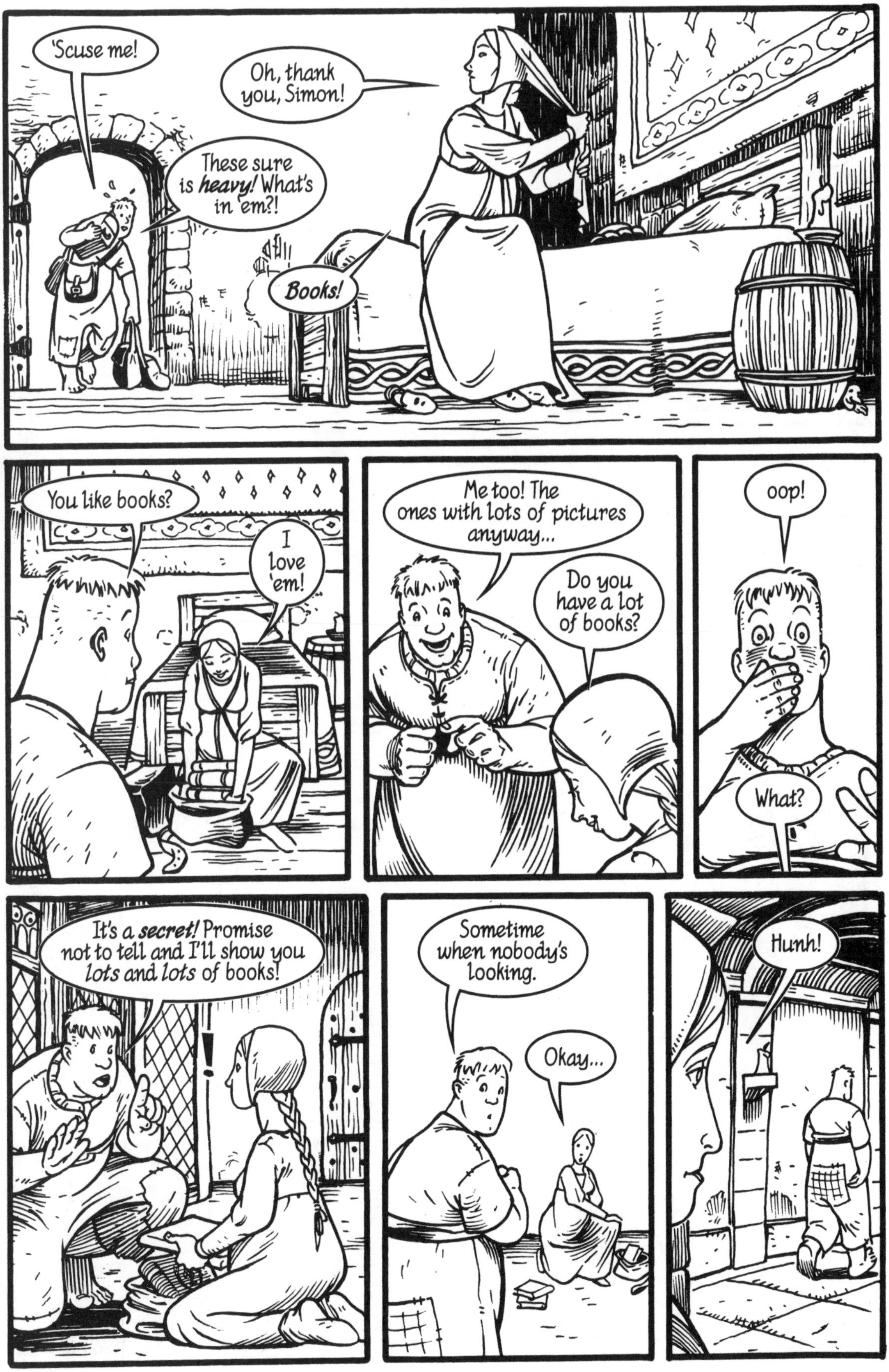
'Scuse me!
Oh, thank you, Simon!
These sure is *heavy!* What's in 'em?!
Books!
You like books?
I love 'em!
Me too! The ones with lots of pictures anyway...
Do you have a lot of books?
oop!
What?
It's a *secret!* Promise not to tell and I'll show you *lots and lots* of books!
!
Sometime when nobody's looking.
Okay...
Hunh!

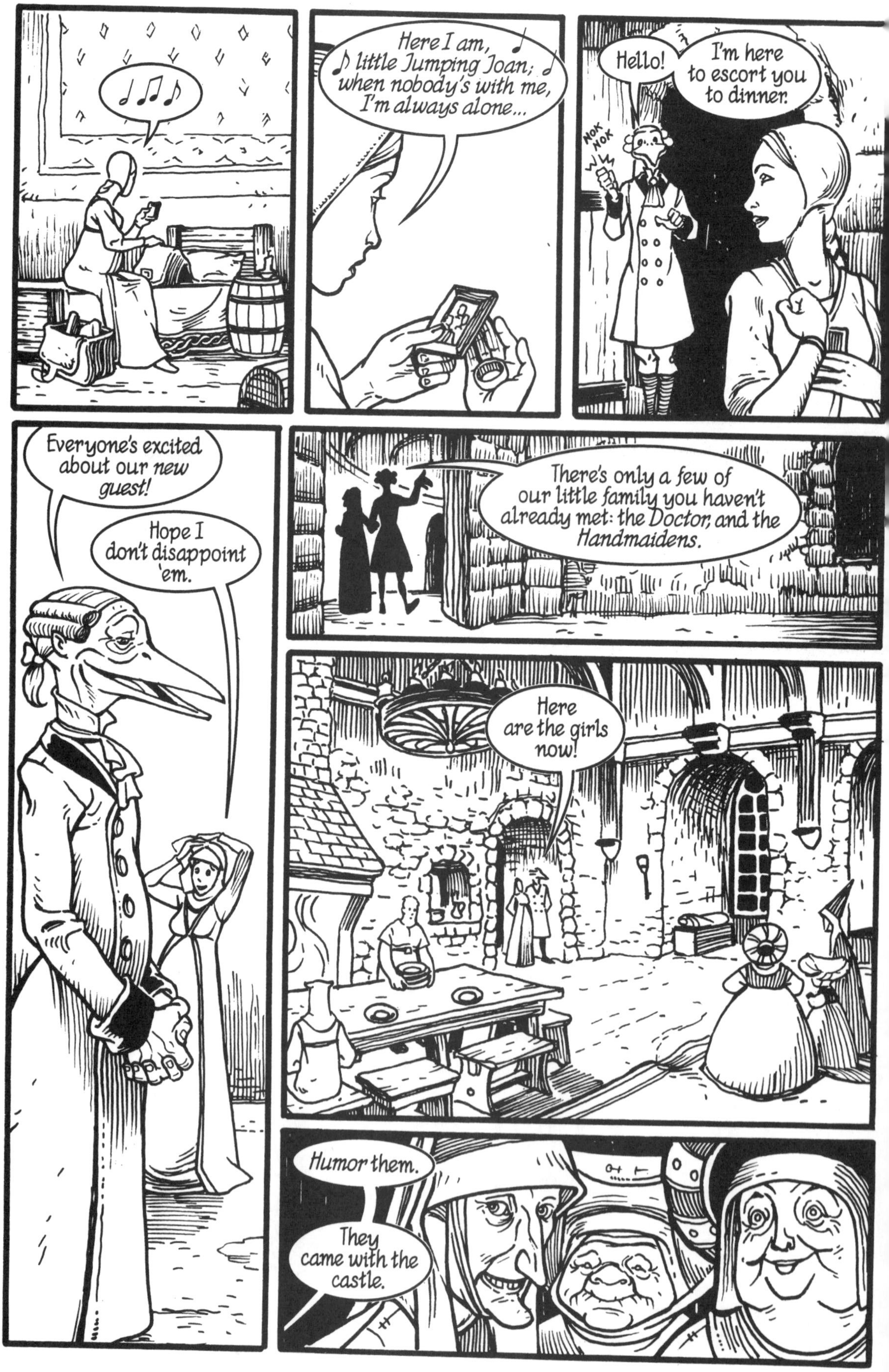
♩♫♪
Here I am, ♪ little Jumping Joan; ♩ when nobody's with me, I'm always alone...
NOK NOK
Hello!
I'm here to escort you to dinner.
Everyone's excited about our *new* guest!
Hope I don't disappoint 'em.
There's only a few of our little family you haven't already met: the *Doctor*, and the *Handmaidens*.
Here are the girls now!
Humor them.
They came with the castle.

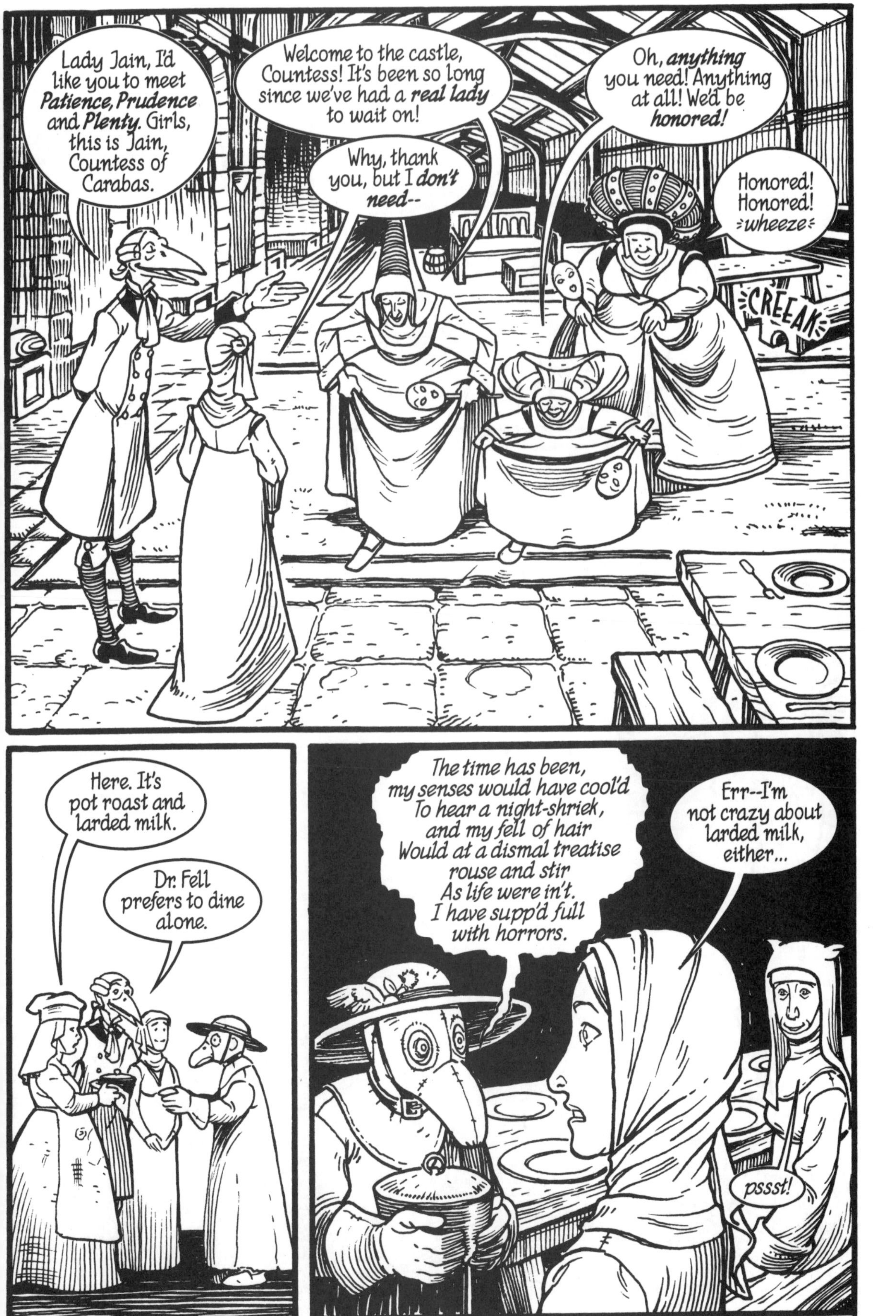
Lady Jain, I'd like you to meet **Patience, Prudence** and **Plenty**. Girls, this is Jain, Countess of Carabas.
Welcome to the castle, Countess! It's been so long since we've had a **real lady** to wait on!
Why, thank you, but I **don't need**--
Oh, **anything** you need! Anything at all! We'd be **honored!**
Honored! Honored! *wheeze*
CREEAK
Here. It's pot roast and larded milk.
Dr. Fell prefers to dine alone.
The time has been, my senses would have cool'd To hear a night-shriek, and my fell of hair Would at a dismal treatise rouse and stir As life were in't. I have supp'd full with horrors.
Err--I'm not crazy about larded milk, either...
pssst!

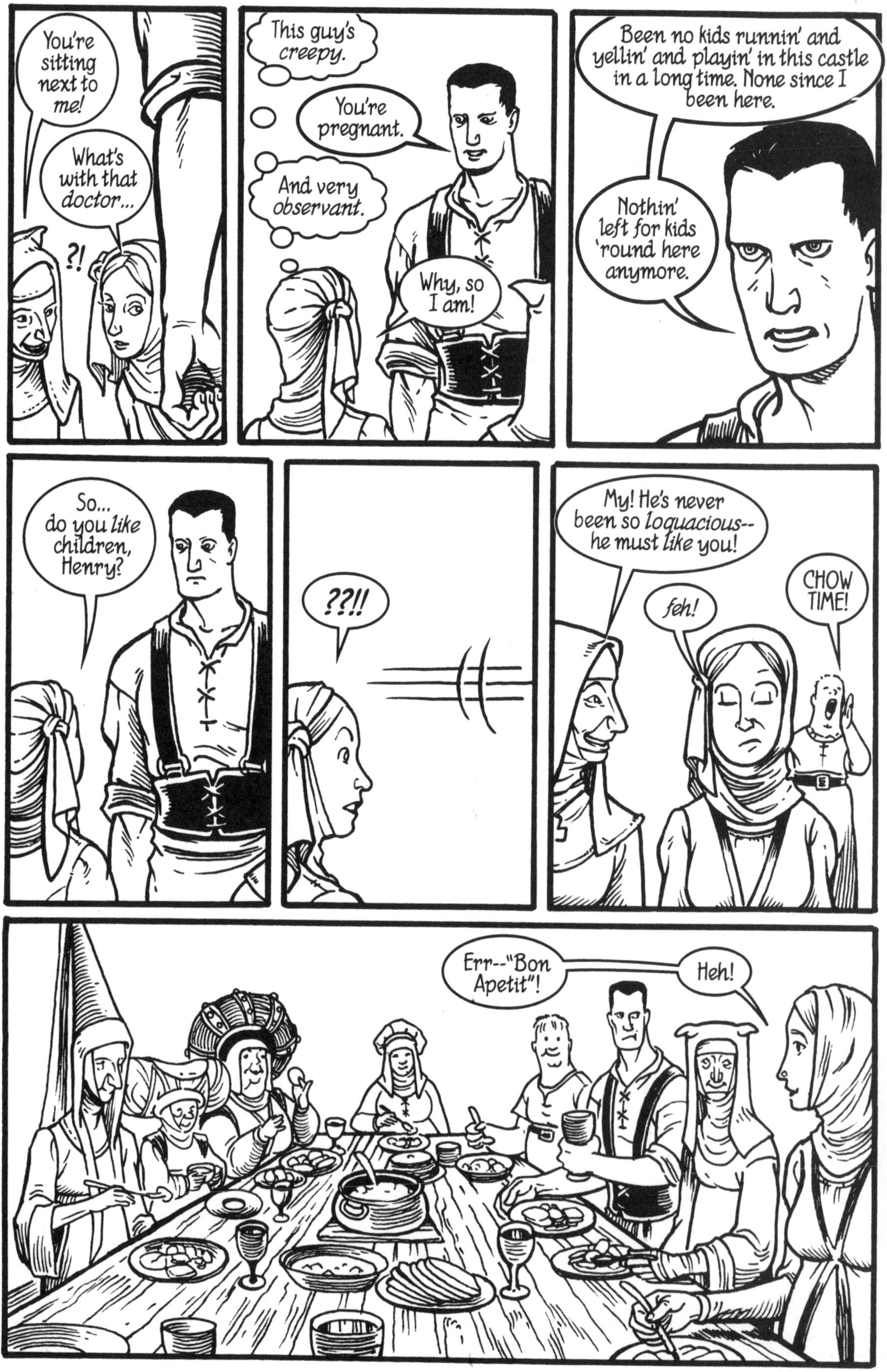

You're sitting next to me!
What's with that doctor...
?!
This guy's creepy.
You're pregnant.
And very observant.
Why, so I am!
Been no kids runnin' and yellin' and playin' in this castle in a long time. None since I been here.
Nothin' left for kids 'round here anymore.
So... do you like children, Henry?
??!!
My! He's never been so loquacious--he must like you!
feh!
CHOW TIME!
Err--"Bon Apetit"!
Heh!

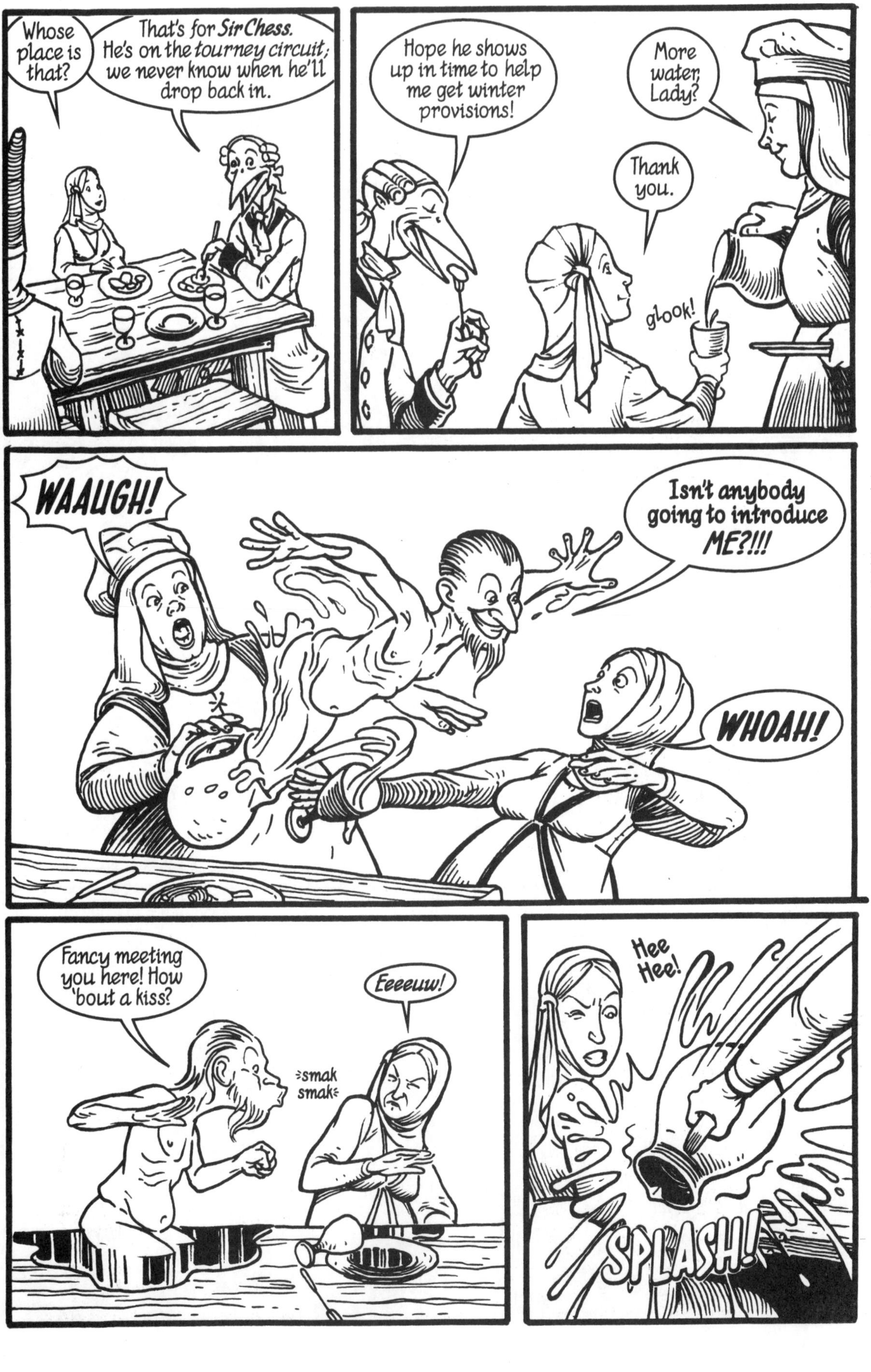
Whose place is that?
That's for Sir Chess. He's on the tourney circuit; we never know when he'll drop back in.
Hope he shows up in time to help me get winter provisions!
More water, Lady?
Thank you.
glook!
WAAUGH!
Isn't anybody going to introduce ME?!!!
WHOAH!
Fancy meeting you here! How 'bout a kiss?
Eeeeuw!
smak smak
Hee Hee!
SPLASH!

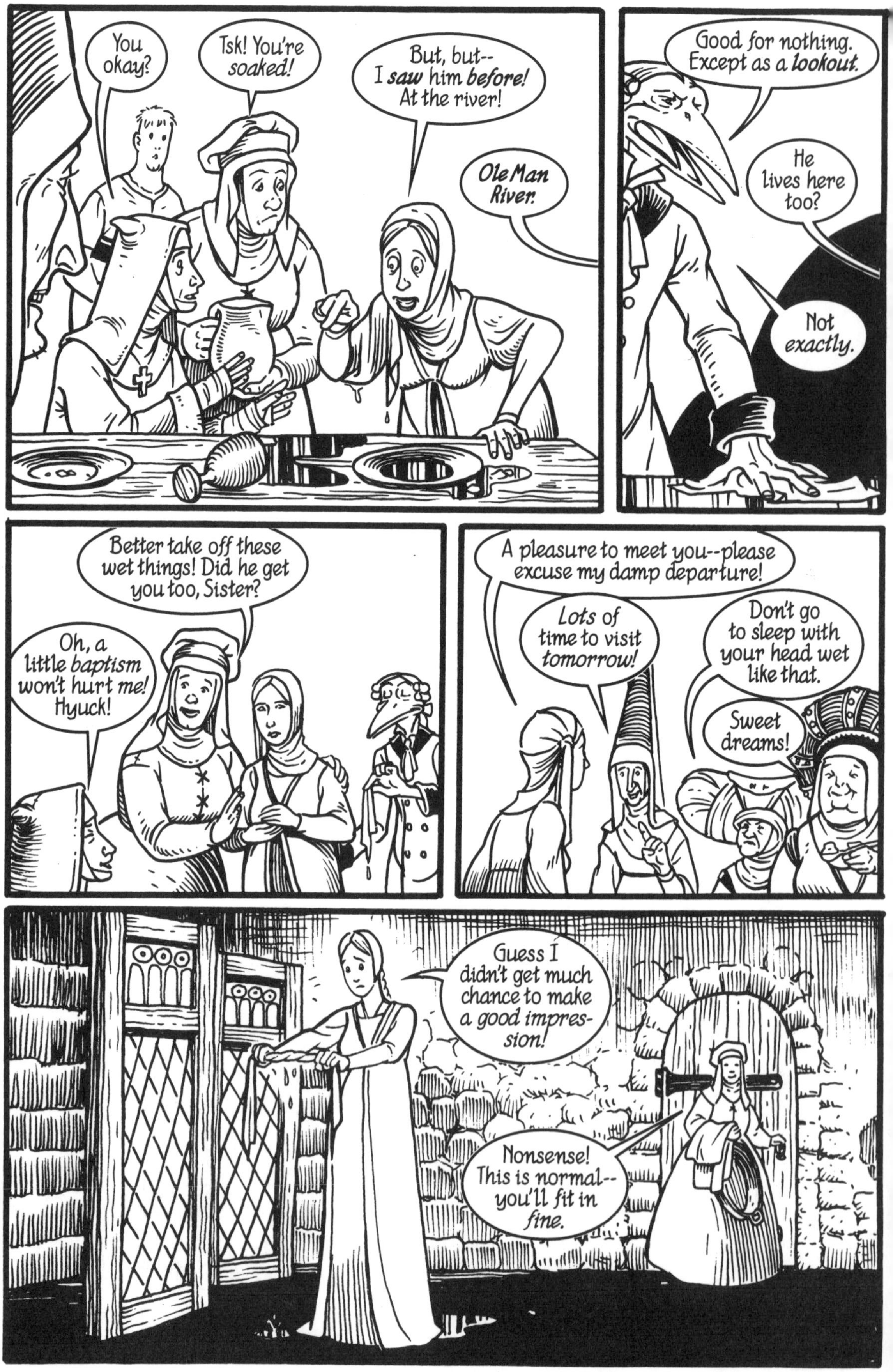
You okay?
Tsk! You're *soaked!*
But, but-- I *saw* him *before!* At the river!
Ole Man River.
Good for nothing. Except as a *lookout.*
He lives here too?
Not *exactly.*
Better take off these wet things! Did he get you too, Sister?
Oh, a little *baptism* won't hurt me! Hyuck!
A pleasure to meet you--please excuse my damp departure!
Lots of time to visit *tomorrow!*
Don't go to sleep with your head wet like that.
Sweet dreams!
Guess I didn't get much chance to make a *good impression!*
Nonsense! This is normal--you'll fit in *fine.*

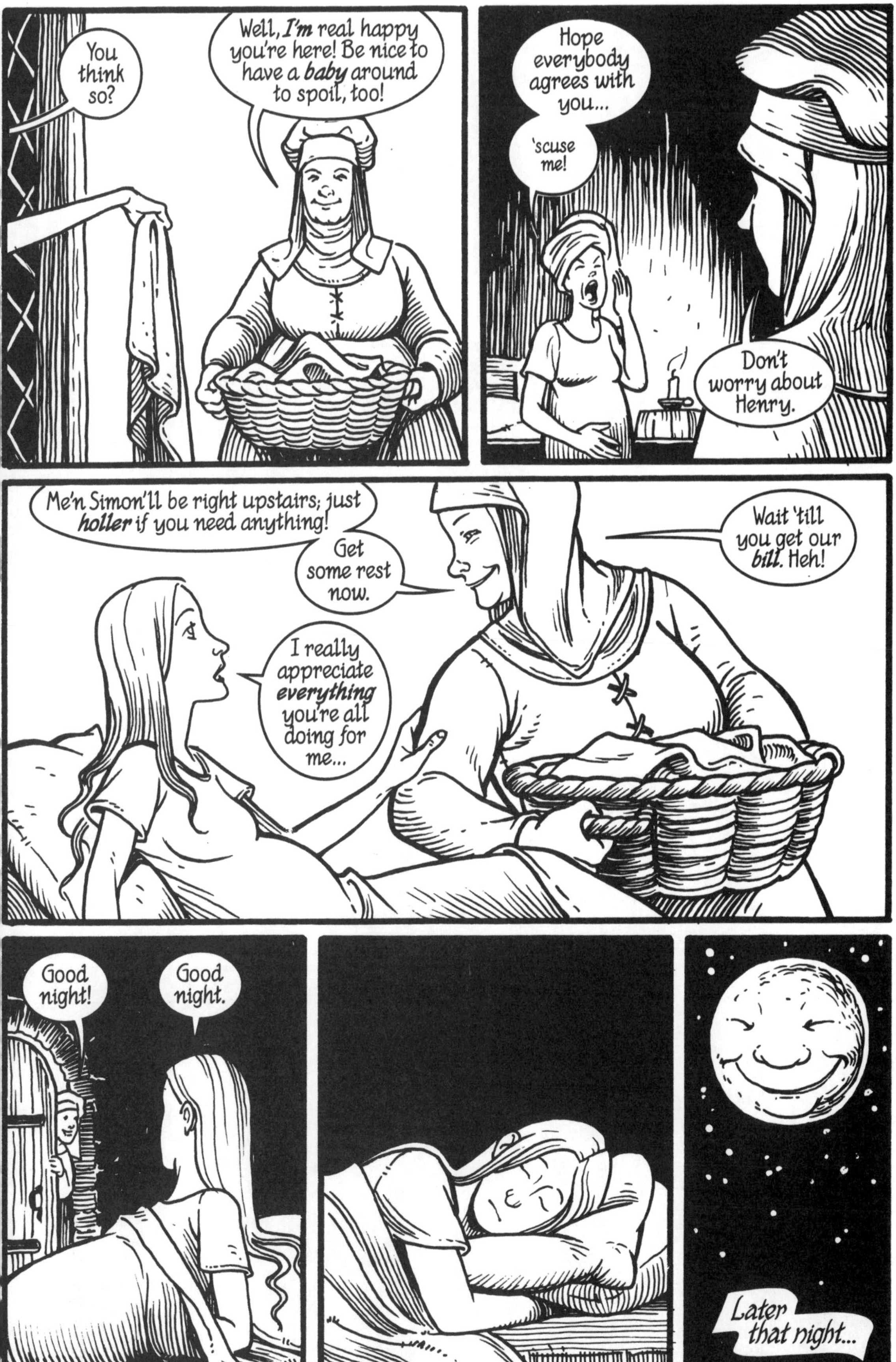
You think so?
Well, I'm real happy you're here! Be nice to have a baby around to spoil, too!
Hope everybody agrees with you...
'scuse me!
Don't worry about Henry.
Me'n Simon'll be right upstairs; just holler if you need anything!
Get some rest now.
Wait 'till you get our bill. Heh!
I really appreciate everything you're all doing for me...
Good night!
Good night.
Later that night...

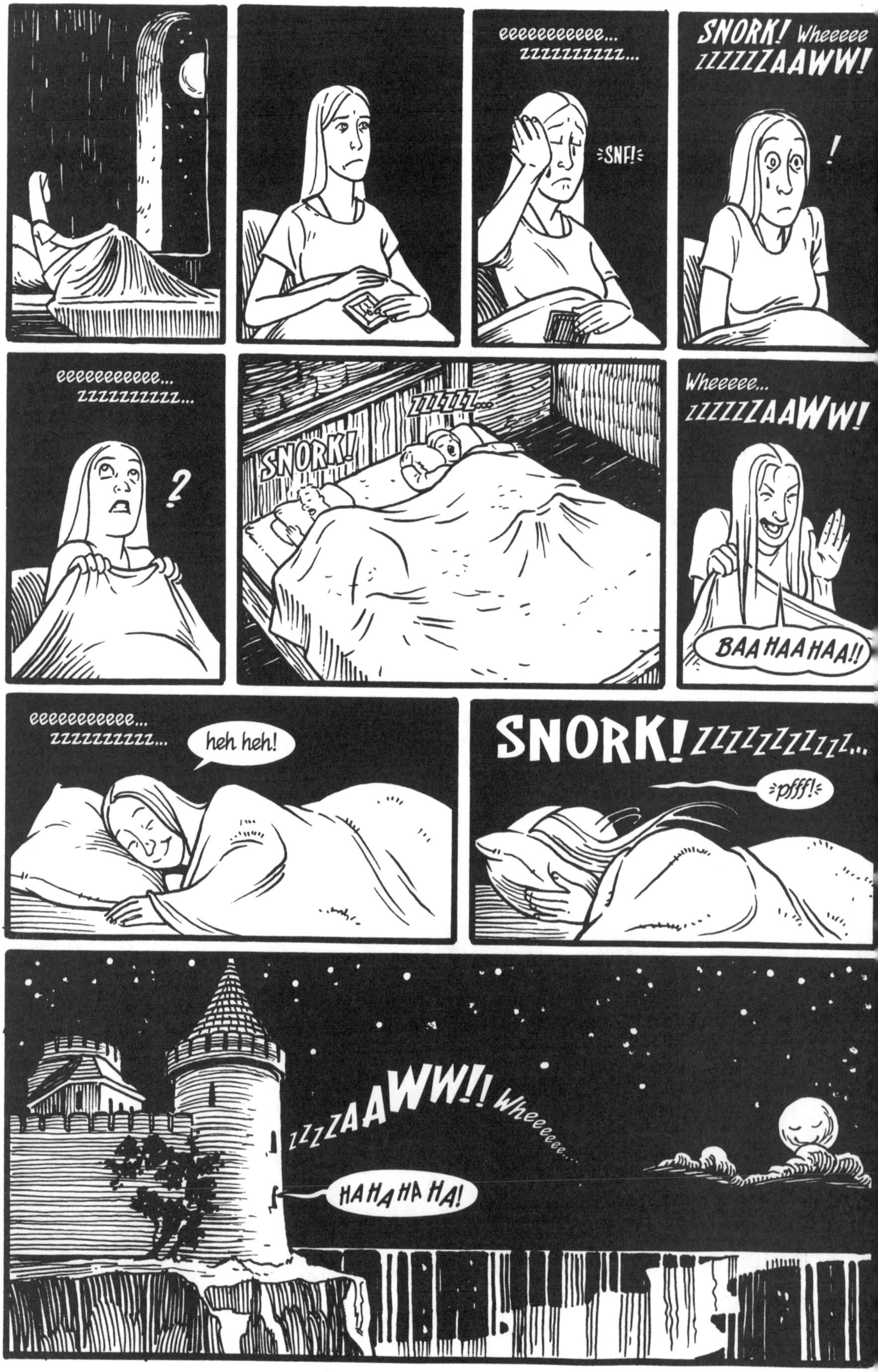
eeeeeeeeeee...
zzzzzzzzzz...
SNF!
SNORK! Wheeeee
zzzzzZAAWW!
!
eeeeeeeeeee...
zzzzzzzzzz...
?
SNORK!
zzzzz...
Wheeeee...
zzzzzZAAWW!
BAA HAA HAA!!
eeeeeeeeeee...
zzzzzzzzzz...
heh heh!
SNORK! zzzzzzzzzz...
pfff!
zzzzAAWW!! Wheeeeee...
HA HA HA HA!

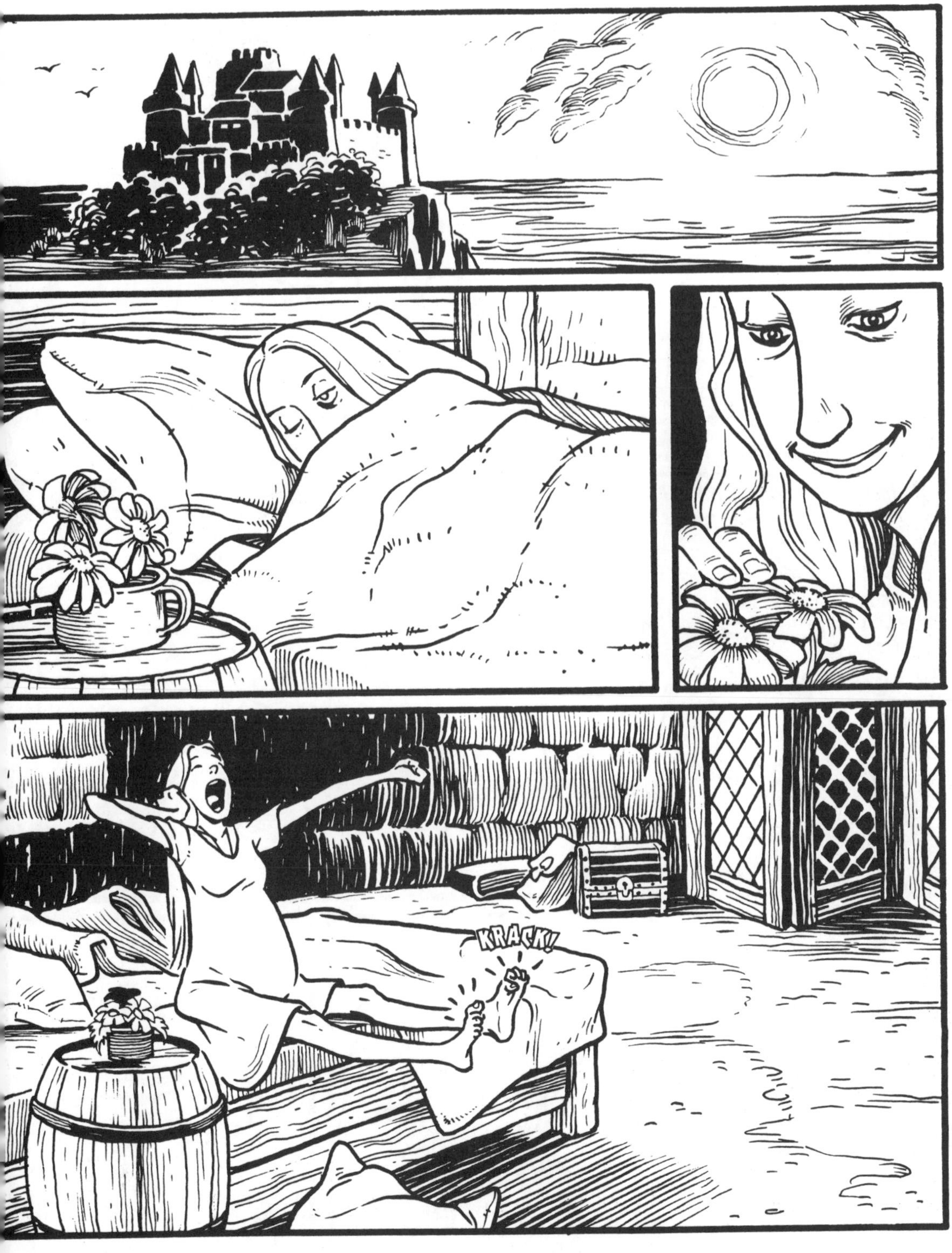
KRACK!

Labors of Love

Story and Art by LINDA MEDLEY ~ Lettering by TODD KLEIN

Rackham will eventually find *something* for you to do, but I doubt it'll be *peeling vegetables.*

Everyone pitches in and helps with the work. Well, except Dr. Fell--he keeps to *himself...*

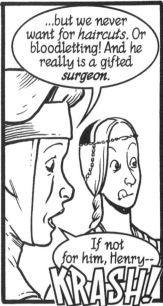

...but we never want for *haircuts.* Or *bloodletting!* And he really is a gifted *surgeon.*

If not for him, Henry--

KRASH!

#@$%!!

*$@+!! #&;%!!

Shoo!

Excuuuse *me!*

Go get some *fresh* air!

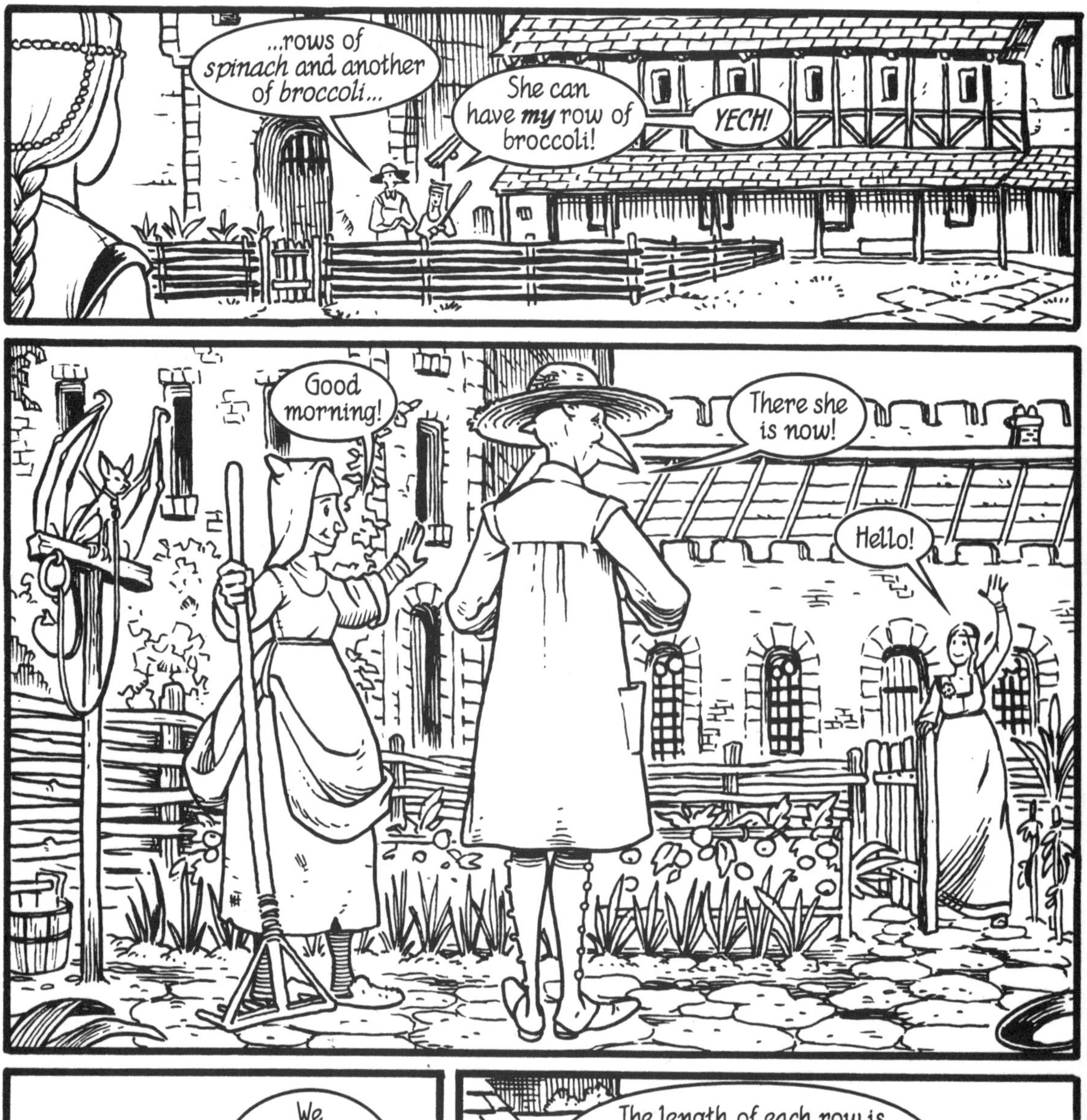
...rows of *spinach* and another of *broccoli*...
She can have ***my*** row of broccoli!
YECH!
Good morning!
There she is now!
Hello!
We were just planning ***your space*** in the garden.
The length of each row is *scientifically* calculated to feed ***one person***...whenever we get a new person, we just add one row of *each!*
Everyone helps out!

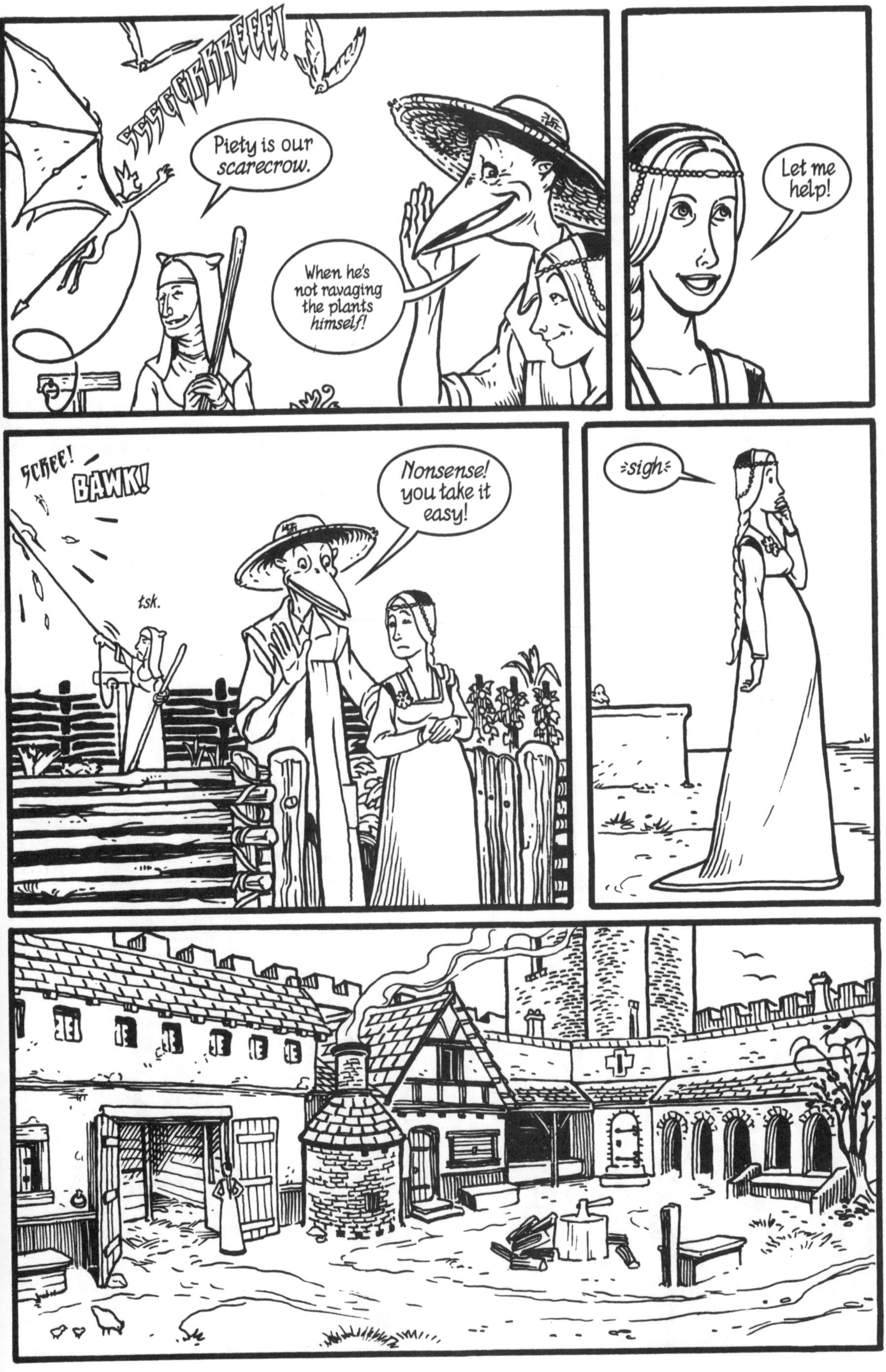
SSSCRRREEE!
Piety is our scarecrow.
When he's not ravaging the plants himself!
Let me help!
SCREE!
BAWK!
Nonsense! you take it easy!
tsk.
sigh

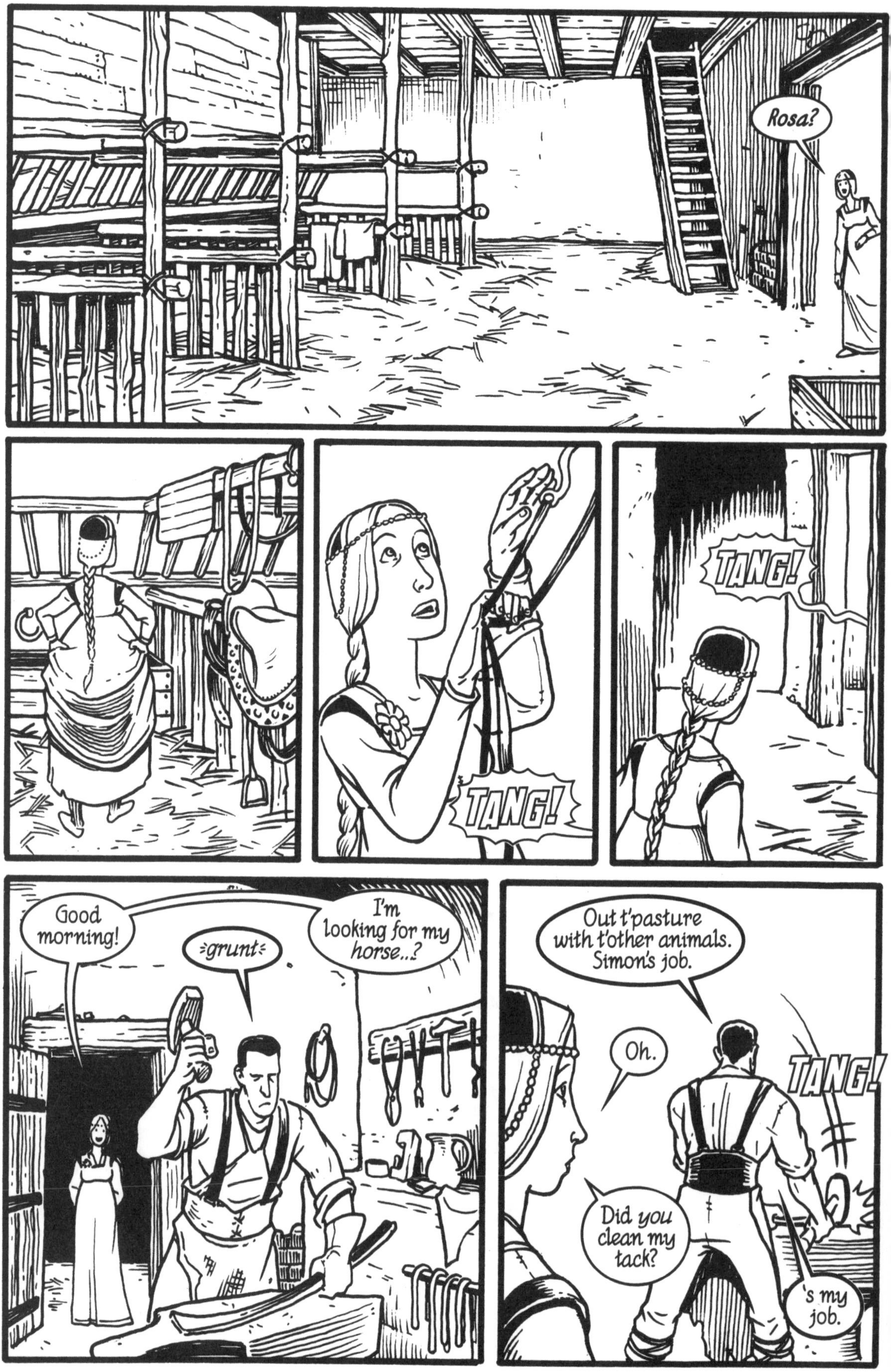
Rosa?
TANG!
TANG!
Good morning!
grunt
I'm looking for my horse...?
Out t'pasture with t'other animals. Simon's job.
Oh.
TANG!
Did you clean my tack?
's my job.

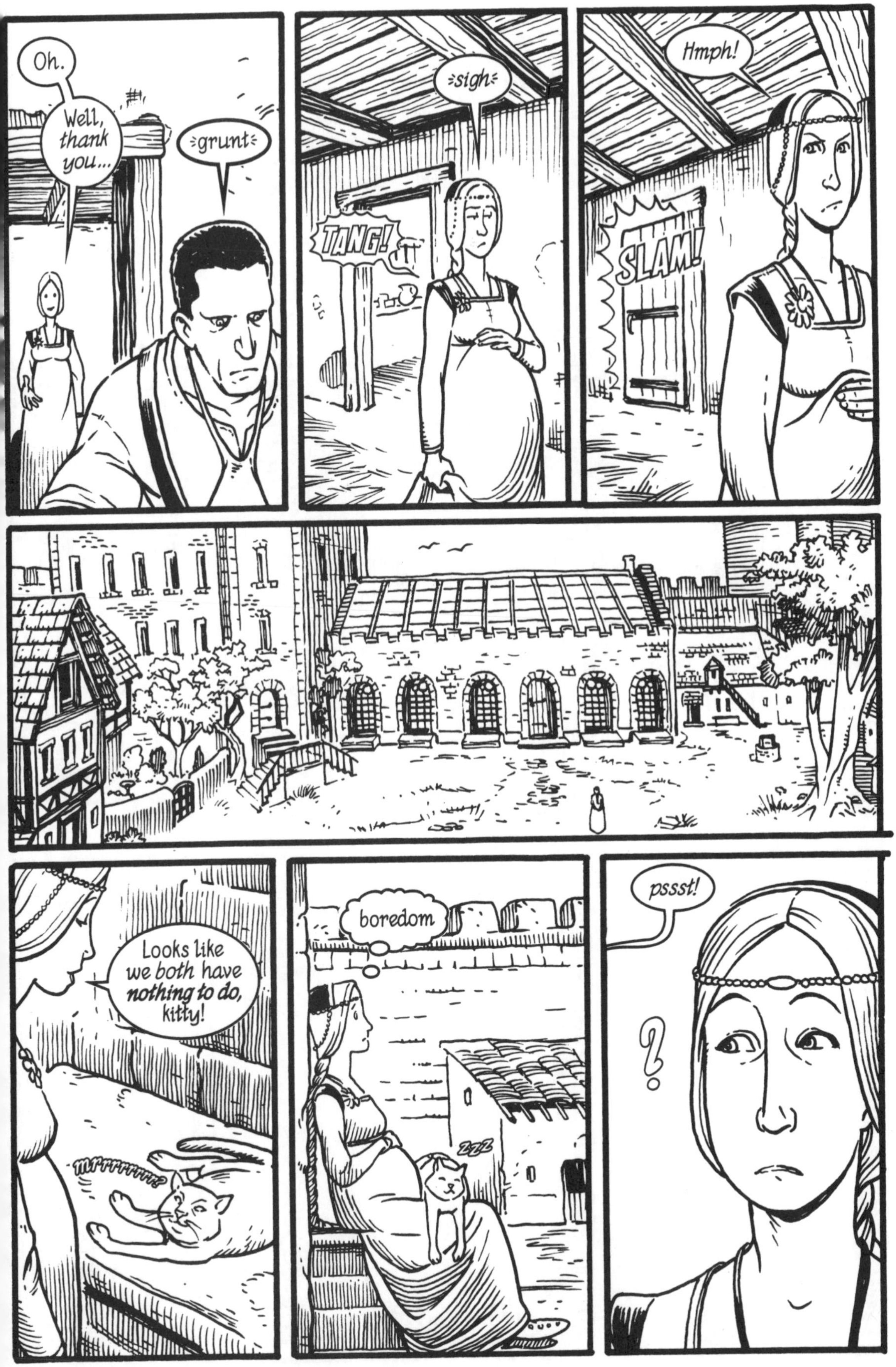
Oh.
Well, thank you...
grunt
sigh
TANG!
Hmph!
SLAM!
Looks like we both have nothing to do, kitty!
mrrrrrrrr?
boredom
zzz
pssst!
?

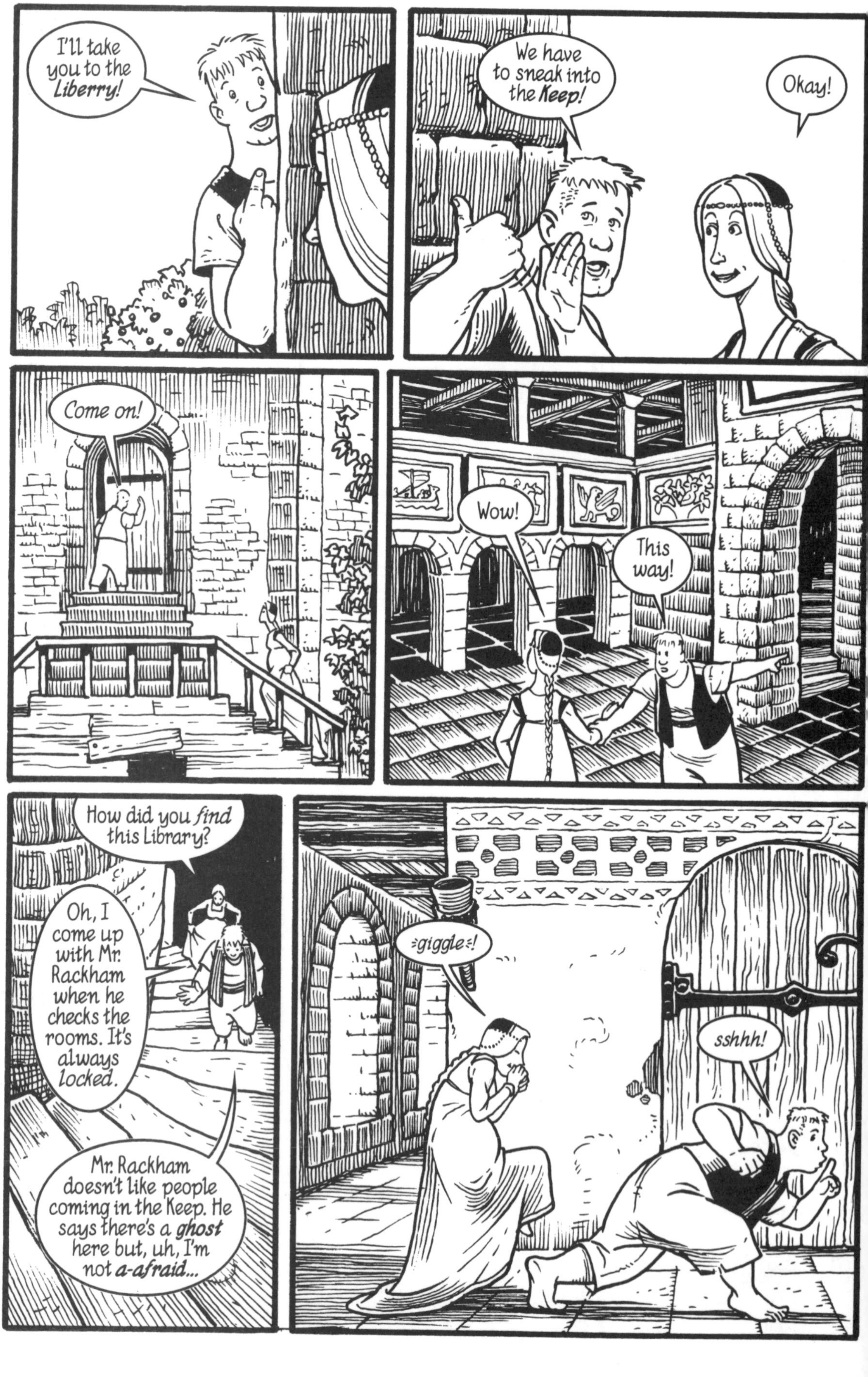
I'll take you to the *Liberry!*
We have to sneak into the *Keep!*
Okay!
Come on!
Wow!
This way!
How did you *find* this Library?
Oh, I come up with Mr. Rackham when he checks the rooms. It's always *locked*.
Mr. Rackham doesn't like people coming in the Keep. He says there's a ***ghost*** here but, uh, I'm not ***a-afraid...***
giggle!
sshhh!

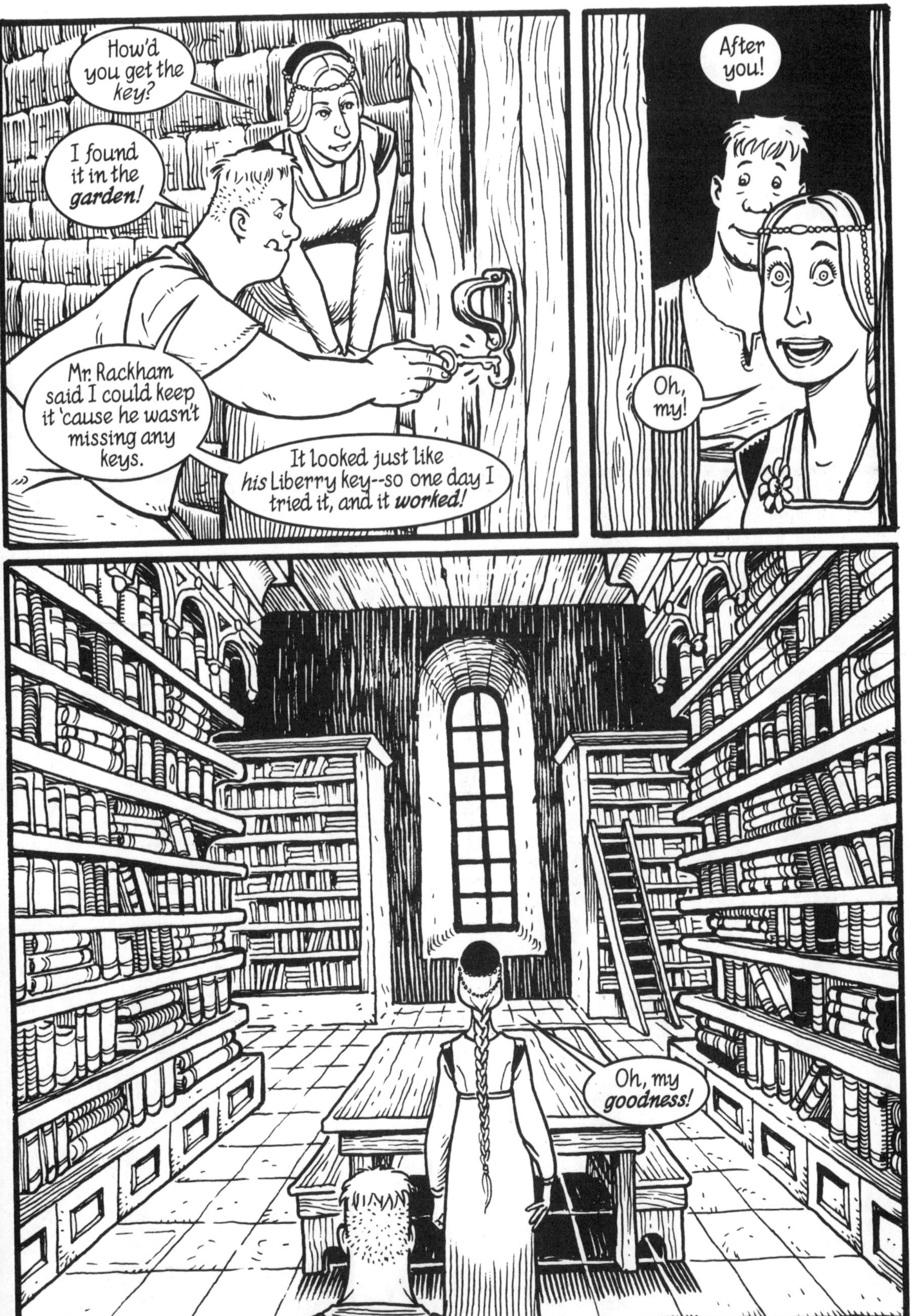
How'd you get the key?
I found it in the *garden!*
Mr. Rackham said I could keep it 'cause he wasn't missing any keys.
It looked just like *his* Liberry key--so one day I tried it, and it *worked!*
After you!
Oh, my!
Oh, my *goodness!*

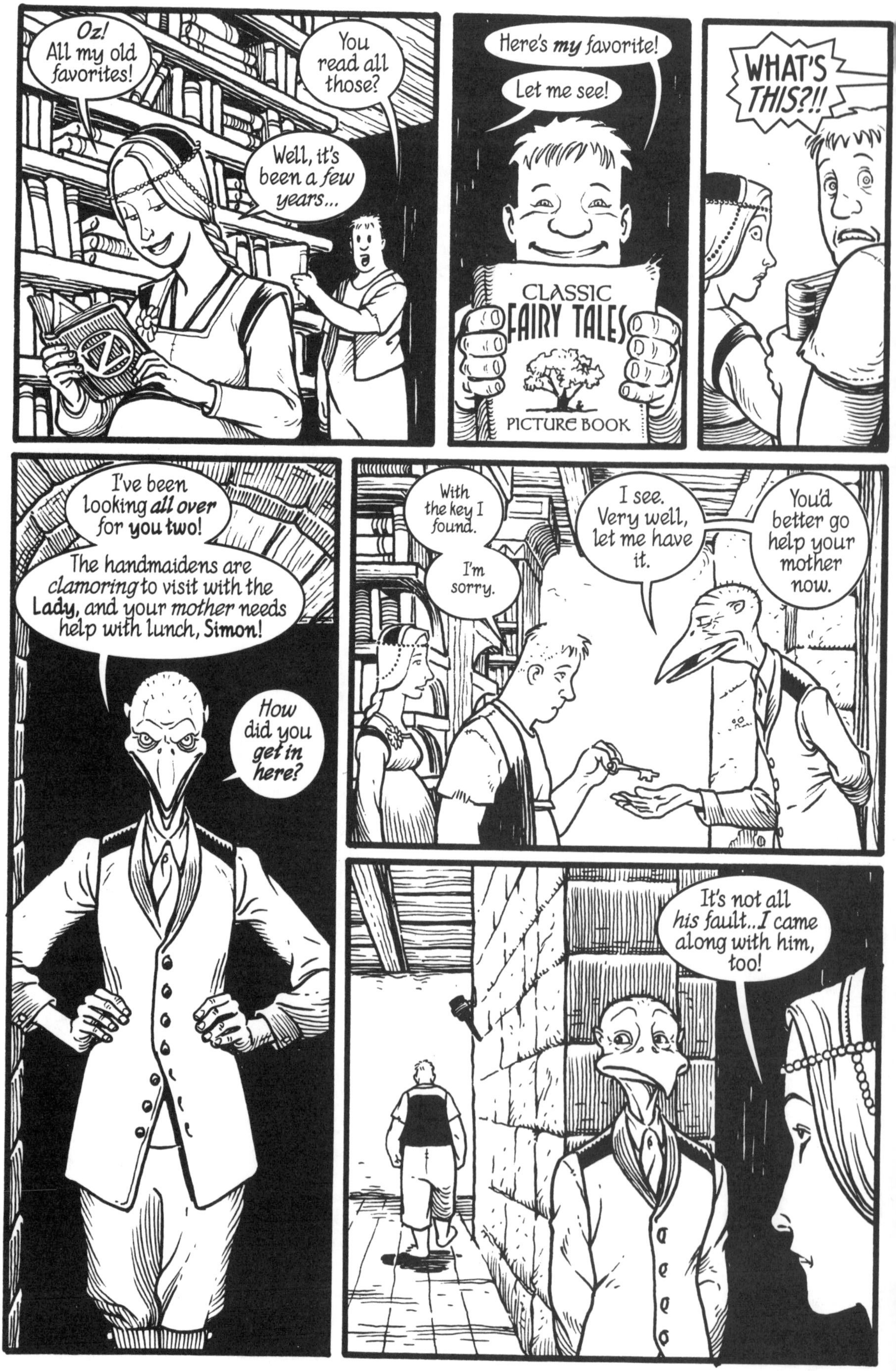
Oz! All my old favorites!
You read all those?
Well, it's been a few years...
Here's my favorite!
Let me see!
CLASSIC FAIRY TALES PICTURE BOOK
WHAT'S THIS?!!
I've been looking all over for you two!
The handmaidens are clamoring to visit with the Lady, and your mother needs help with lunch, Simon!
How did you get in here?
With the key I found.
I'm sorry.
I see. Very well, let me have it.
You'd better go help your mother now.
It's not all his fault...I came along with him, too!

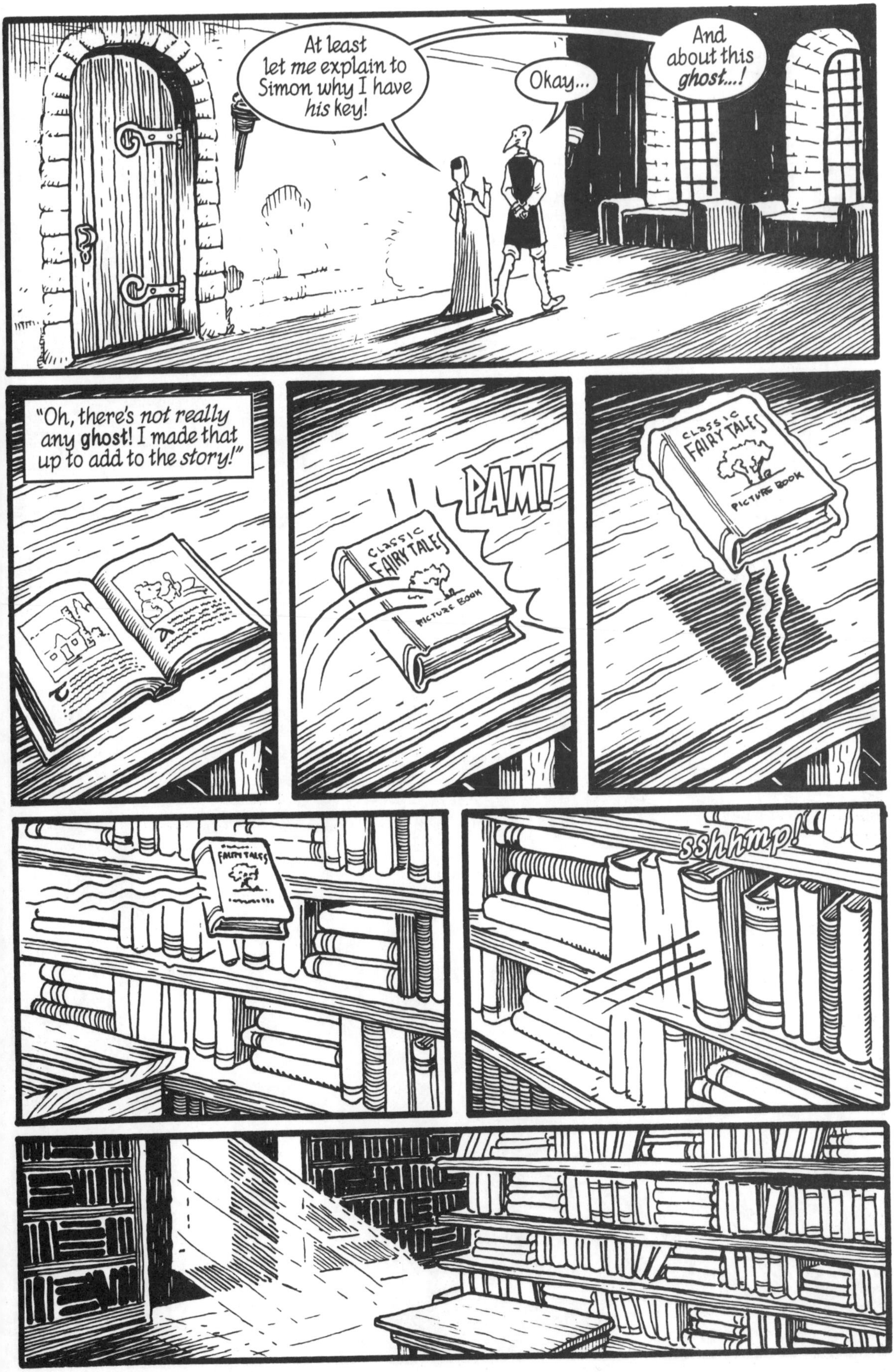
At least let me explain to Simon why I have his key!
Okay...
And about this ghost...!
"Oh, there's not really any ghost! I made that up to add to the story!"
PAM!
CLASSIC FAIRY TALES PICTURE BOOK
sshhmp!

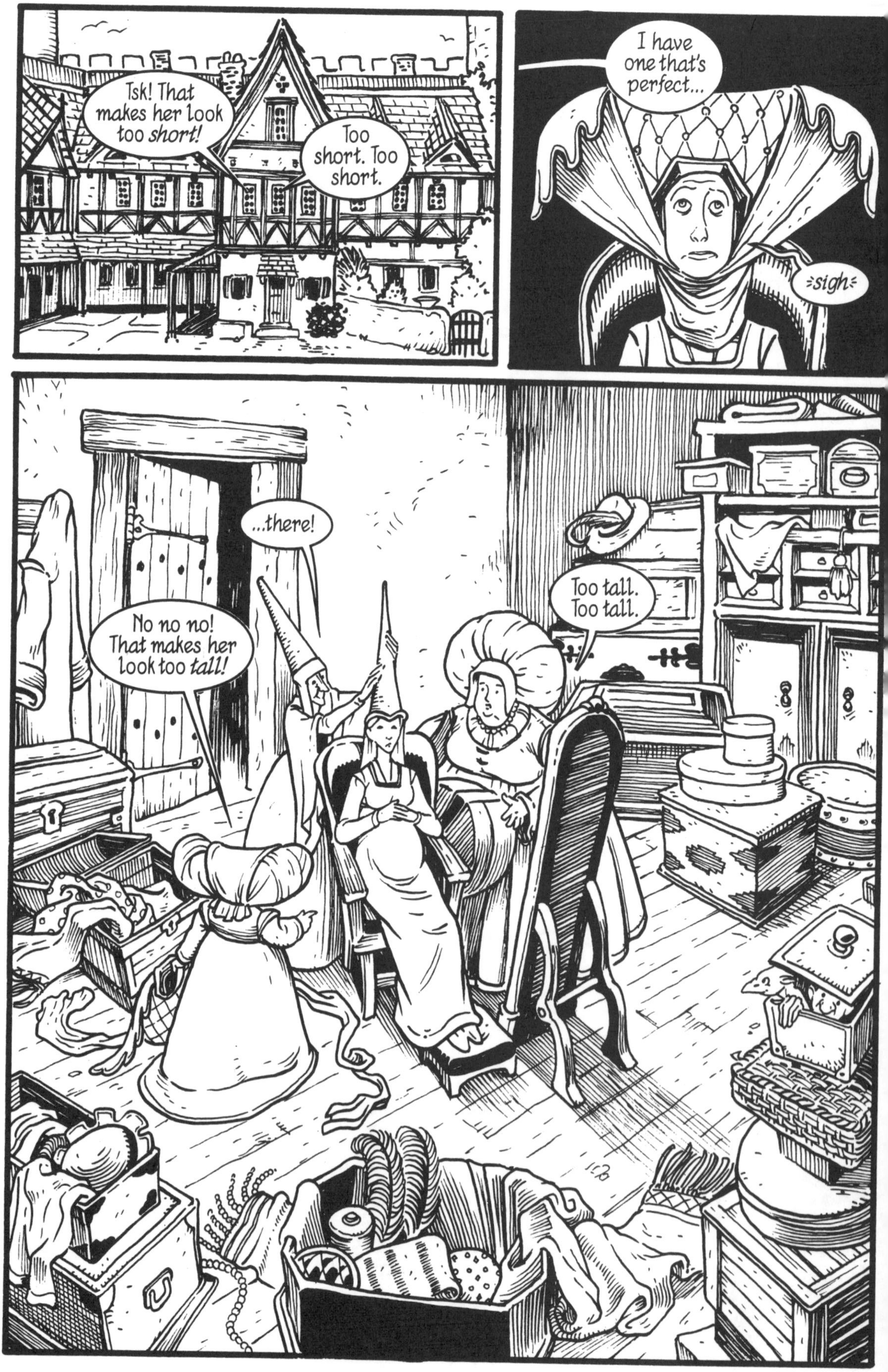
Tsk! That makes her look too *short!*
Too short. Too short.
I have one that's perfect...
sigh
...there!
No no no! That makes her look too *tall!*
Too tall. Too tall.

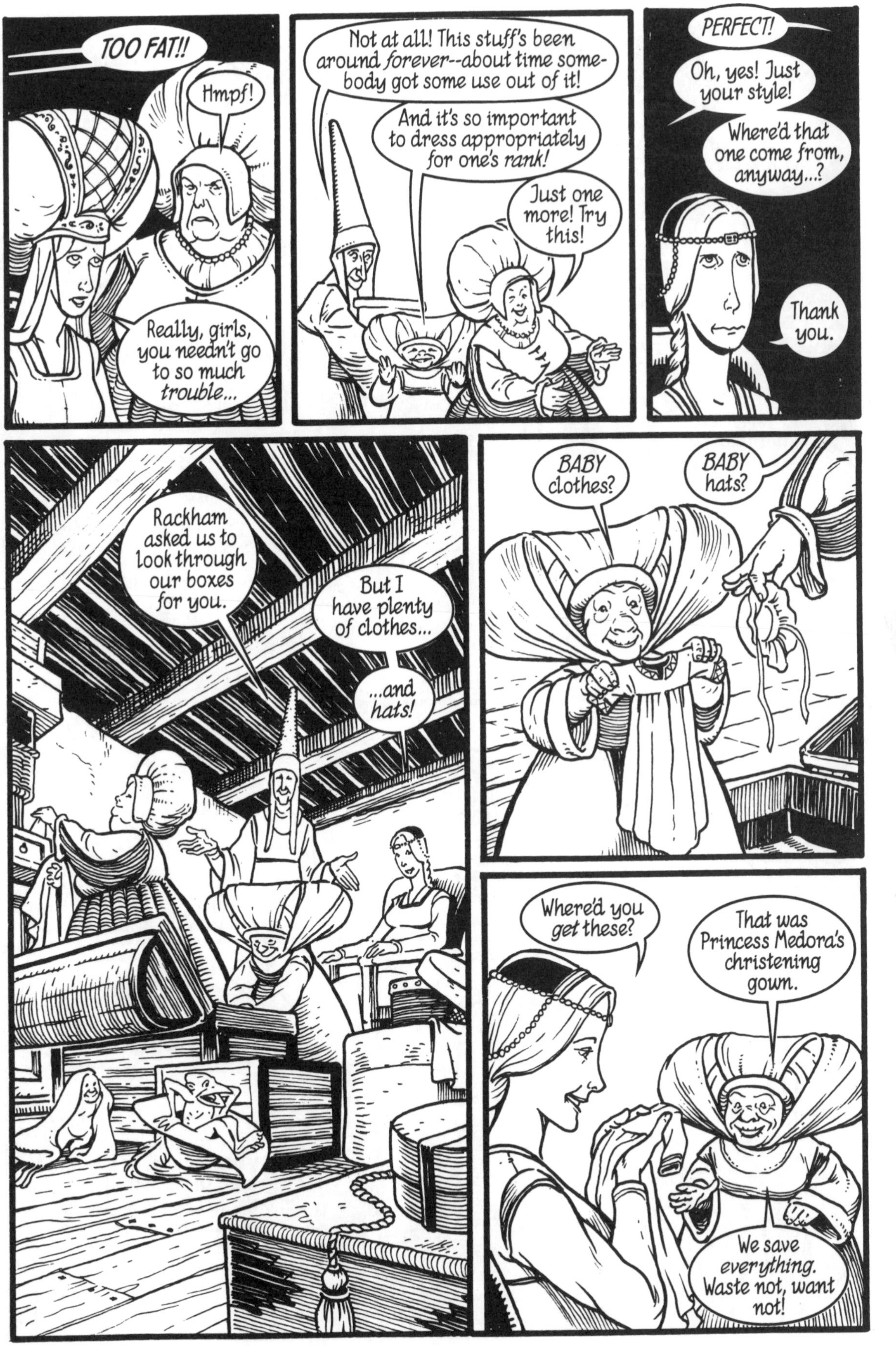
TOO FAT!!
Hmpf!
Really, girls, you needn't go to so much *trouble*...
Not at all! This stuff's been around *forever*--about time somebody got some use out of it!
And it's so important to dress appropriately for one's *rank*!
Just one more! Try this!
PERFECT!
Oh, yes! Just your style!
Where'd that one come from, anyway...?
Thank you.
Rackham asked us to look through our boxes for you.
But I have plenty of clothes...
...and *hats*!
BABY clothes?
BABY hats?
Where'd you *get* these?
That was Princess Medora's christening gown.
We save *everything*. Waste not, want not!

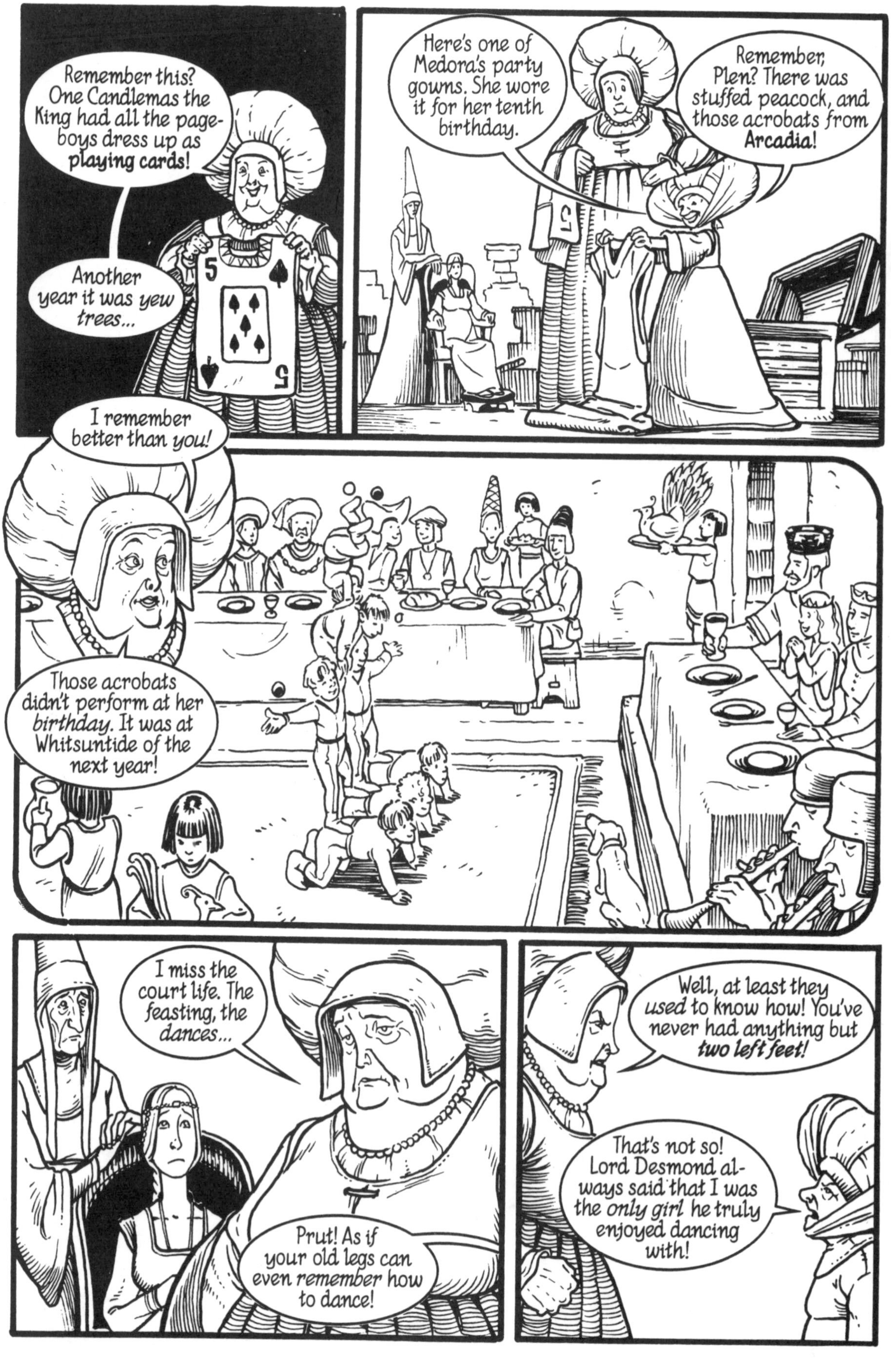
Remember this? One Candlemas the King had all the page-boys dress up as **playing cards**!
Another year it was *yew trees*...
Here's one of Medora's party gowns. She wore it for her tenth birthday.
Remember, Plen? There was stuffed peacock, and those acrobats from **Arcadia**!
I remember better than *you*!
Those acrobats didn't perform at her *birthday*. It was at Whitsuntide of the next year!
I miss the court life. The feasting, the *dances*...
Prut! As *if* your old legs can even *remember* how to dance!
Well, at least they *used* to know how! You've never had anything but ***two left feet!***
That's not so! Lord Desmond always said that I was the *only girl* he truly enjoyed dancing with!

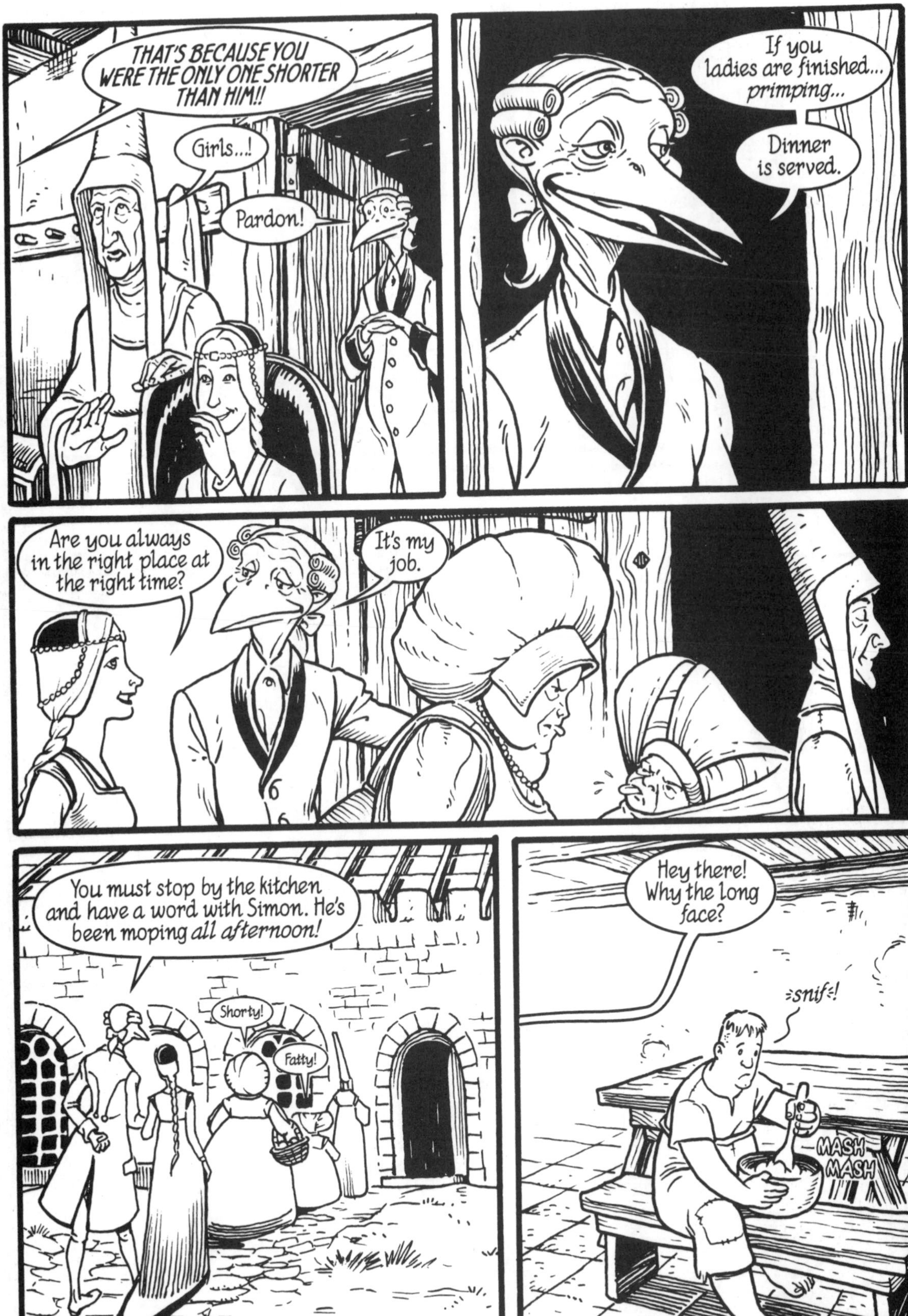

THAT'S BECAUSE YOU WERE THE ONLY ONE SHORTER THAN HIM!!
Girls...!
Pardon!
If you ladies are finished... *primping...*
Dinner is served.
Are you always in the right place at the right time?
It's my job.
You must stop by the kitchen and have a word with Simon. He's been moping *all afternoon!*
Shorty!
Fatty!
Hey there! Why the long face?
snif!
MASH MASH

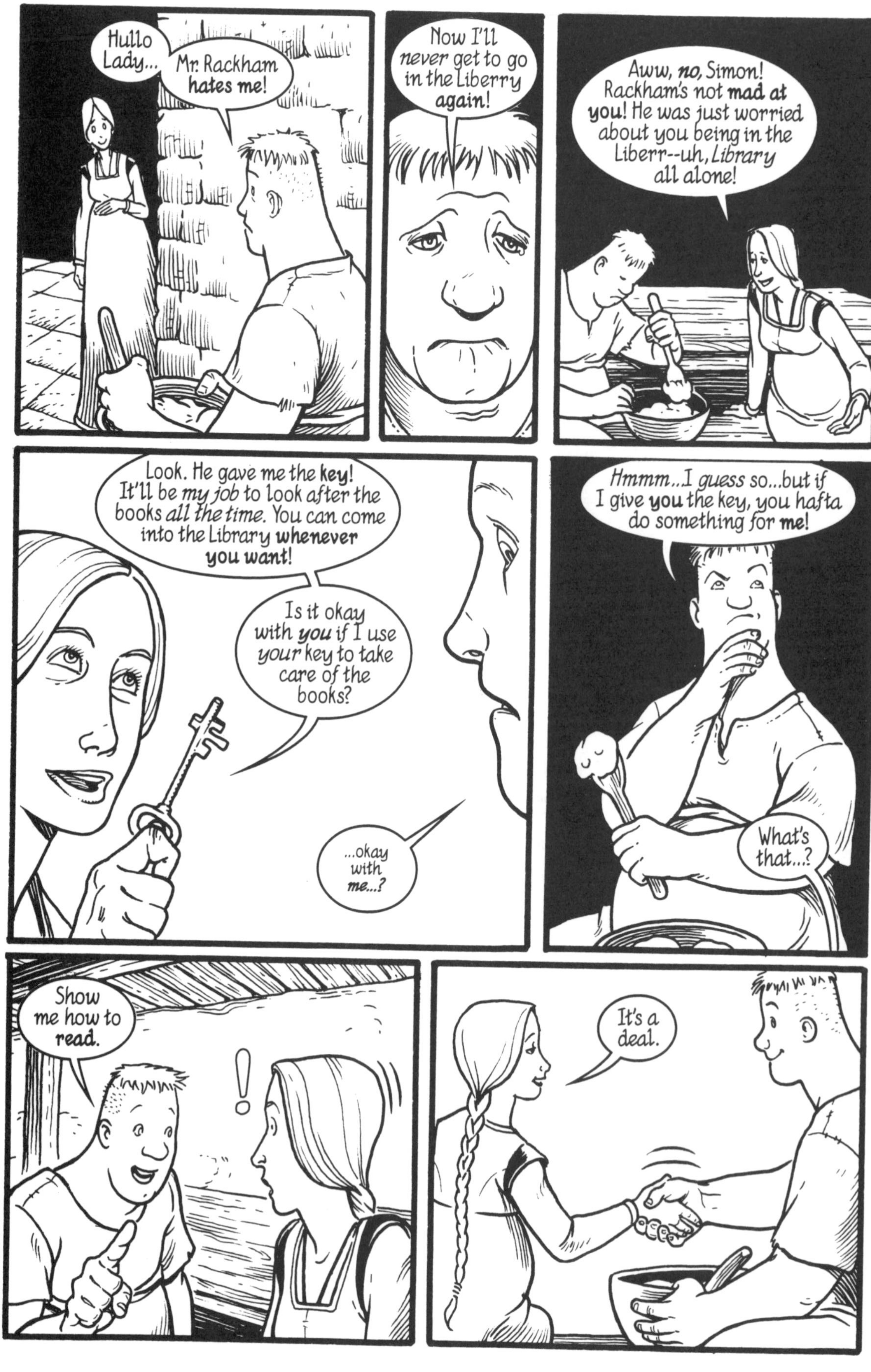
Hullo Lady...
Mr. Rackham hates me!
Now I'll never get to go in the Liberry again!
Aww, no, Simon! Rackham's not mad at you! He was just worried about you being in the Liberr--uh, Library all alone!
Look. He gave me the key! It'll be my job to look after the books all the time. You can come into the Library whenever you want!
Is it okay with you if I use your key to take care of the books?
...okay with me...?
Hmmm...I guess so...but if I give you the key, you hafta do something for me!
What's that...?
Show me how to read.
!
It's a deal.

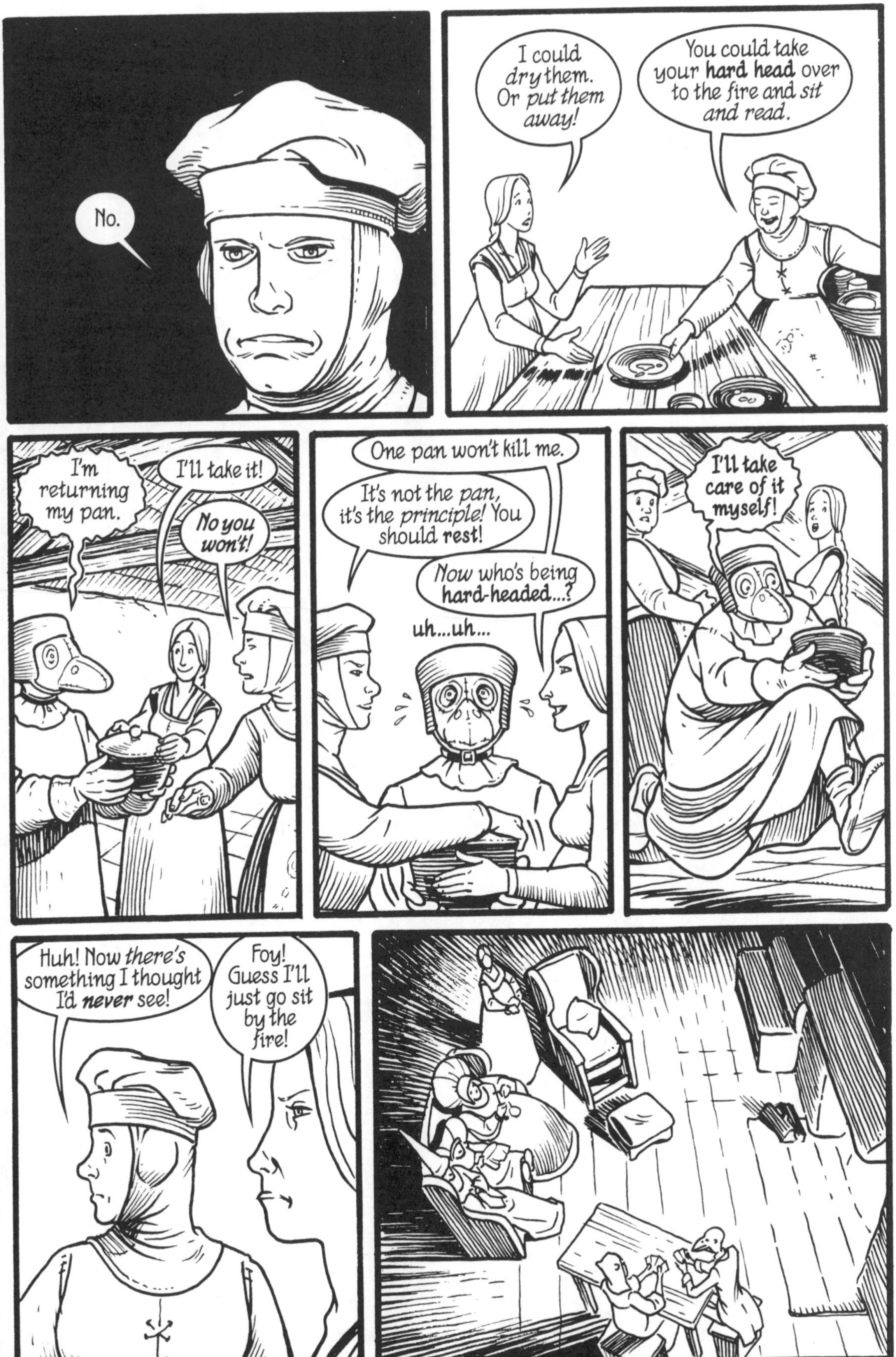
No.
I could dry them. Or put them away!
You could take your hard head over to the fire and sit and read.
I'm returning my pan.
I'll take it!
No you won't!
One pan won't kill me.
It's not the pan, it's the principle! You should rest!
Now who's being hard-headed...?
uh...uh...
I'll take care of it myself!
Huh! Now there's something I thought I'd never see!
Foy! Guess I'll just go sit by the fire!

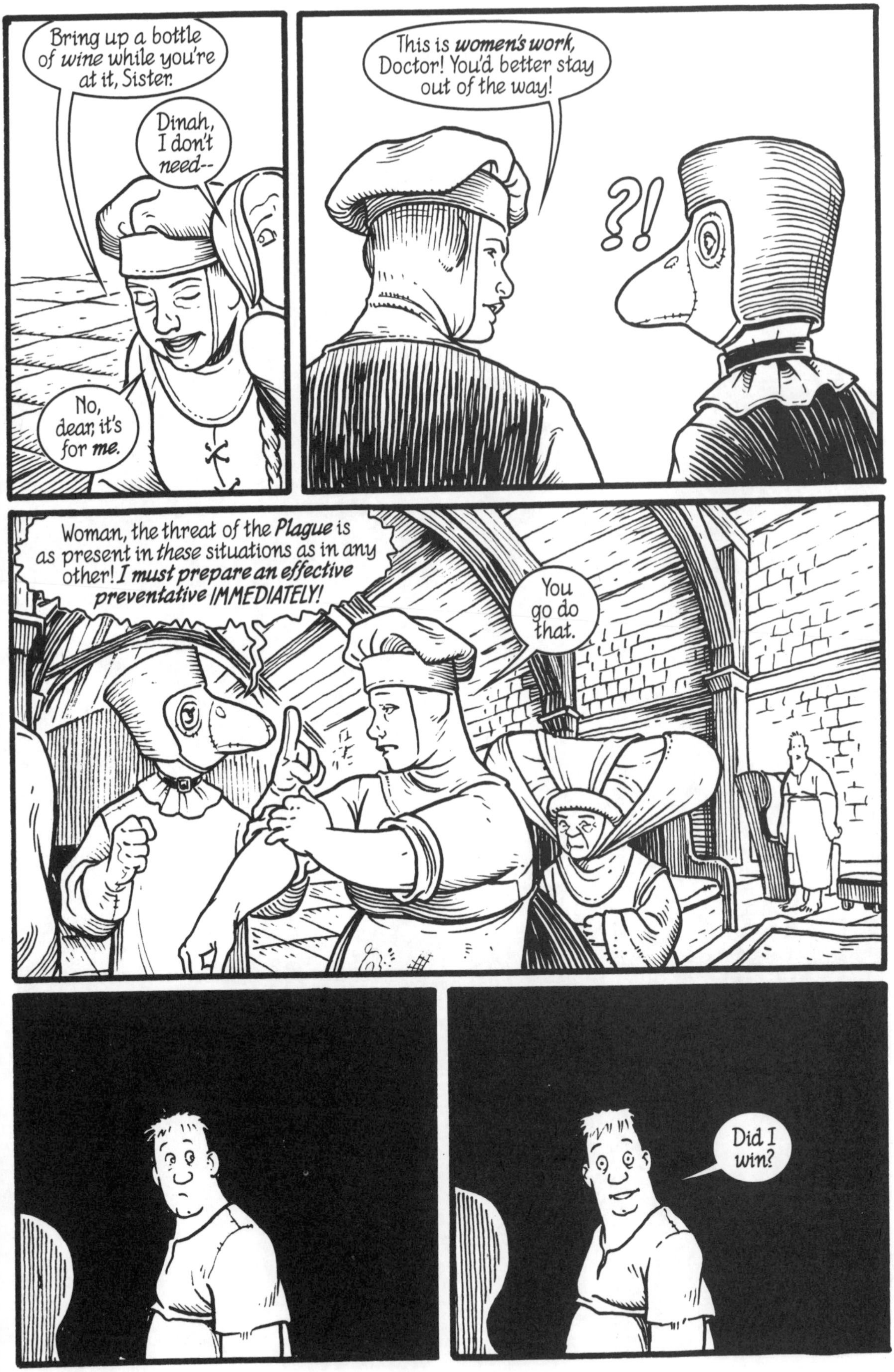
Bring up a bottle of *wine* while you're at it, Sister.
Dinah, I don't *need*--
No, dear, it's for *me*.
This is ***women's work***, Doctor! You'd better stay out of the way!
?!
Woman, the threat of the *Plague* is as present in *these* situations as in any other! ***I must prepare an effective preventative*** *IMMEDIATELY!*
You go do that.
Did I win?

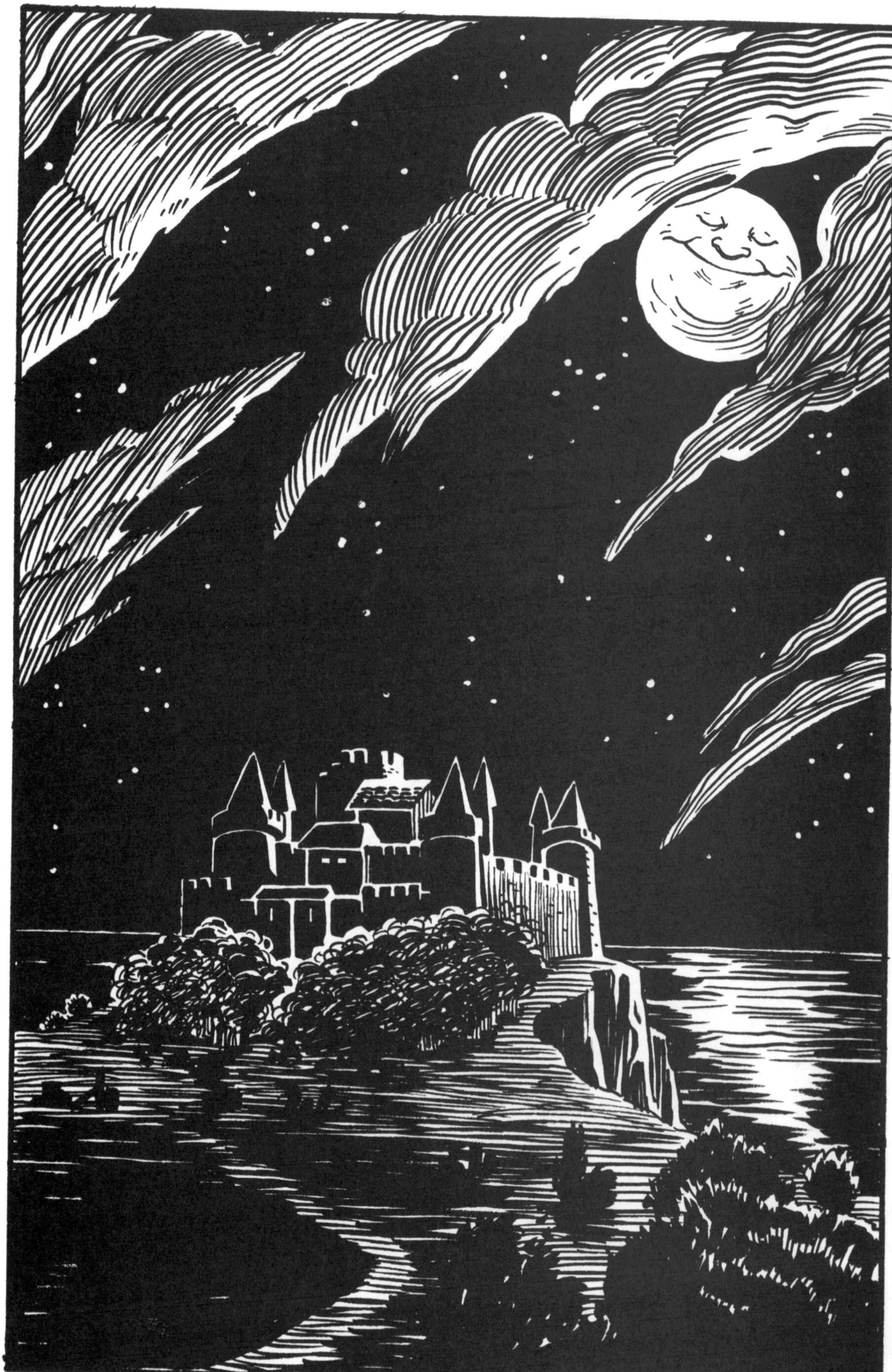

The Caged Heart
Story and Art by Linda Medley —
Lettering by Todd Klein

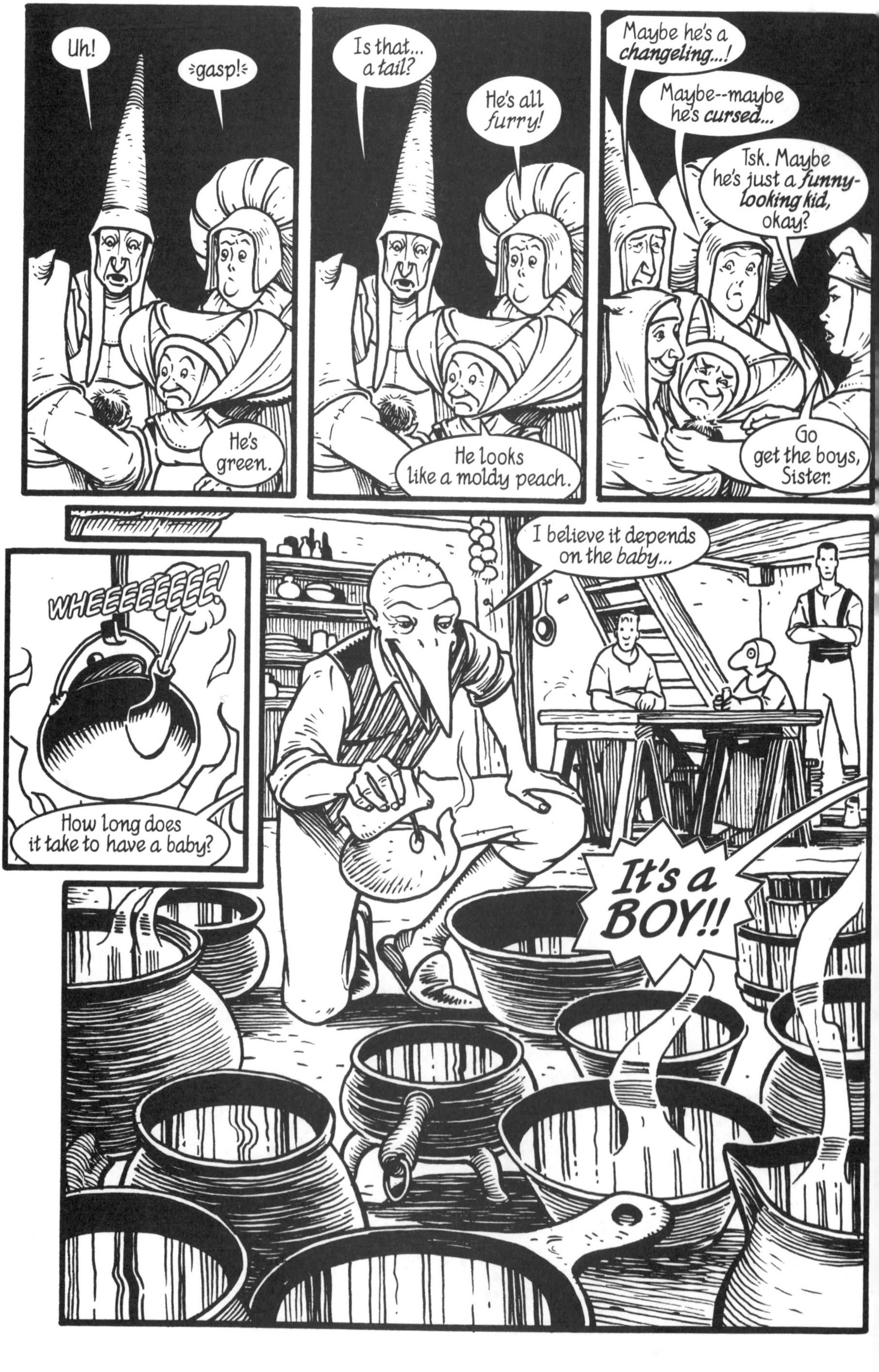
Uh!
gasp!
He's green.
Is that... a tail?
He's all furry!
He looks like a moldy peach.
Maybe he's a changeling...!
Maybe--maybe he's cursed...
Tsk. Maybe he's just a funny-looking kid, okay?
Go get the boys, Sister.
WHEEEEEEEEE!
How long does it take to have a baby?
I believe it depends on the baby...
It's a BOY!!

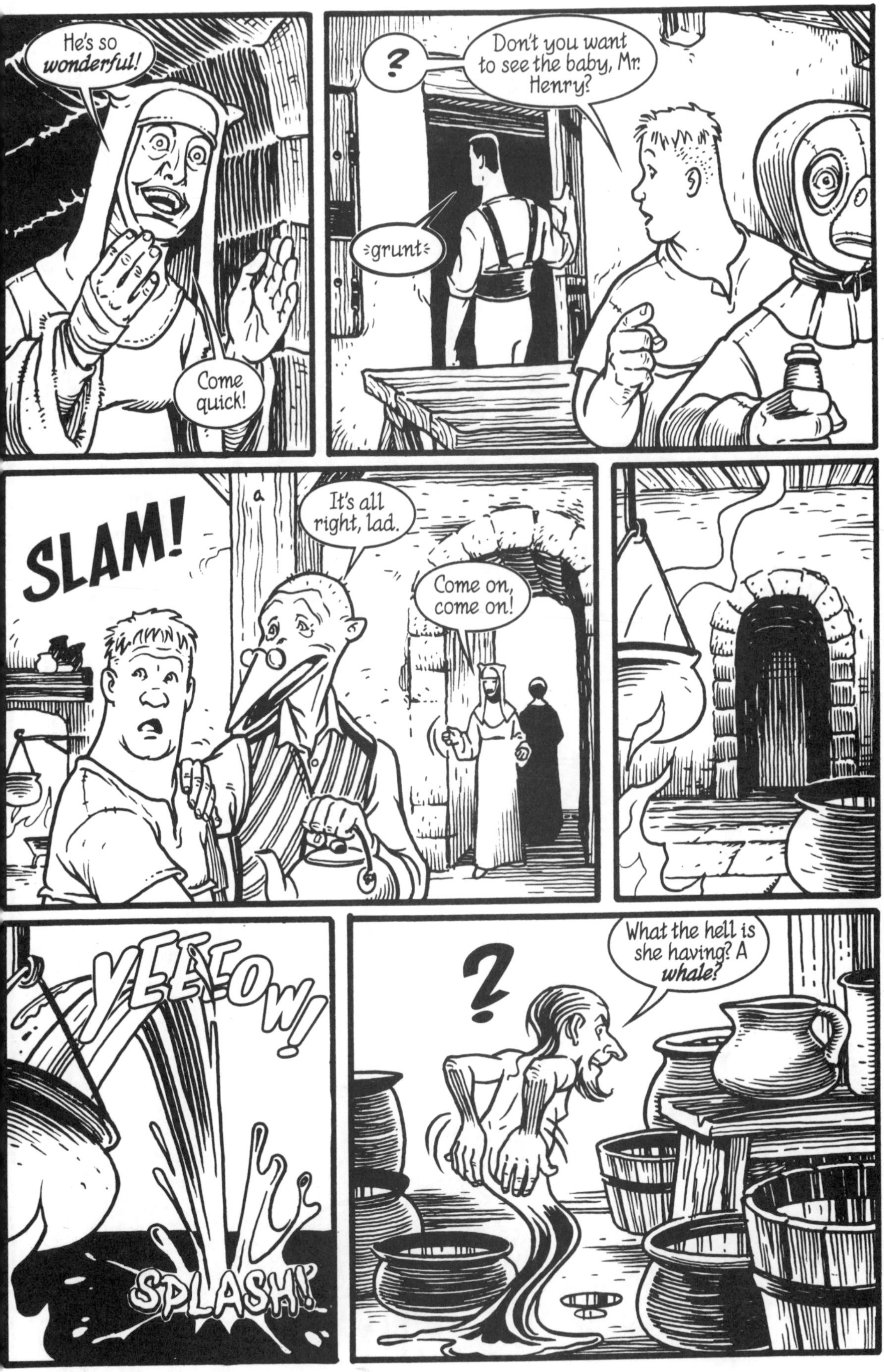
He's so *wonderful!*
Come quick!
?
Don't you want to see the baby, Mr. Henry?
grunt
SLAM!
It's all right, lad.
Come on, come on!
YEEEOW!
SPLASH!
?
What the hell is she having? A *whale?*

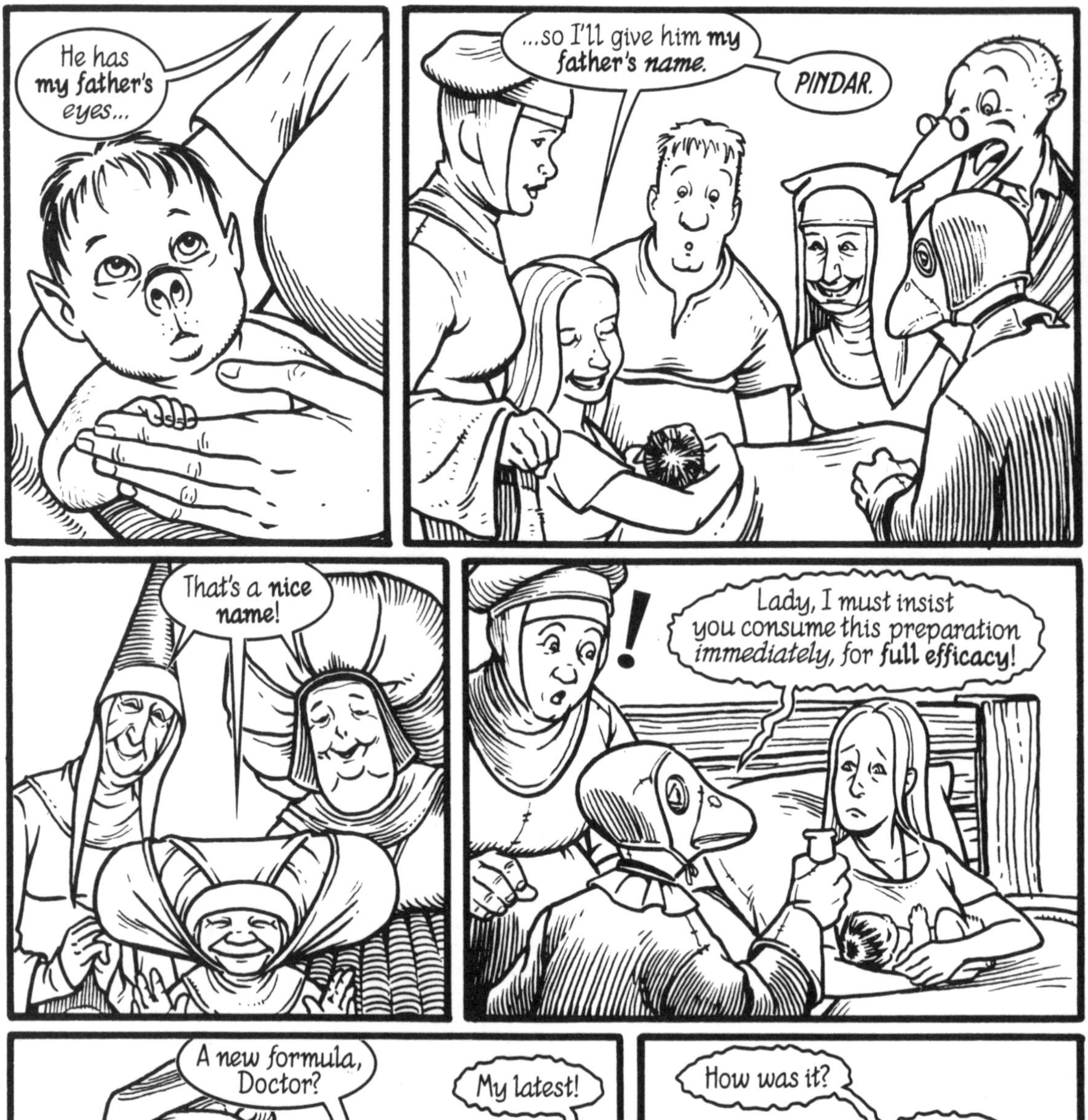
He has my father's eyes...
...so I'll give him my father's name.
PINDAR.
That's a nice name!
!
Lady, I must insist you consume this preparation immediately, for full efficacy!
A new formula, Doctor?
My latest!
How was it?
Kinda bitter.
Ah, that would be the sulfur.

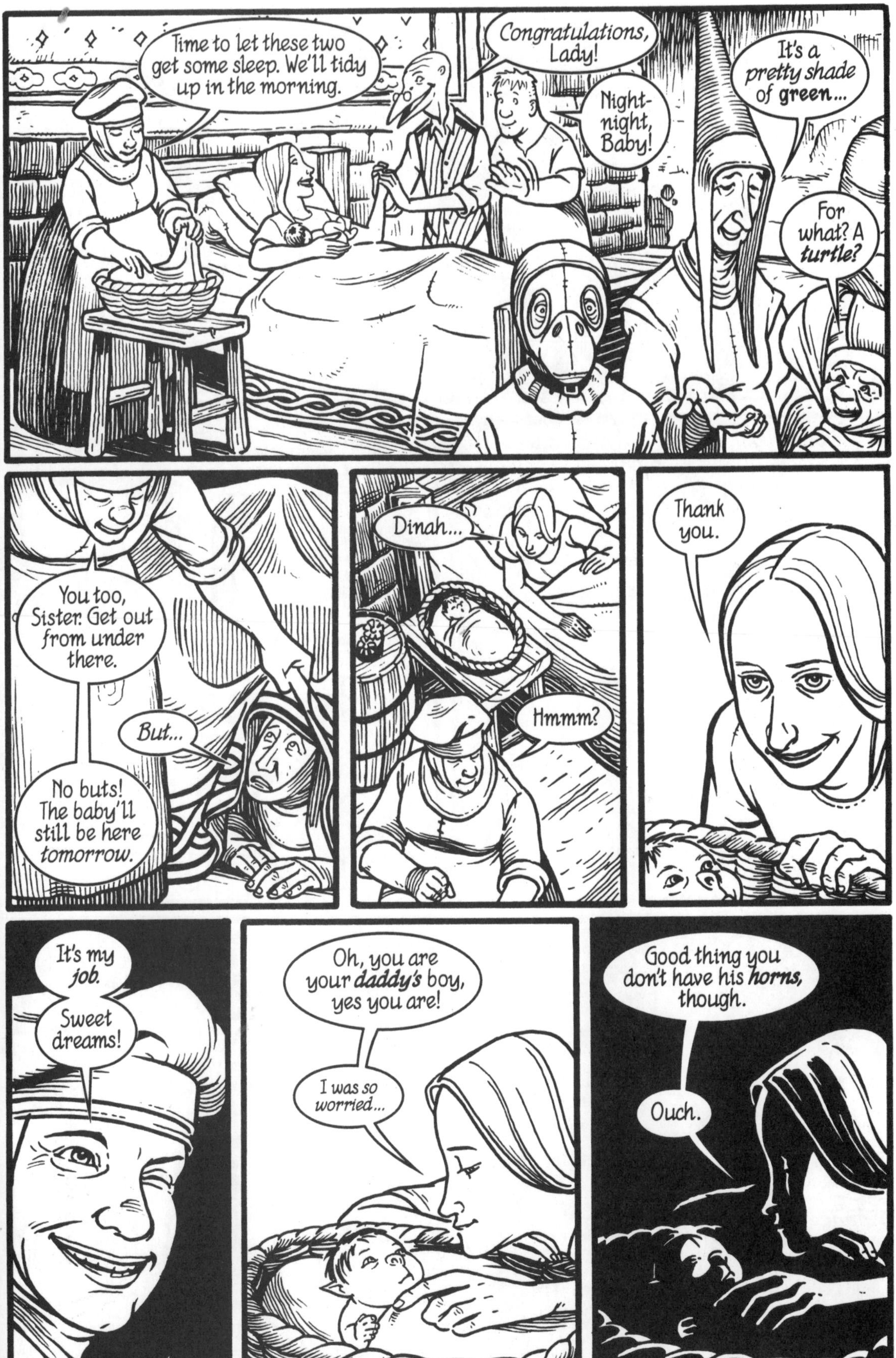
Time to let these two get some sleep. We'll tidy up in the morning.
Congratulations, Lady!
Night-night, Baby!
It's a *pretty shade* of **green...**
For what? A ***turtle?***
You too, Sister. Get out from under there.
But...
No buts! The baby'll still be here *tomorrow.*
Dinah...
Hmmm?
Thank you.
It's my *job.*
Sweet dreams!
Oh, you are your ***daddy's*** boy, yes you are!
I was so worried...
Good thing you don't have his ***horns,*** though.
Ouch.

Long ago and far away...

What do you think of your daughter, Pindar?

Our daughter, Tomasina.

That is the *ugliest* baby I've ever seen.

AGGIE!

She's even uglier than *you* were, Master Pindar.

Ha ha! "*Ugly babies make pretty ladies,*" Agatha!

Phew! Little *Iain* ought to be quite a *beauty*, then.

Tsk. Please bring in the children now, Aggie.

Well, if you really want to *frighten* them...

Christian? Galen? Come meet your sister Iain!

ZZZZ....

Not 'nother *sister!*

This one's *different.* This one's *ours.*

Aimee! Andreia!

Your mother and father want you to come in and meet your *new sister.*

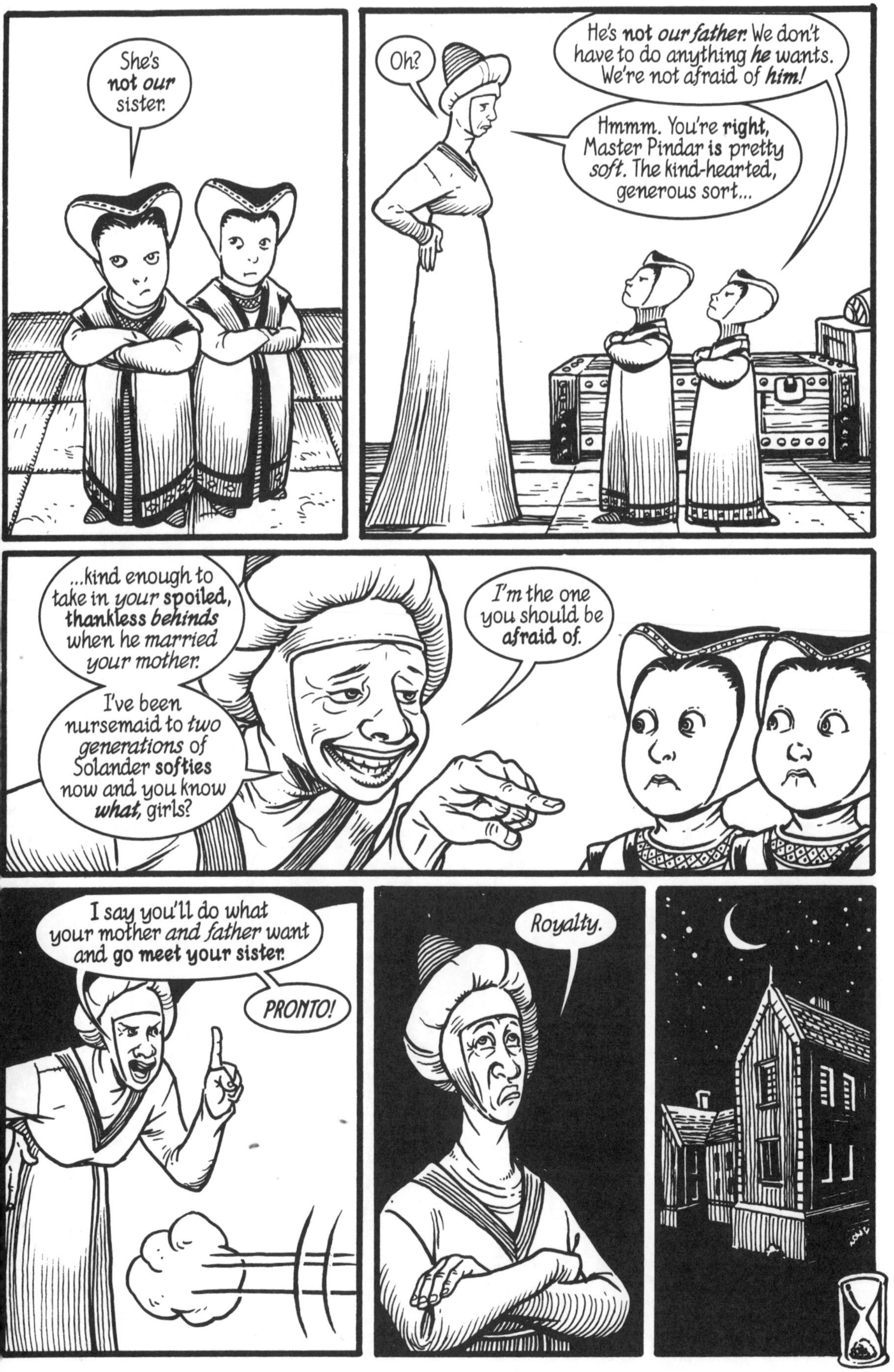
She's **not our** sister.
Oh?
He's **not *our father.*** We don't have to do anything ***he*** wants. We're not afraid of ***him!***
Hmmm. You're **right,** Master Pindar **is** pretty *soft*. The kind-hearted, generous sort...
...kind enough to take in *your* **spoiled, thankless *behinds*** when he married your mother.
I've been nursemaid to *two generations* of Solander **softies** now and you know ***what,*** girls?
I'm the one you should be **afraid of.**
I say you'll do what your mother *and father* want and **go meet your sister.**
PRONTO!
Royalty.

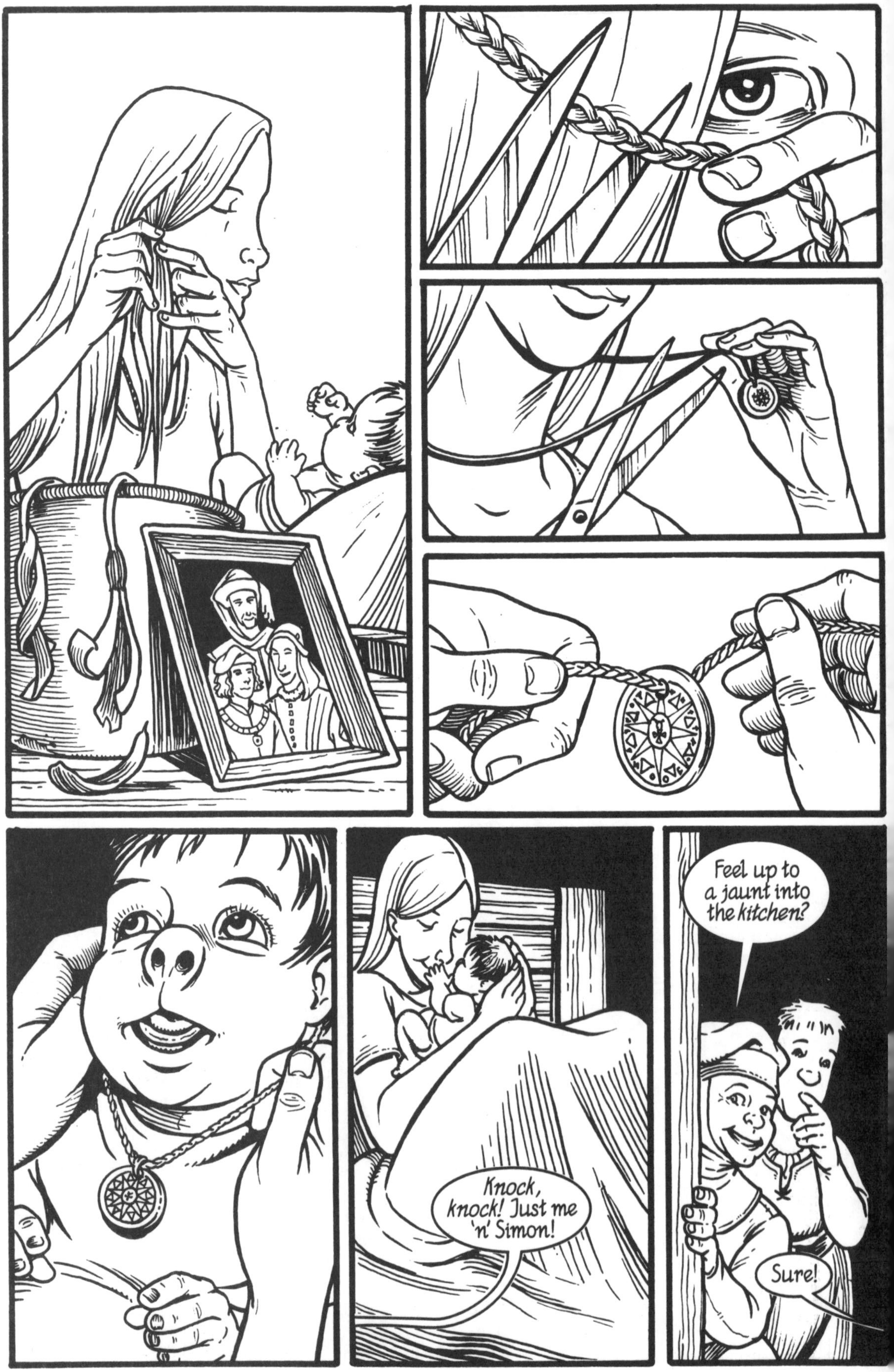
Knock, knock! Just me 'n' Simon!
Feel up to a jaunt into the kitchen?
Sure!

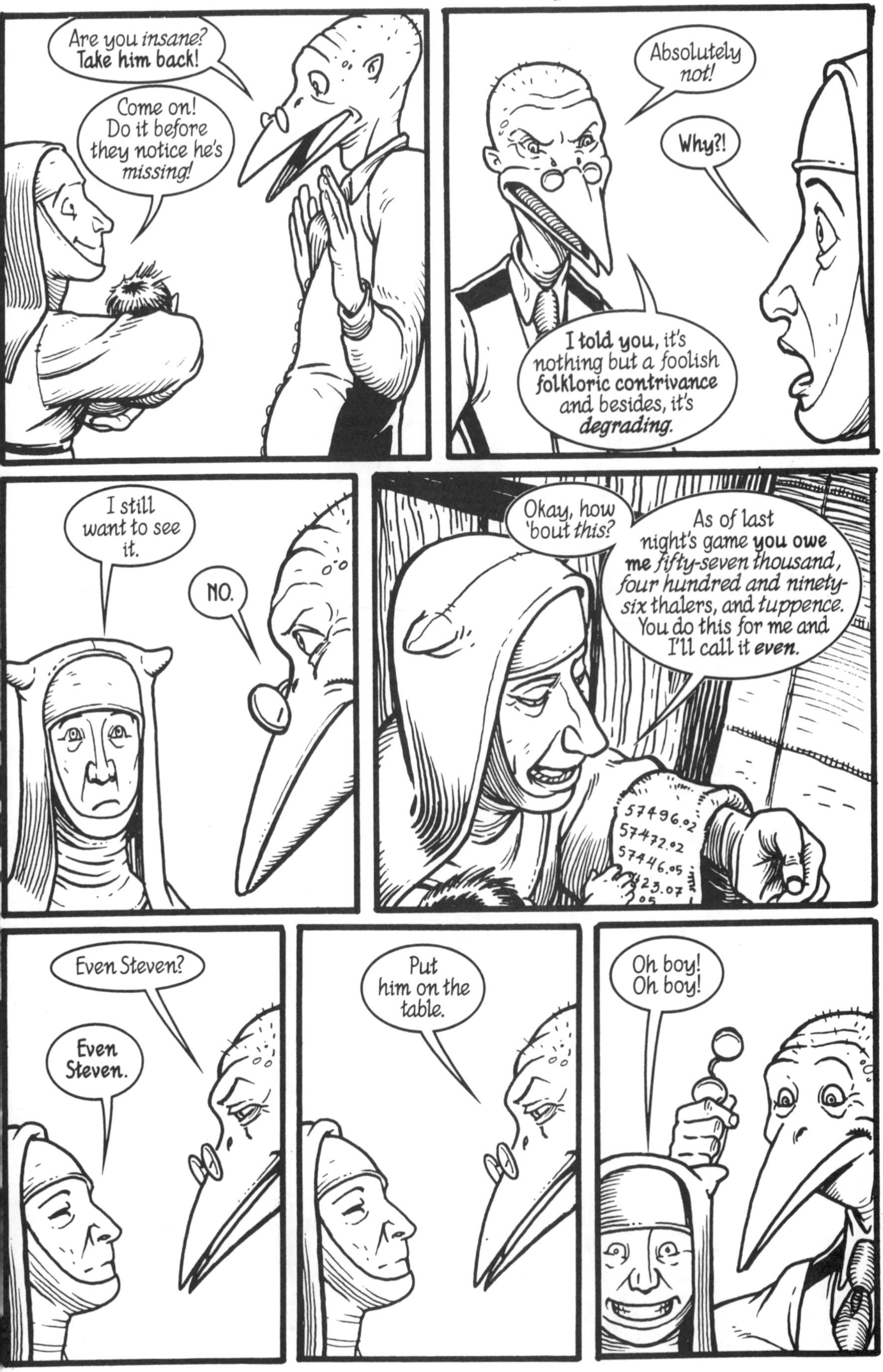
Are you *insane?* **Take him back!**
Come on! Do it before they notice he's *missing!*
Absolutely *not!*
Why?!
I told you, it's nothing but a foolish **folkloric contrivance** and besides, it's ***degrading***.
I still want to see it.
NO.
Okay, how 'bout *this?*
As of last night's game **you owe me** *fifty-seven thousand, four hundred and ninety-six* thalers, and *tuppence*. You do this for me and I'll call it ***even***.
57496.02
57472.02
57446.05
Even Steven?
Even Steven.
Put him on the table.
Oh boy! Oh boy!

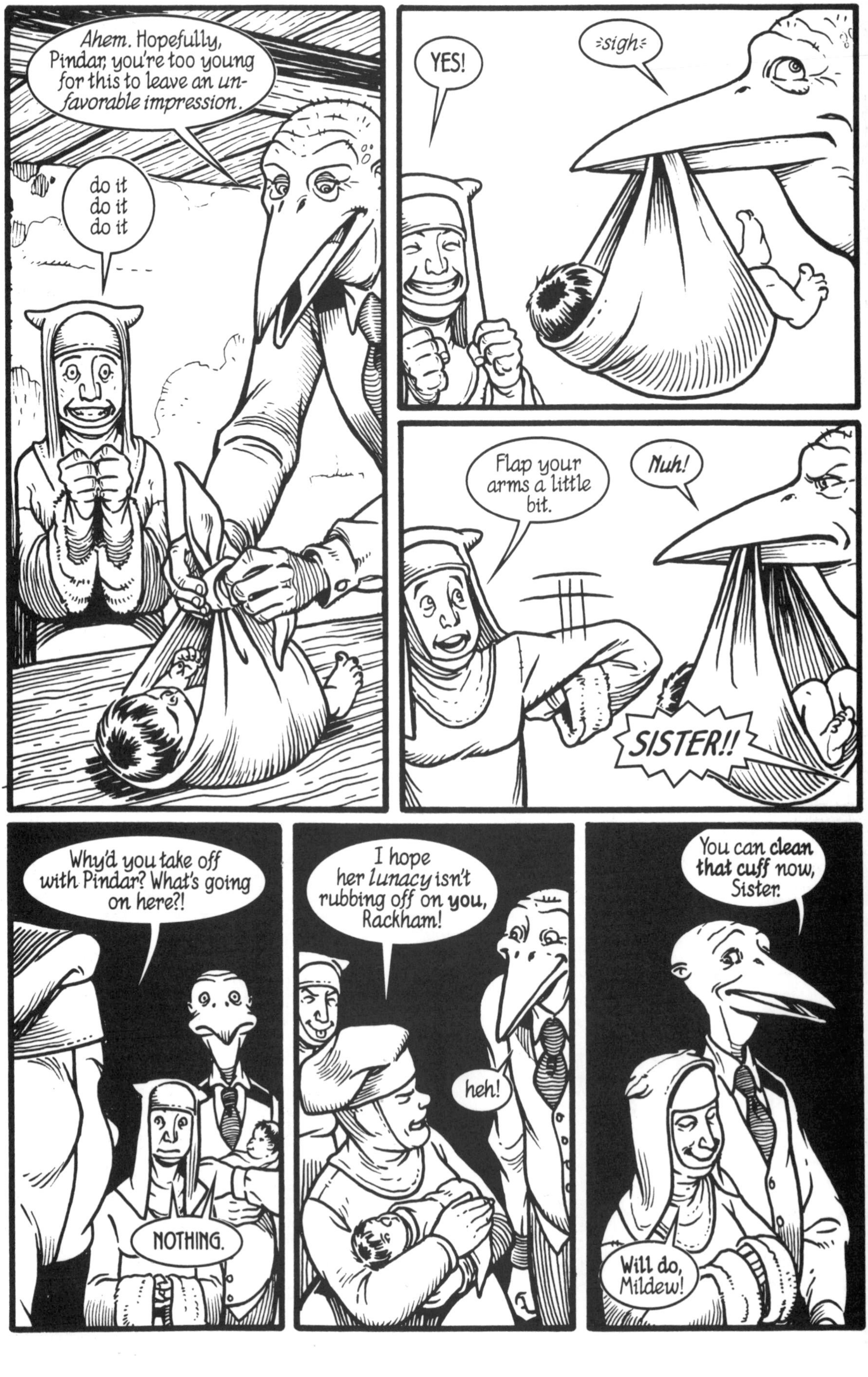

Ahem. Hopefully, Pindar, you're too young for this to leave an *un-favorable impression*.
do it do it do it
YES!
sigh
Flap your arms a little bit.
Nuh!
SISTER!!
Why'd you take off with Pindar? What's going on here?!
NOTHING.
I hope her *lunacy* isn't rubbing off on **you**, Rackham!
heh!
You can **clean that cuff** now, Sister.
Will do, Mildew!

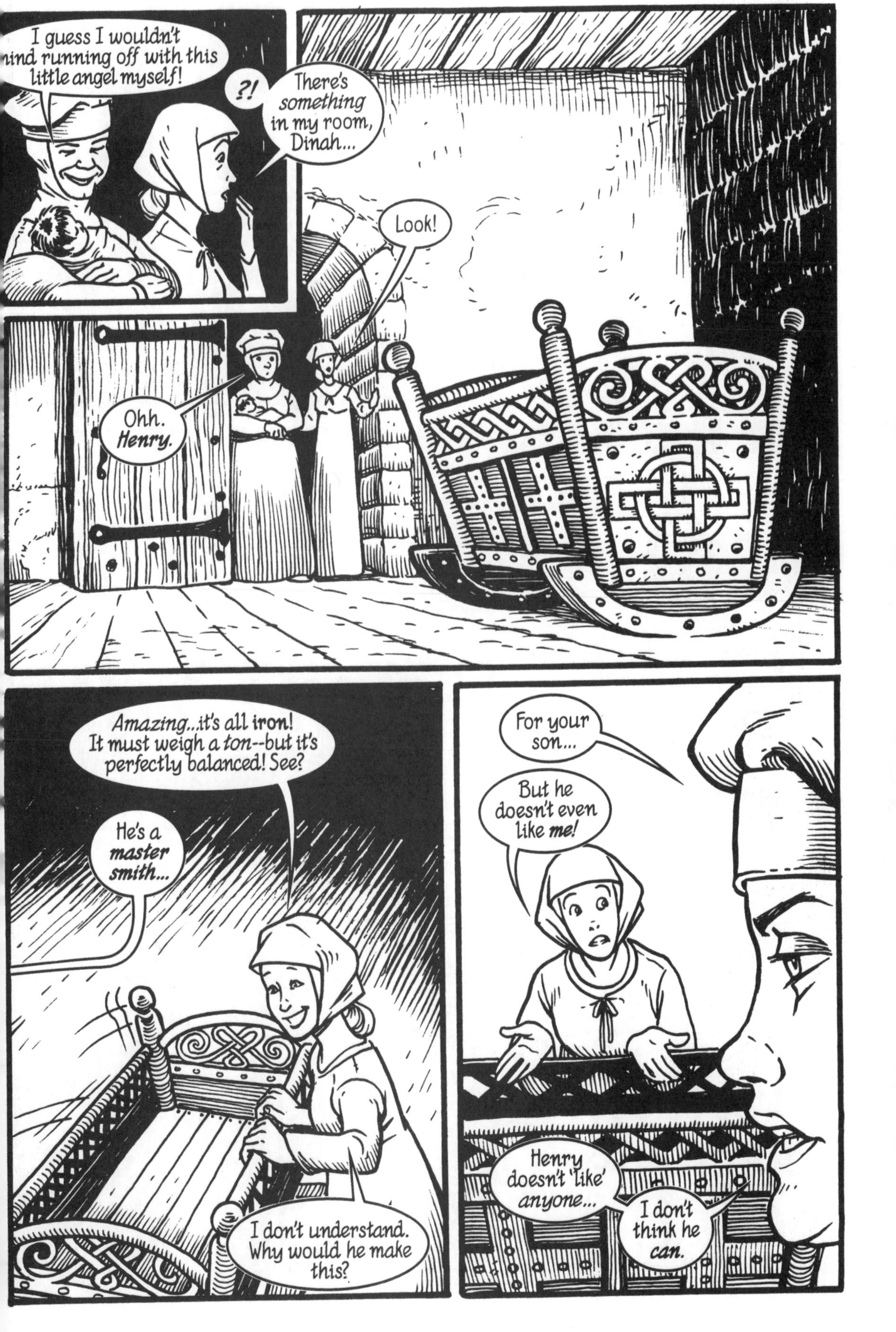

I guess I wouldn't mind running off with this little angel myself!
?!
There's *something* in my room, Dinah...
Look!
Ohh. ***Henry.***
Amazing...it's all **iron**! It must weigh a *ton*--but it's perfectly balanced! See?
He's a ***master smith...***
I don't understand. Why would he make this?
For your son...
But he doesn't even like ***me!***
Henry doesn't 'like' *anyone*...
I don't think he ***can.***

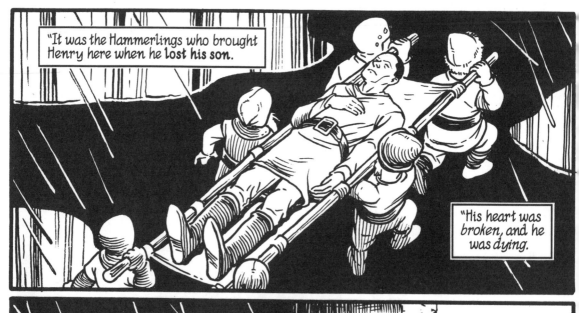

"It was the Hammerlings who brought Henry here when he lost his son.

"His heart was broken, and he was dying.

"Henry was like a **brother** to the Dwarves. They *begged* us to help *save him*.

"They worked in the forge all **night long**.

"In the morning, they brought out *three iron bands*..."

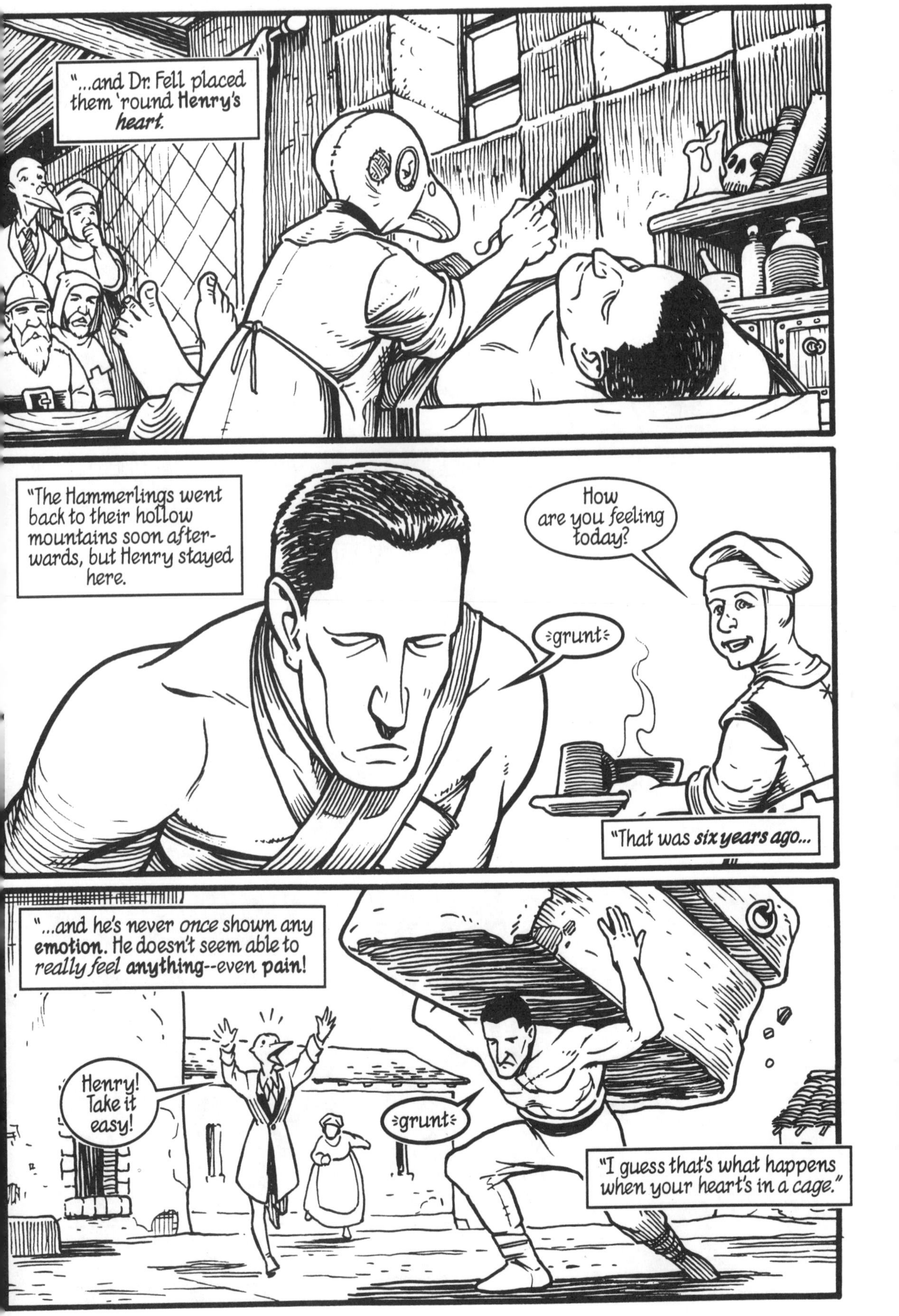
"...and Dr. Fell placed them 'round Henry's *heart*.
"The Hammerlings went back to their hollow mountains soon afterwards, but Henry stayed here.
How are you feeling today?
grunt
"That was *six years ago*...
"...and he's never *once* shown any **emotion**. He doesn't seem able to *really feel* **anything**--even **pain**!
Henry! Take it easy!
grunt
"I guess that's what happens when your heart's in a cage."

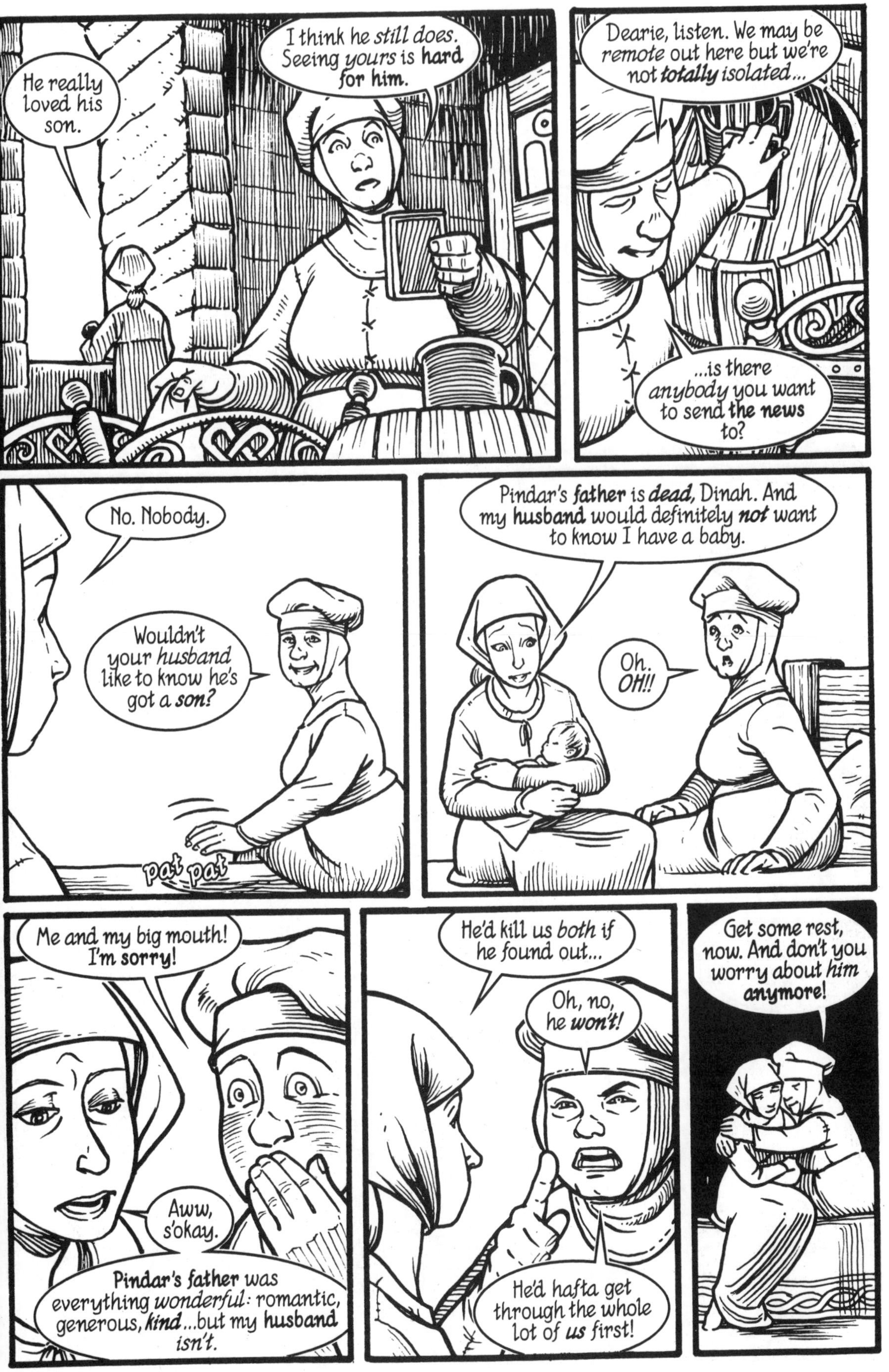
He really loved his son.
I think he *still does*. Seeing *yours* is **hard for him.**
Dearie, listen. We may be *remote* out here but we're not ***totally*** isolated...
...is there *anybody* you want to send **the news** to?
No. Nobody.
Wouldn't your *husband* like to know he's got a ***son?***
pat pat
Pindar's **father** is ***dead,*** Dinah. And my **husband** would definitely ***not*** want to know I have a baby.
Oh. *OH!!*
Me and my big mouth! I'm **sorry!**
Aww, s'okay.
Pindar's father was everything *wonderful*: romantic, generous, ***kind***...but my **husband** *isn't*.
He'd kill us *both* if he found out...
Oh, no, he ***won't!***
He'd hafta get through the whole lot of ***us*** first!
Get some rest, now. And don't you worry about ***him*** **anymore!**

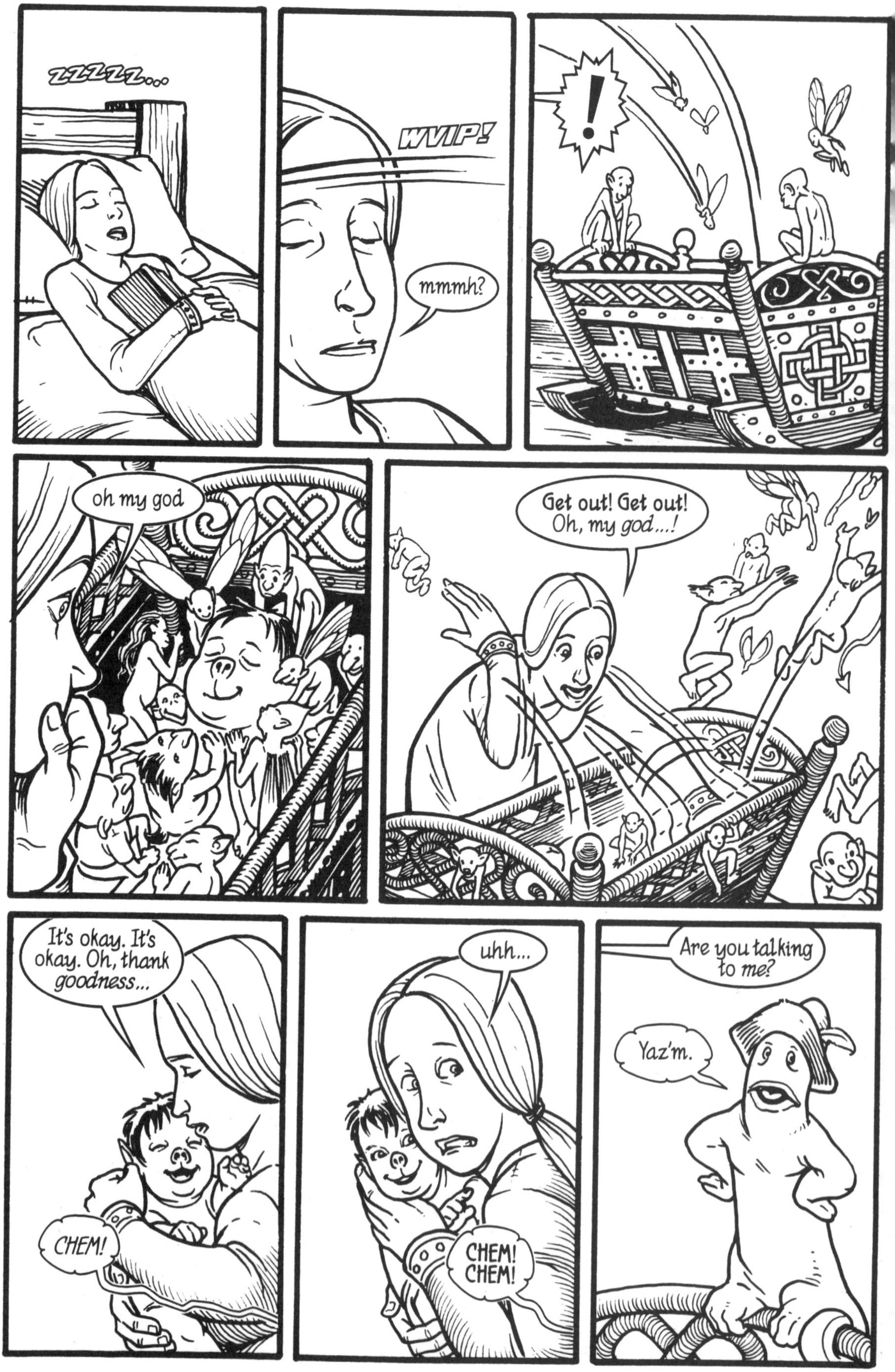
ZZZZZZ...
WVIP!
mmmh?
!
oh my god
Get out! Get out! Oh, my god...!
It's okay. It's okay. Oh, thank goodness...
CHEM!
uhh...
CHEM! CHEM!
Are you talking to me?
Yaz'm.

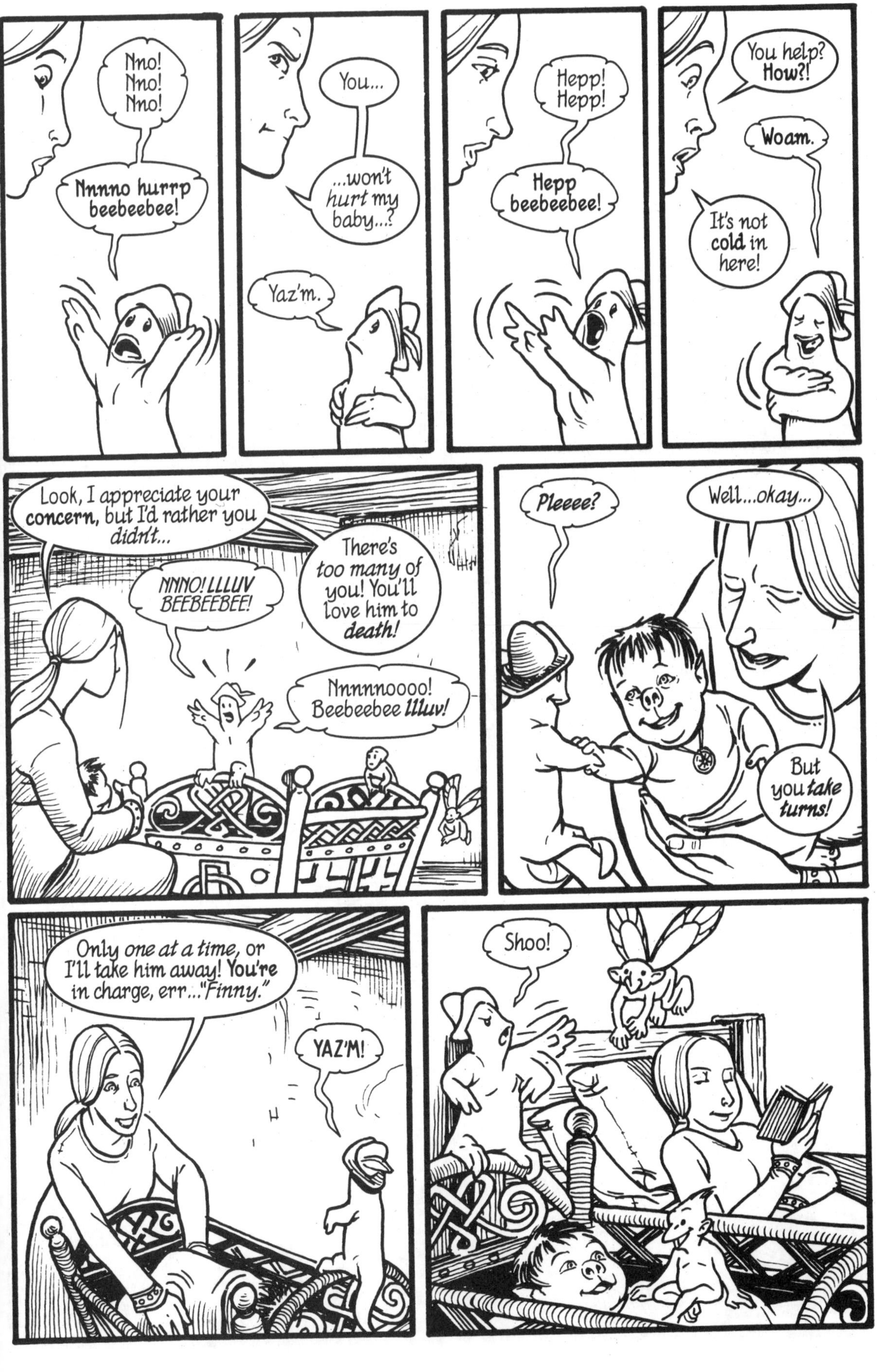

Nno! Nno! Nno!
Nnnno hurrp beebeebee!
You...
...won't *hurt* my baby...?
Yaz'm.
Hepp! Hepp!
Hepp beebeebee!
You help? **How?!**
Woam.
It's not **cold** in here!
Look, I appreciate your **concern**, but I'd rather you *didn't*...
NNNO! LLLUV BEEBEEBEE!
There's *too many* of you! You'll love him to ***death!***
Nnnnnoooo! Beebeebee ***Llluv!***
Pleeee?
Well...*okay*...
But you ***take turns!***
Only *one at a time*, or I'll take him away! **You're** in charge, err..."*Finny*."
YAZ'M!
Shoo!

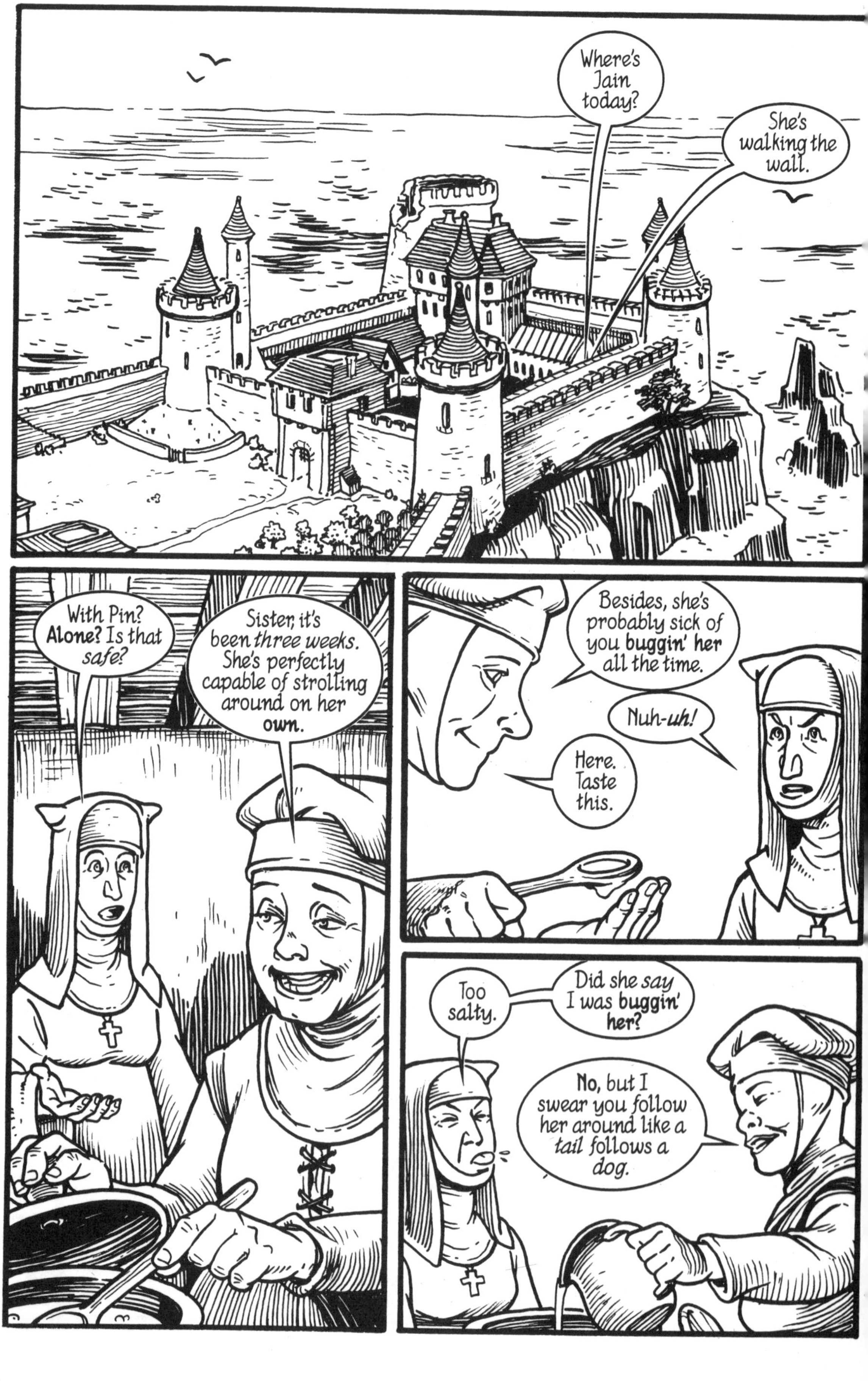
Where's Jain today?
She's walking the wall.
With Pin? **Alone?** Is that *safe?*
Sister, it's been *three weeks.* She's perfectly capable of strolling around on her **own.**
Besides, she's probably sick of you **buggin' her** all the time.
Nuh-*uh!*
Here. Taste this.
Too salty.
Did she *say* I was **buggin' her?**
No, but I swear you follow her around like a *tail* follows a dog.

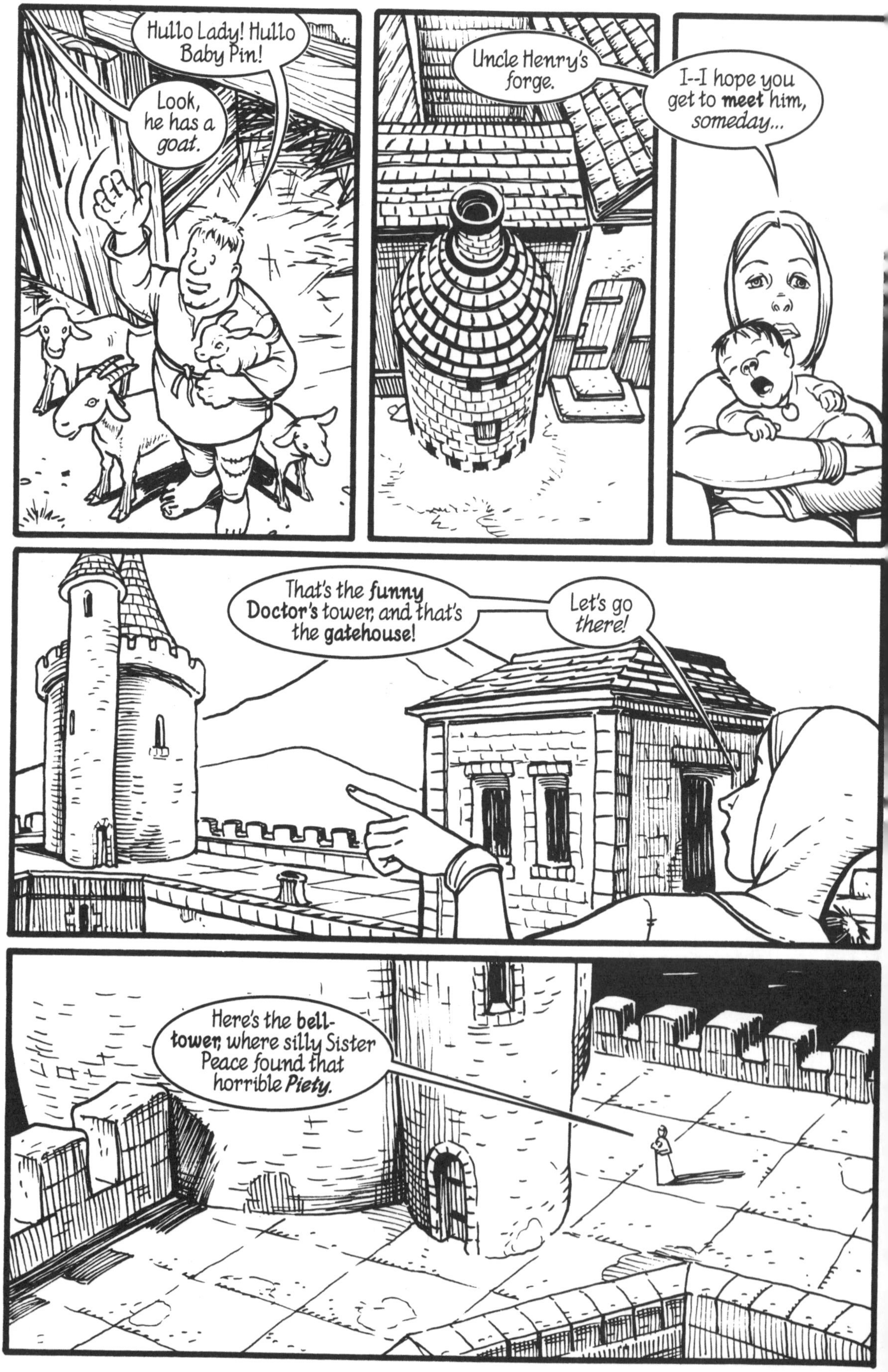
Hullo Lady! Hullo Baby Pin!
Look, he has a goat.
Uncle Henry's forge.
I--I hope you get to **meet** him, *someday...*
That's the **funny Doctor's** tower, and that's the **gatehouse!**
Let's go *there!*
Here's the **bell-tower,** where silly Sister Peace found that horrible ***Piety.***

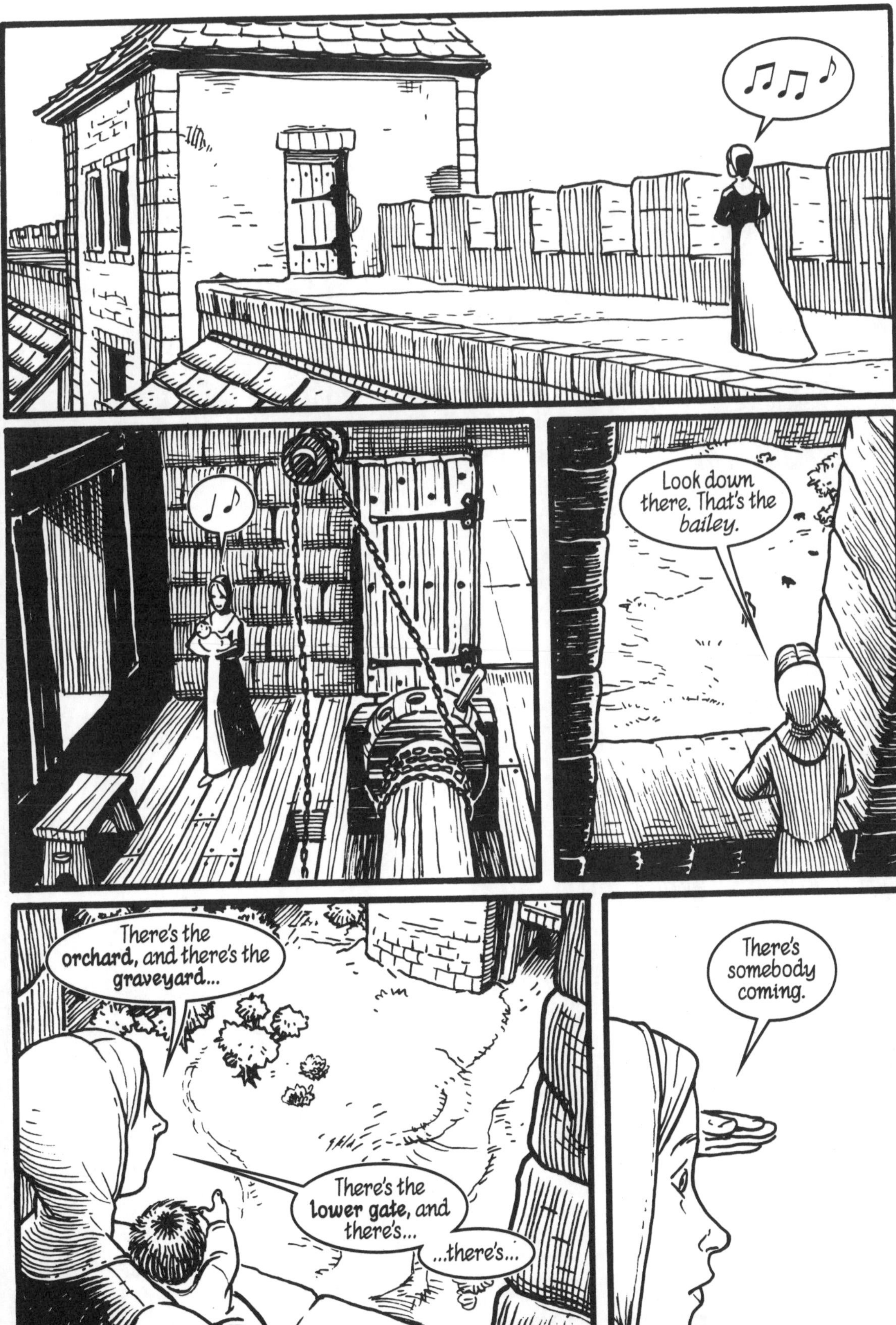
♫♫♪
♪♪
Look down there. That's the *bailey.*
There's the **orchard**, and there's the **graveyard**...
There's the **lower gate**, and there's...
...there's...
There's somebody coming.

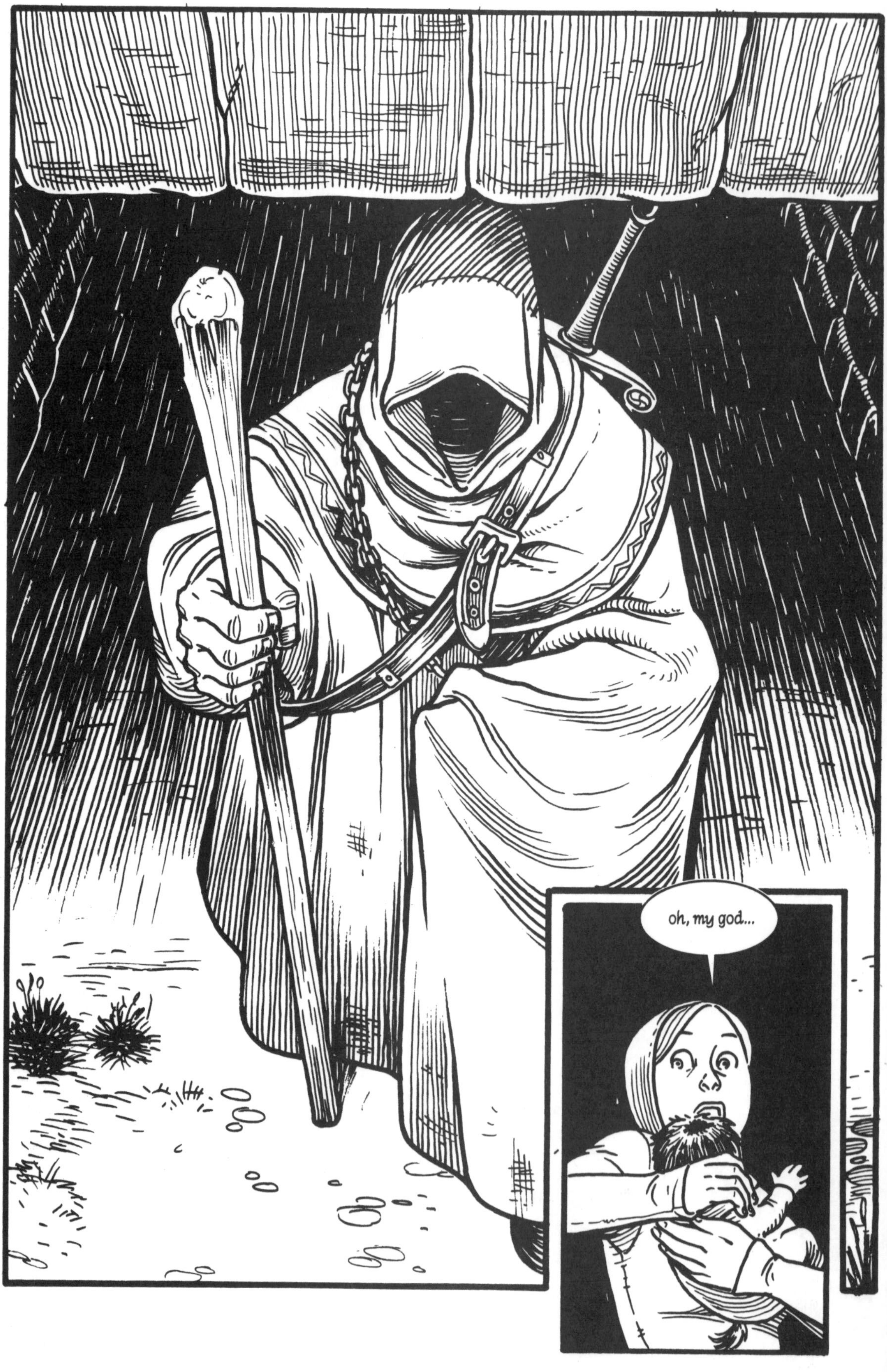
oh, my god...

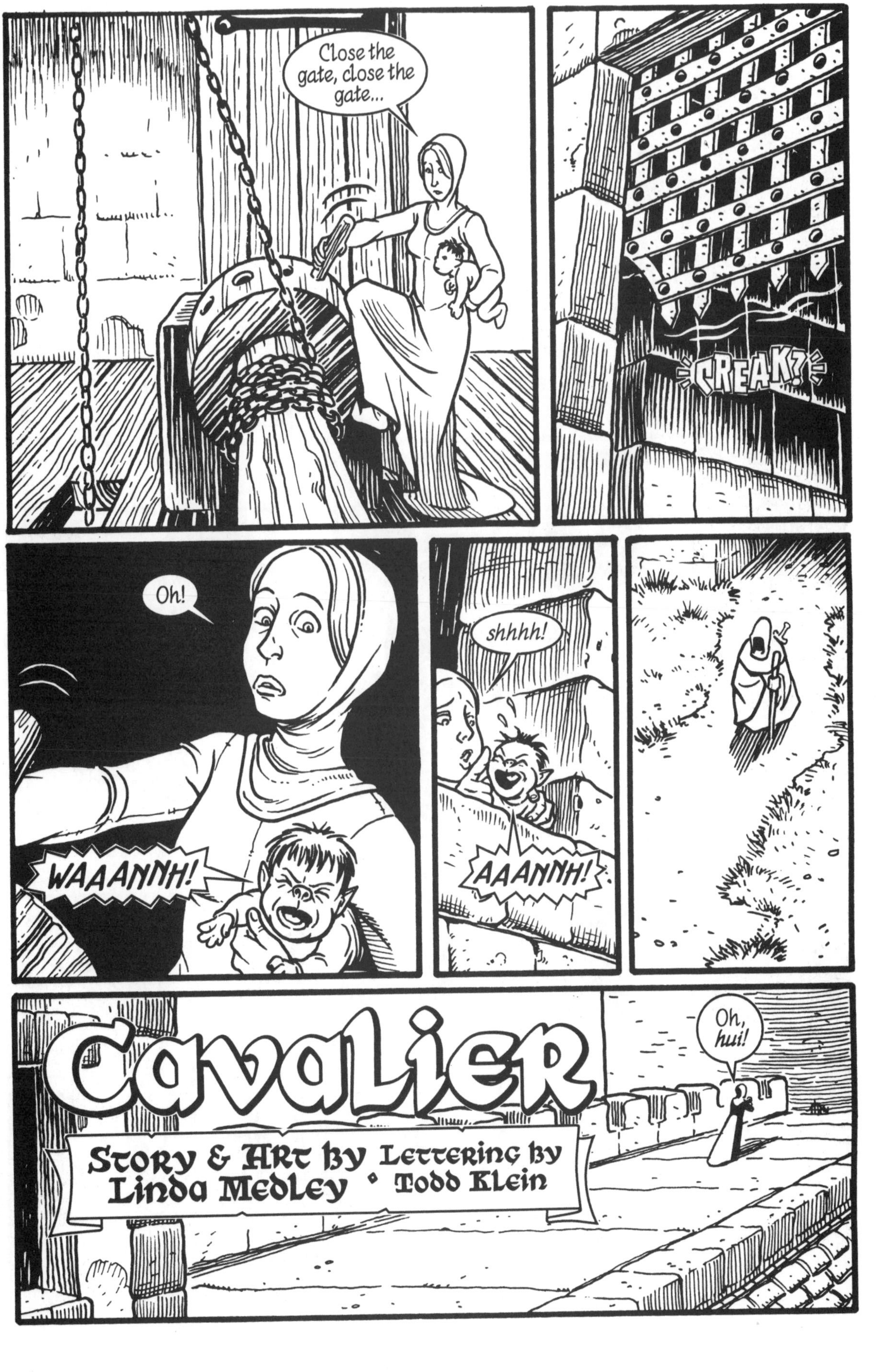
Close the gate, close the gate...
CREAK?
Oh!
WAAANNH!
shhhh!
AAANNH!
Oh, hui!
Cavalier
Story & Art by Linda Medley
Lettering by Todd Klein

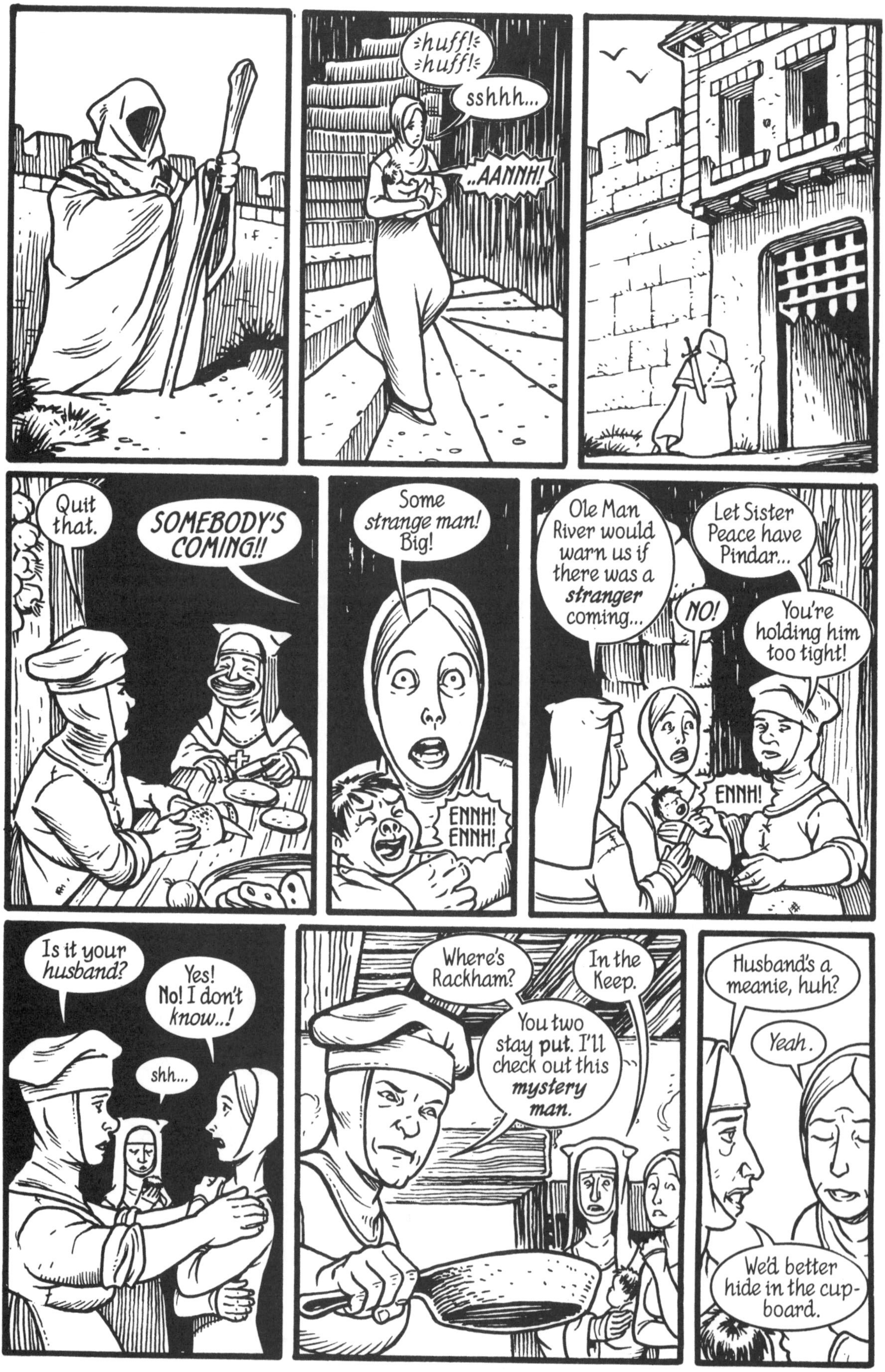
huff! huff!
sshhh...
..AANNH!
Quit that.
SOMEBODY'S COMING!!
Some strange man! Big!
ENNH! ENNH!
Ole Man River would warn us if there was a stranger coming...
NO!
Let Sister Peace have Pindar...
You're holding him too tight!
ENNH!
Is it your husband?
Yes! No! I don't know...!
shh...
Where's Rackham?
In the Keep.
You two stay put. I'll check out this mystery man.
Husband's a meanie, huh?
Yeah.
We'd better hide in the cupboard.

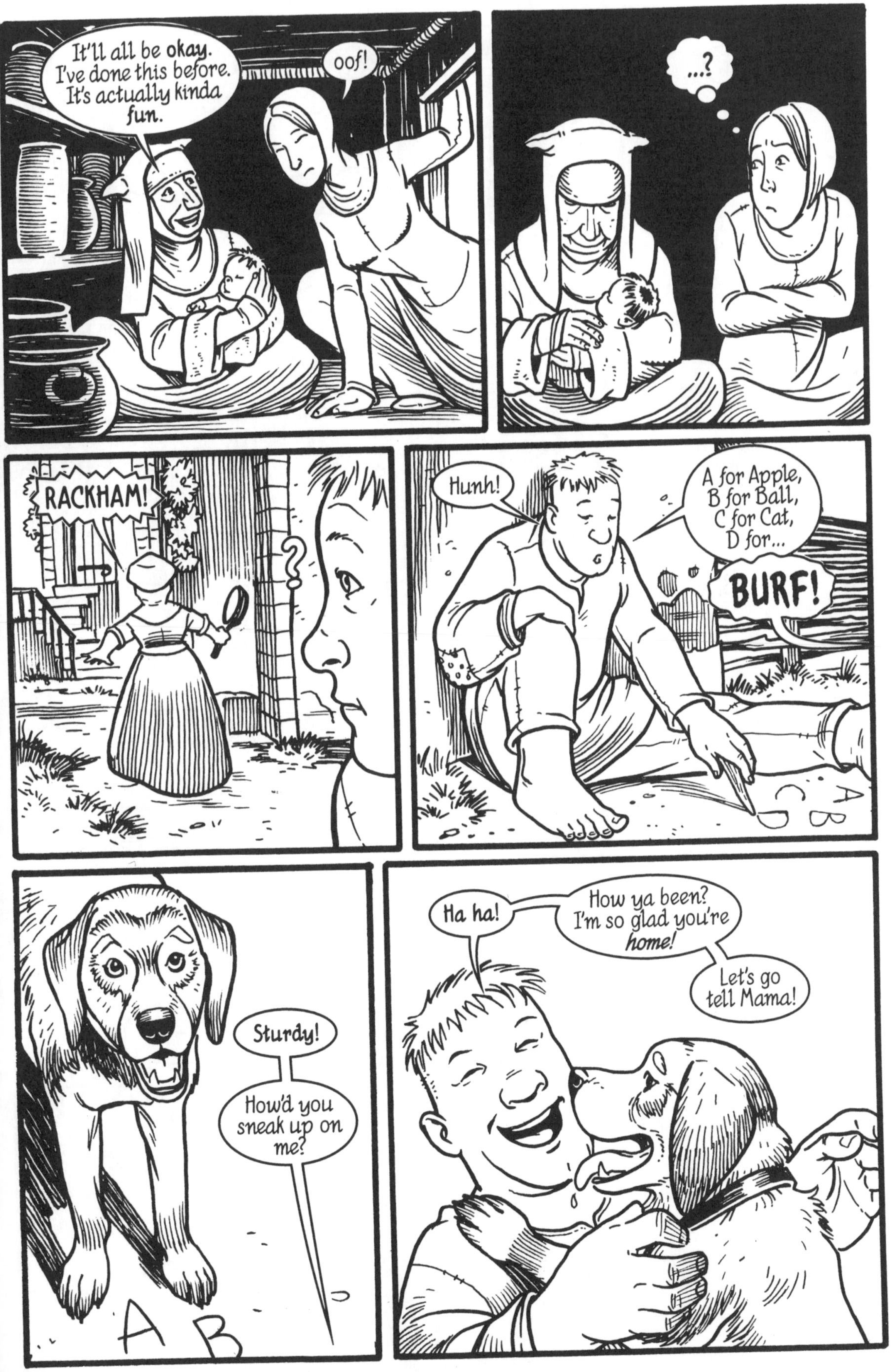
It'll all be okay. I've done this before. It's actually kinda fun.
oof!
...?
RACKHAM!
?
Hunh!
A for Apple, B for Ball, C for Cat, D for...
BURF!
Sturdy!
How'd you sneak up on me?
Ha ha!
How ya been? I'm so glad you're home!
Let's go tell Mama!

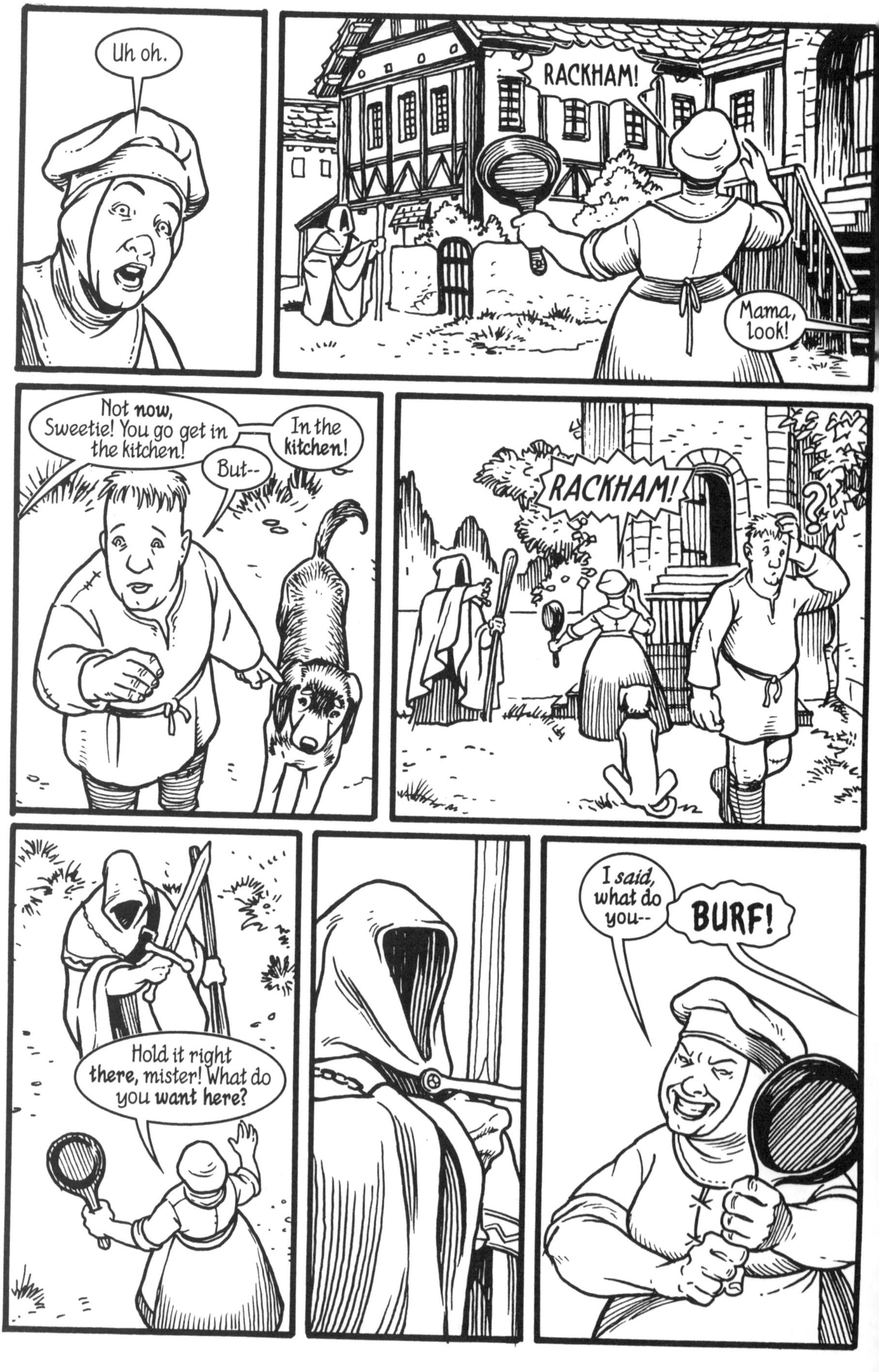

Uh oh.
RACKHAM!
Mama, look!
Not now, Sweetie! You go get in the kitchen!
But--
In the kitchen!
RACKHAM!
?
Hold it right there, mister! What do you want here?
I said, what do you--
BURF!

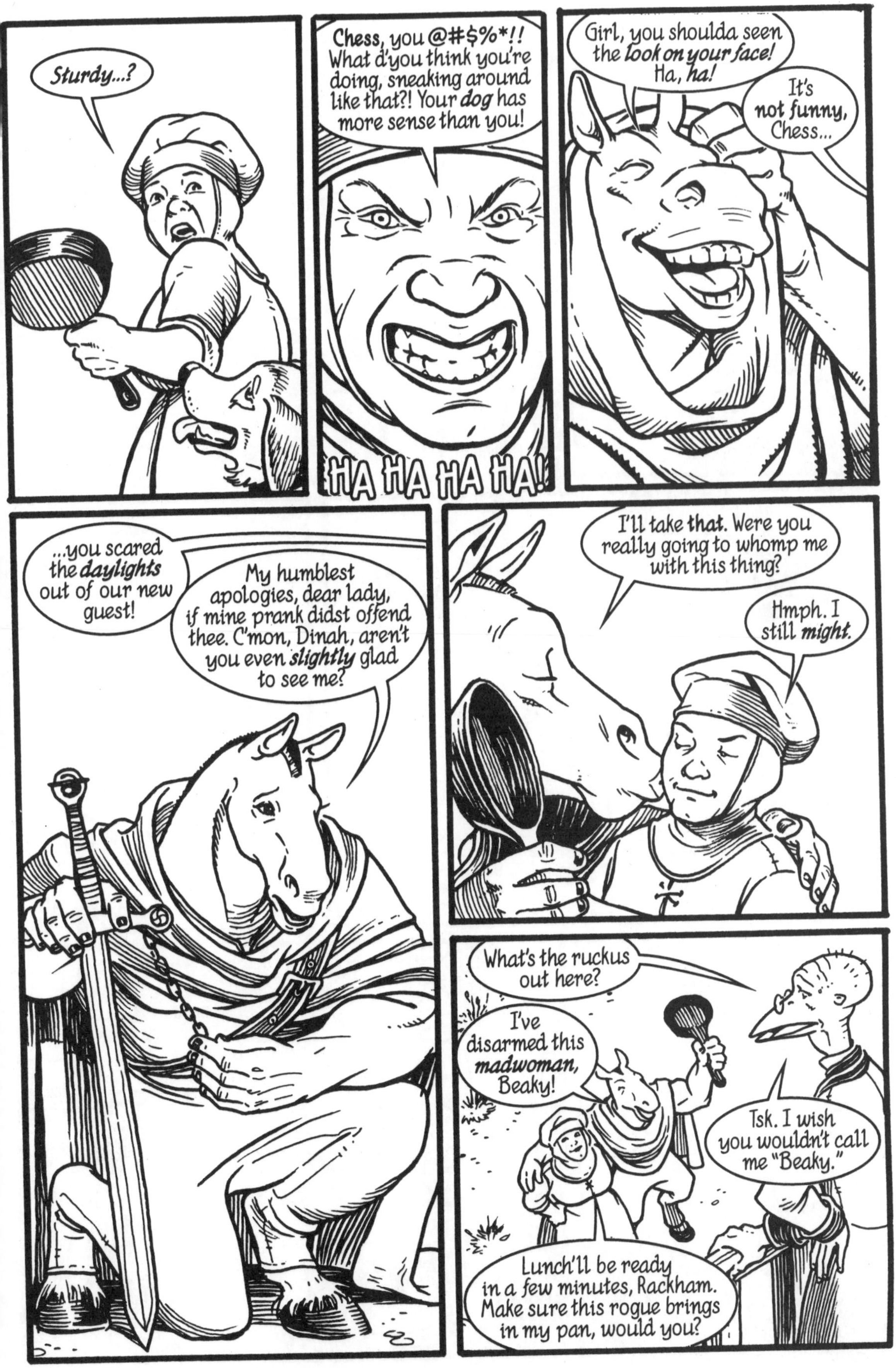
Sturdy...?
Chess, you @#$%*!! What d'you think you're doing, sneaking around like that?! Your dog has more sense than you!
HA HA HA HA!
Girl, you shoulda seen the look on your face! Ha, ha!
It's not funny, Chess...
...you scared the daylights out of our new guest!
My humblest apologies, dear lady, if mine prank didst offend thee. C'mon, Dinah, aren't you even slightly glad to see me?
I'll take that. Were you really going to whomp me with this thing?
Hmph. I still might.
What's the ruckus out here?
I've disarmed this madwoman, Beaky!
Tsk. I wish you wouldn't call me "Beaky."
Lunch'll be ready in a few minutes, Rackham. Make sure this rogue brings in my pan, would you?

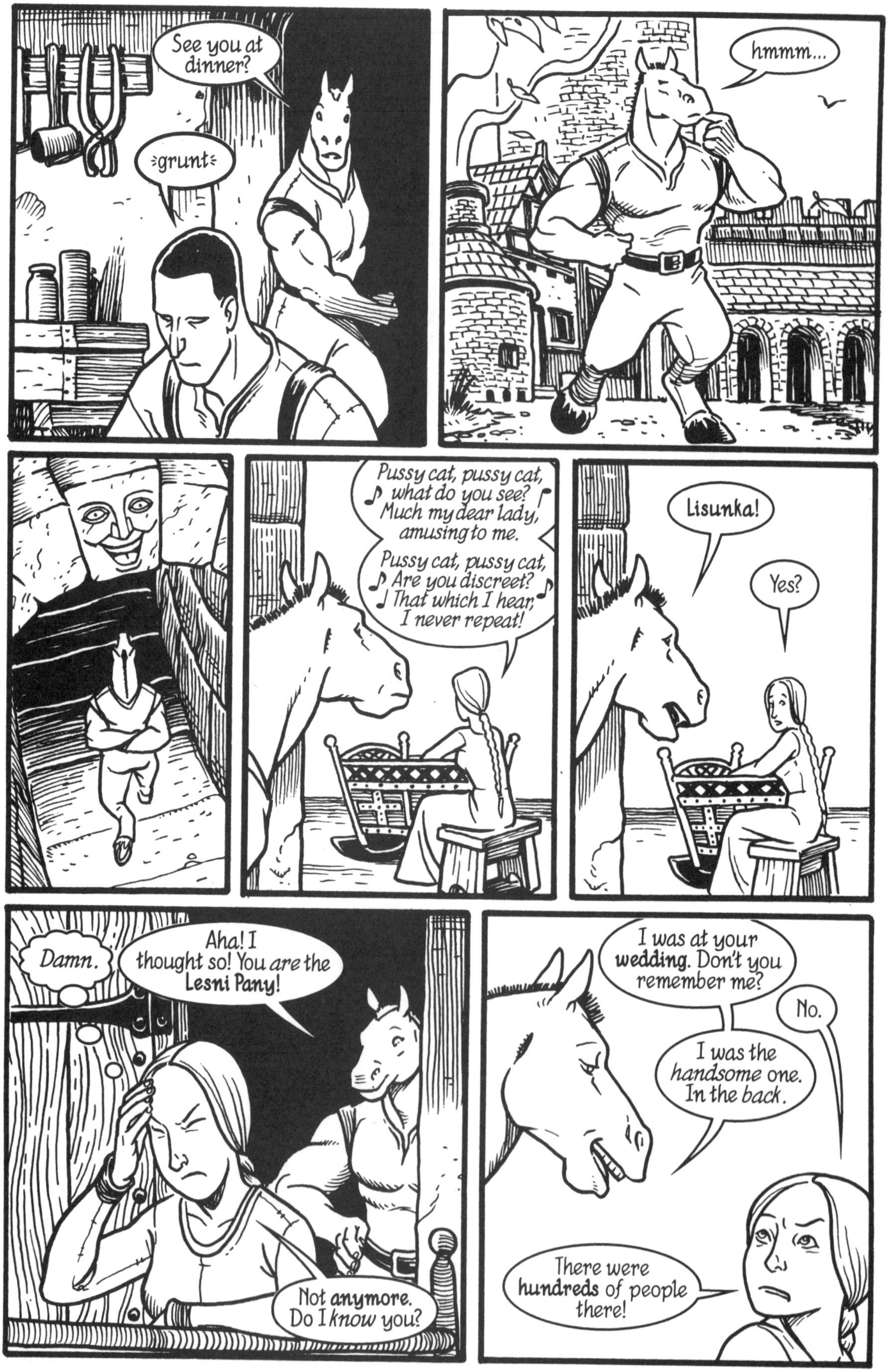
See you at dinner?
grunt
hmmm...
Pussy cat, pussy cat, what do you see? Much my dear lady, amusing to me.
Pussy cat, pussy cat, Are you discreet? That which I hear, I never repeat!
Lisunka!
Yes?
Damn.
Aha! I thought so! You *are* the **Lesni Pany**!
Not **anymore**. Do I *know* you?
I was at your **wedding**. Don't you remember me?
No.
I was the *handsome* one. In the *back*.
There were **hundreds** of people there!

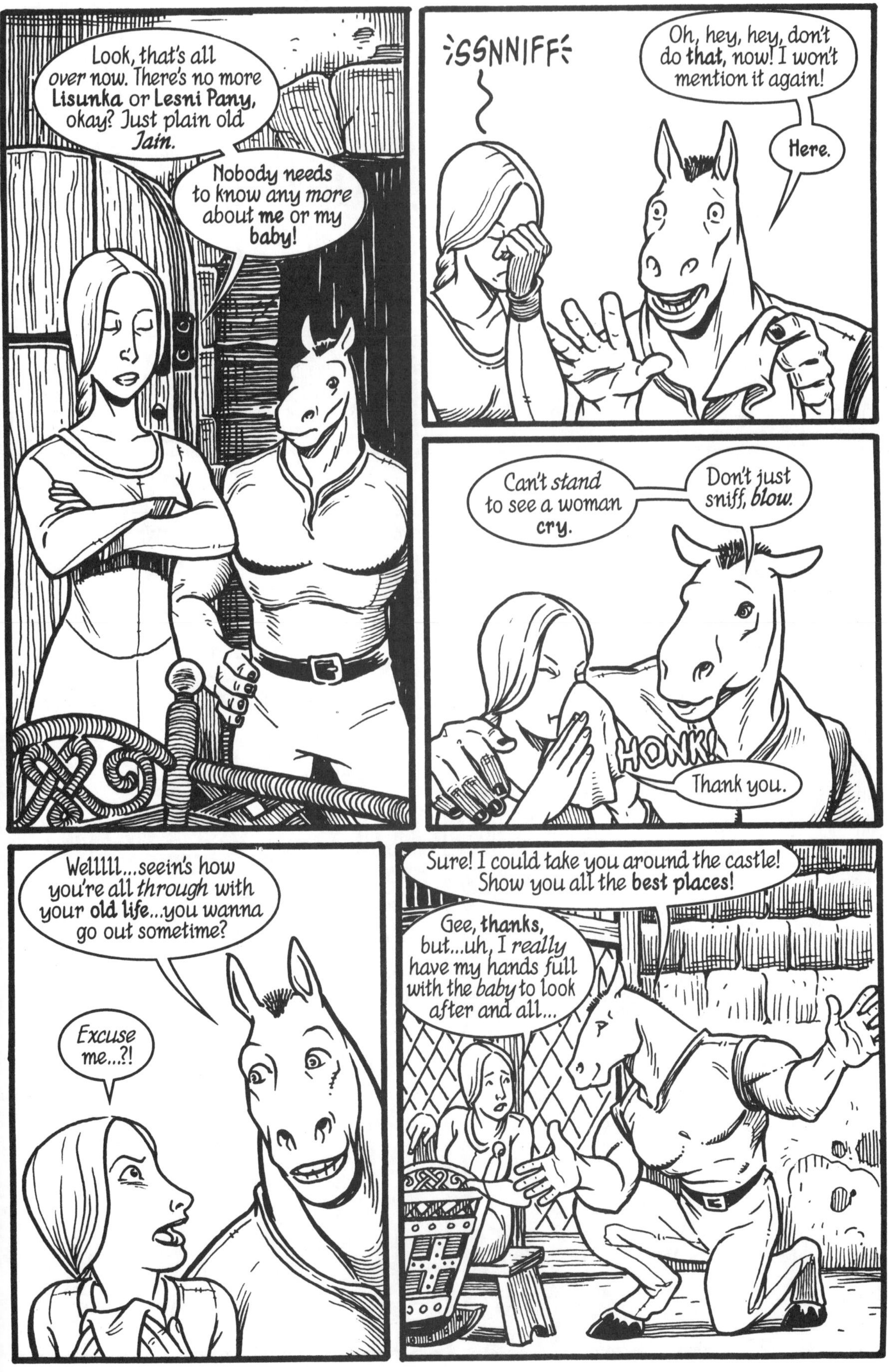
Look, that's all over now. There's no more Lisunka or Lesni Pany, okay? Just plain old Jain.
Nobody needs to know any more about me or my baby!
SSNNIFF
Oh, hey, hey, don't do that, now! I won't mention it again!
Here.
Can't stand to see a woman cry.
Don't just sniff, blow.
HONK!
Thank you.
Wellllll...seein's how you're all through with your old life...you wanna go out sometime?
Excuse me...?!
Sure! I could take you around the castle! Show you all the best places!
Gee, thanks, but...uh, I really have my hands full with the baby to look after and all...

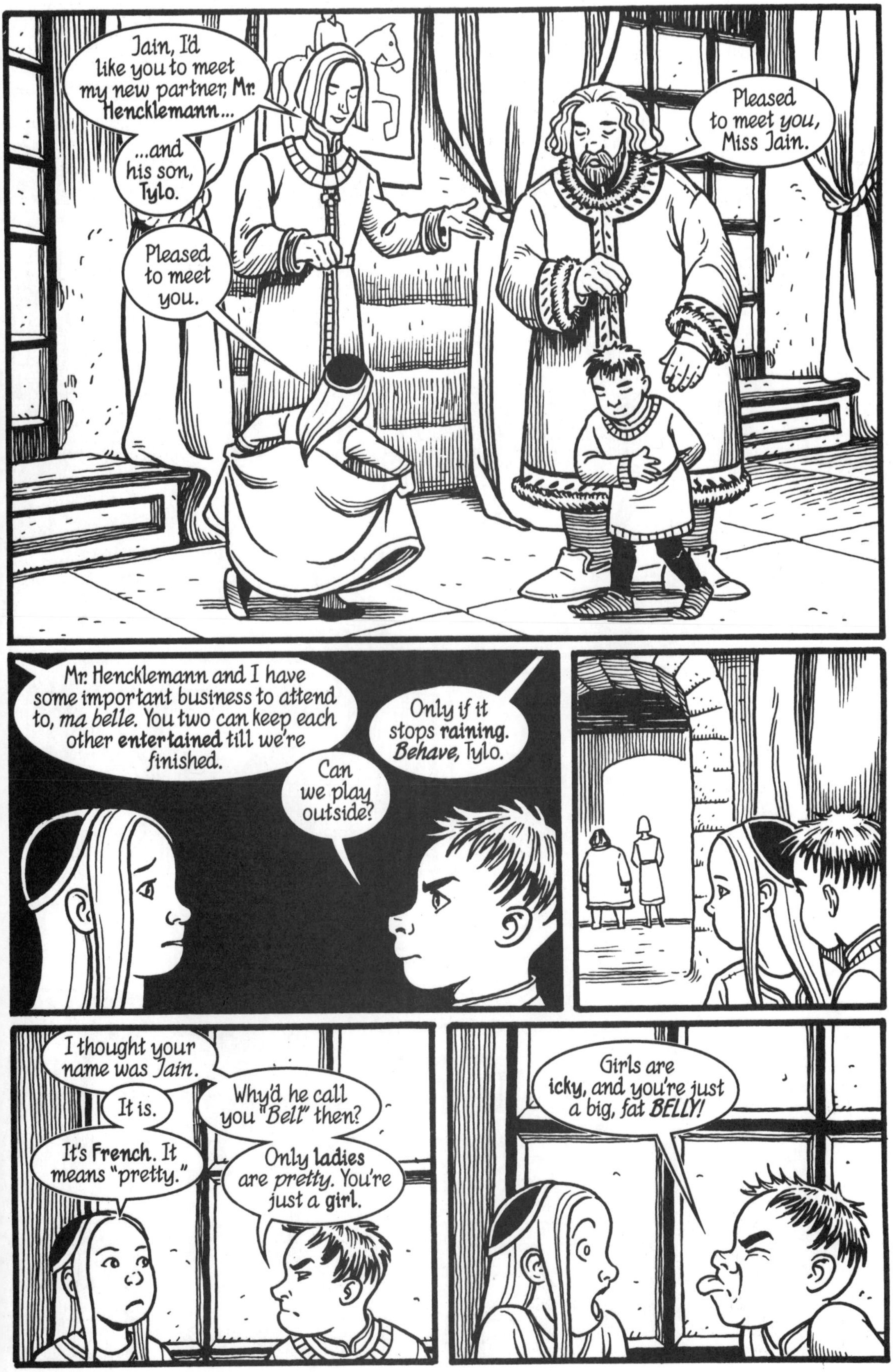
Jain, I'd like you to meet my new partner, Mr. **Hencklemann**...
...and his son, Tylo.
Pleased to meet you, Miss Jain.
Pleased to meet you.
Mr. Hencklemann and I have some important business to attend to, *ma belle*. You two can keep each other **entertained** till we're finished.
Can we play outside?
Only if it stops **raining**. *Behave*, Tylo.
I thought your name was *Jain*.
It is.
Why'd he call you "*Bell*" then?
It's **French**. It means "pretty."
Only **ladies** are *pretty*. You're just a **girl**.
Girls are **icky**, and you're just a big, fat ***BELLY!***

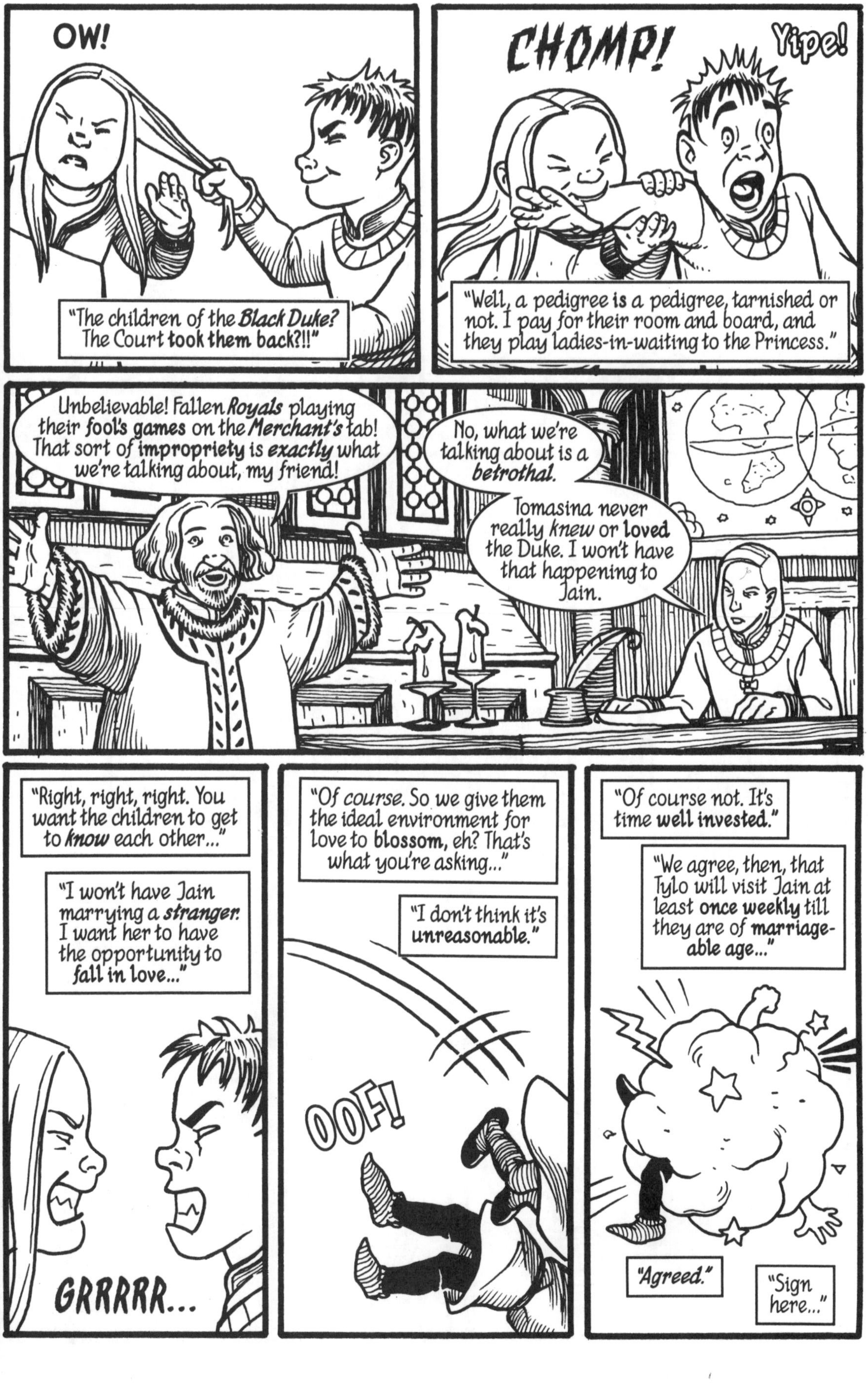
OW!
"The children of the Black Duke? The Court took them back?!!"
CHOMP!
Yipe!
"Well, a pedigree is a pedigree, tarnished or not. I pay for their room and board, and they play ladies-in-waiting to the Princess."
Unbelievable! Fallen Royals playing their fool's games on the Merchant's tab! That sort of impropriety is exactly what we're talking about, my friend!
No, what we're talking about is a betrothal.
Tomasina never really knew or loved the Duke. I won't have that happening to Jain.
"Right, right, right. You want the children to get to know each other..."
"I won't have Jain marrying a stranger. I want her to have the opportunity to fall in love..."
GRRRRR...
"Of course. So we give them the ideal environment for love to blossom, eh? That's what you're asking..."
"I don't think it's unreasonable."
OOF!
"Of course not. It's time well invested."
"We agree, then, that Tylo will visit Jain at least once weekly till they are of marriage-able age..."
"Agreed."
"Sign here..."

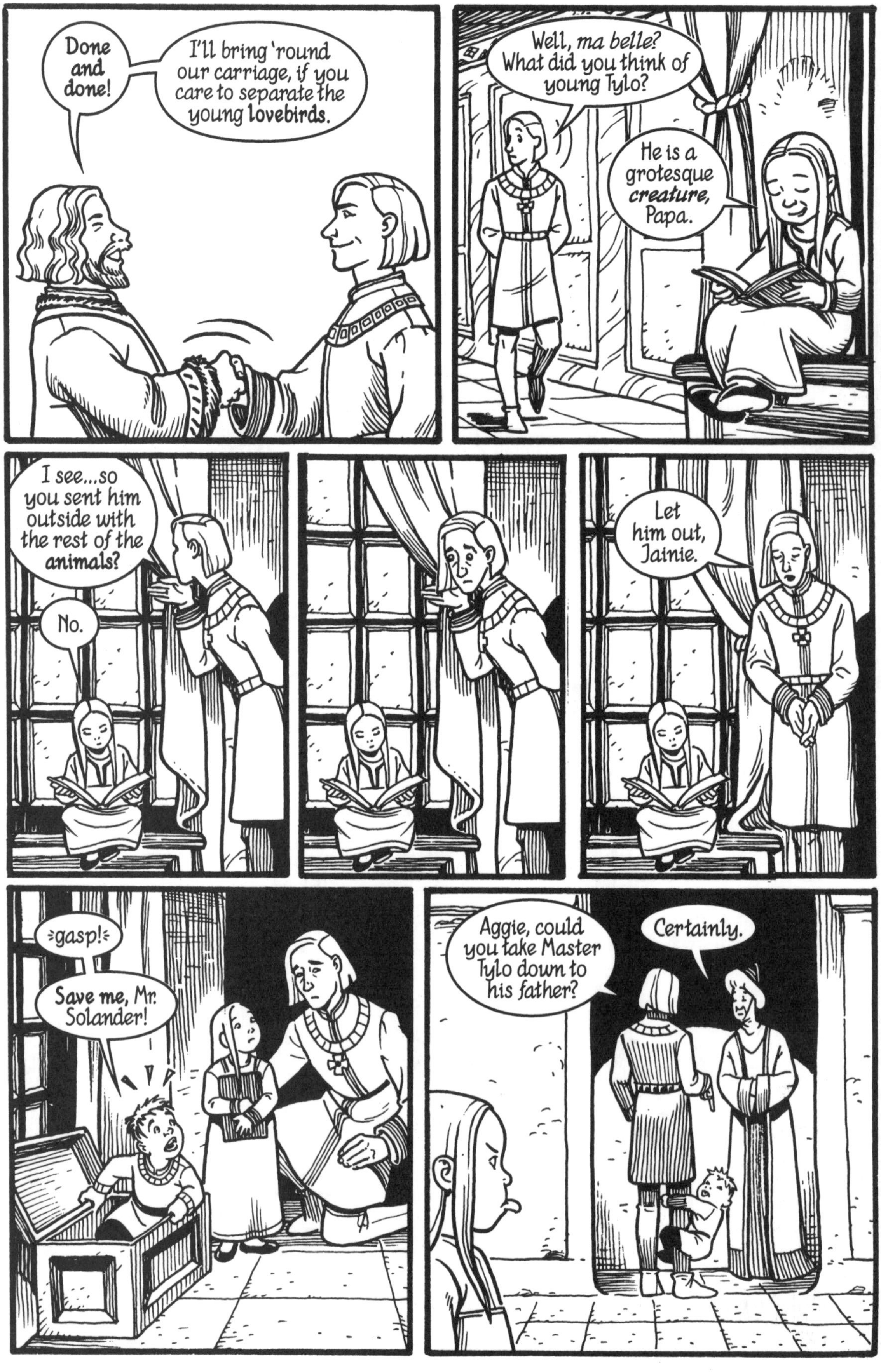
Done and done!
I'll bring 'round our carriage, if you care to separate the young lovebirds.
Well, *ma belle?* What did you think of young Tylo?
He is a grotesque *creature,* Papa.
I see...so you sent him outside with the rest of the animals?
No.
Let him out, Jainie.
gasp!
Save me, Mr. Solander!
Aggie, could you take Master Tylo down to his father?
Certainly.

He started it.

Oh, I don't doubt it.

It's important you learn to get along with Tylo, *cherie*. You'll be spending a lot of time to-gether.

Bleah!

Will you *try*, for *me*? You're such a *good* girl, Jainie. I'm sure he'll *learn* to be good by your example.

I'll try, Papa.

That's my girl!

BELLY!

See you next week, Belly!

≈sigh≈

Excuse me, Rackham?

Come in, Lady, **come** in!

Dinah told me you were planning a trip into **town**. Could you pick up a *few* **baby things** for me?

I'll add them to the list!

I have plenty of **money**--

Nonsense! We had a good year. There's more than enough surplus in the coffers to cover *these*. You keep your money.

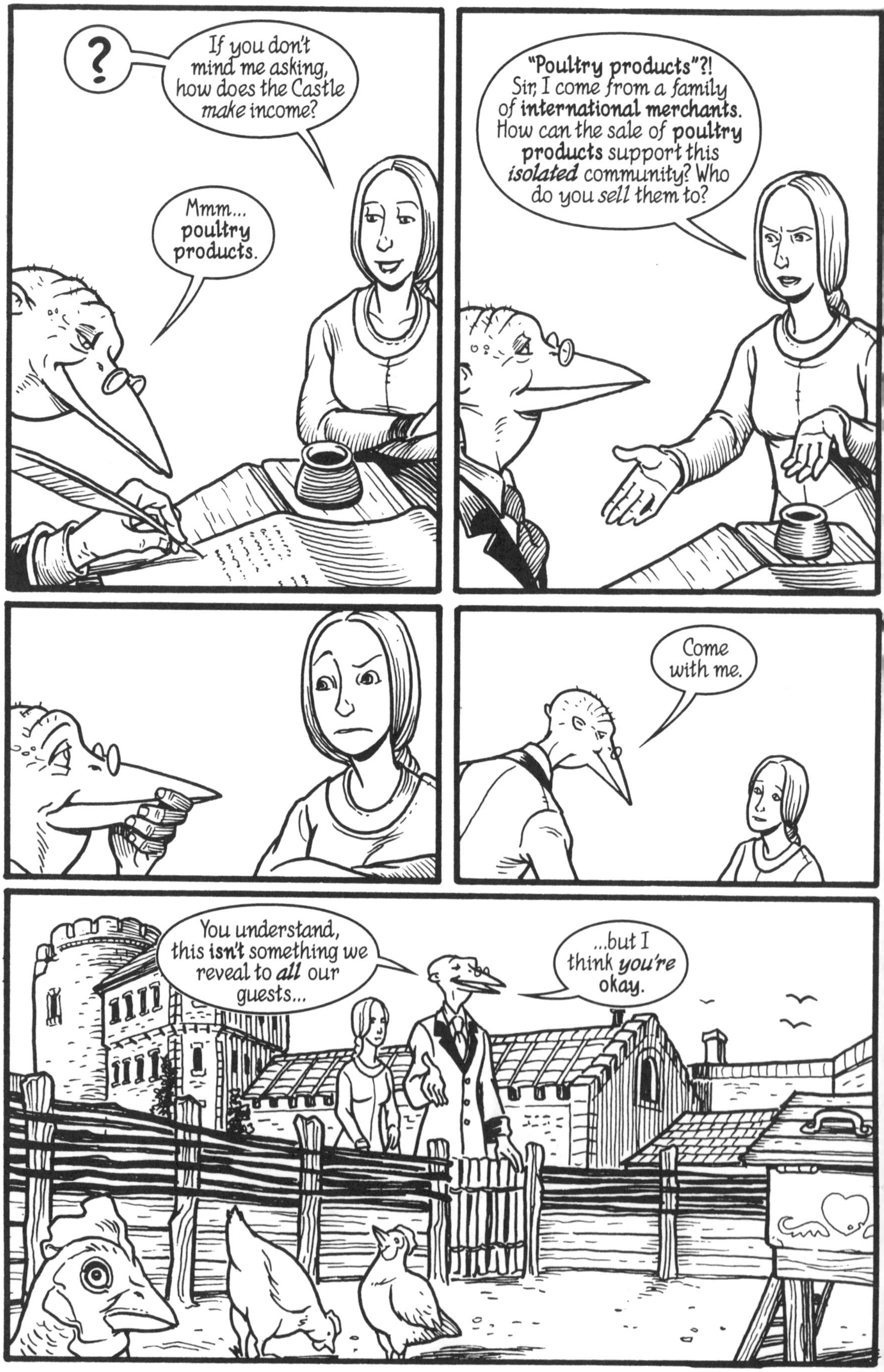
?
If you don't mind me asking, how does the Castle *make* income?
Mmm... **poultry products**.
"**Poultry products**"?! Sir, I come from a family of **international merchants**. How can the sale of **poultry products** support this ***isolated*** community? Who do you *sell* them to?
Come with me.
You understand, this **isn't** something we reveal to ***all*** our guests...
...but I think ***you're*** **okay**.

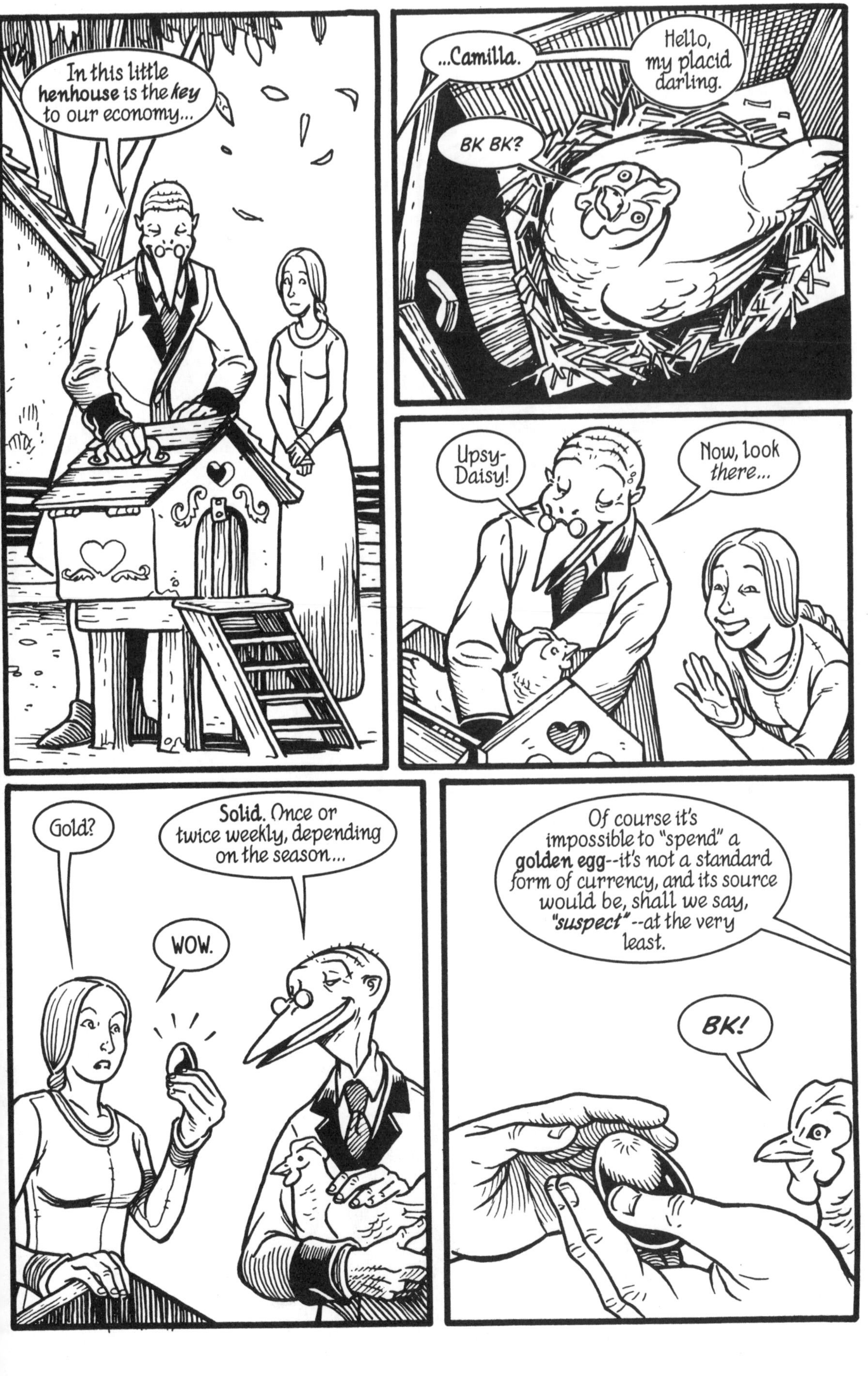
In this little **henhouse** is the ***key*** to our economy...
...Camilla.
Hello, my placid darling.
BK BK?
Upsy-Daisy!
Now, look *there*...
Gold?
Solid. Once or twice weekly, depending on the season...
WOW.
Of course it's impossible to "spend" a **golden egg**--it's not a standard form of currency, and its source would be, shall we say, ***"suspect"***--at the very least.
BK!

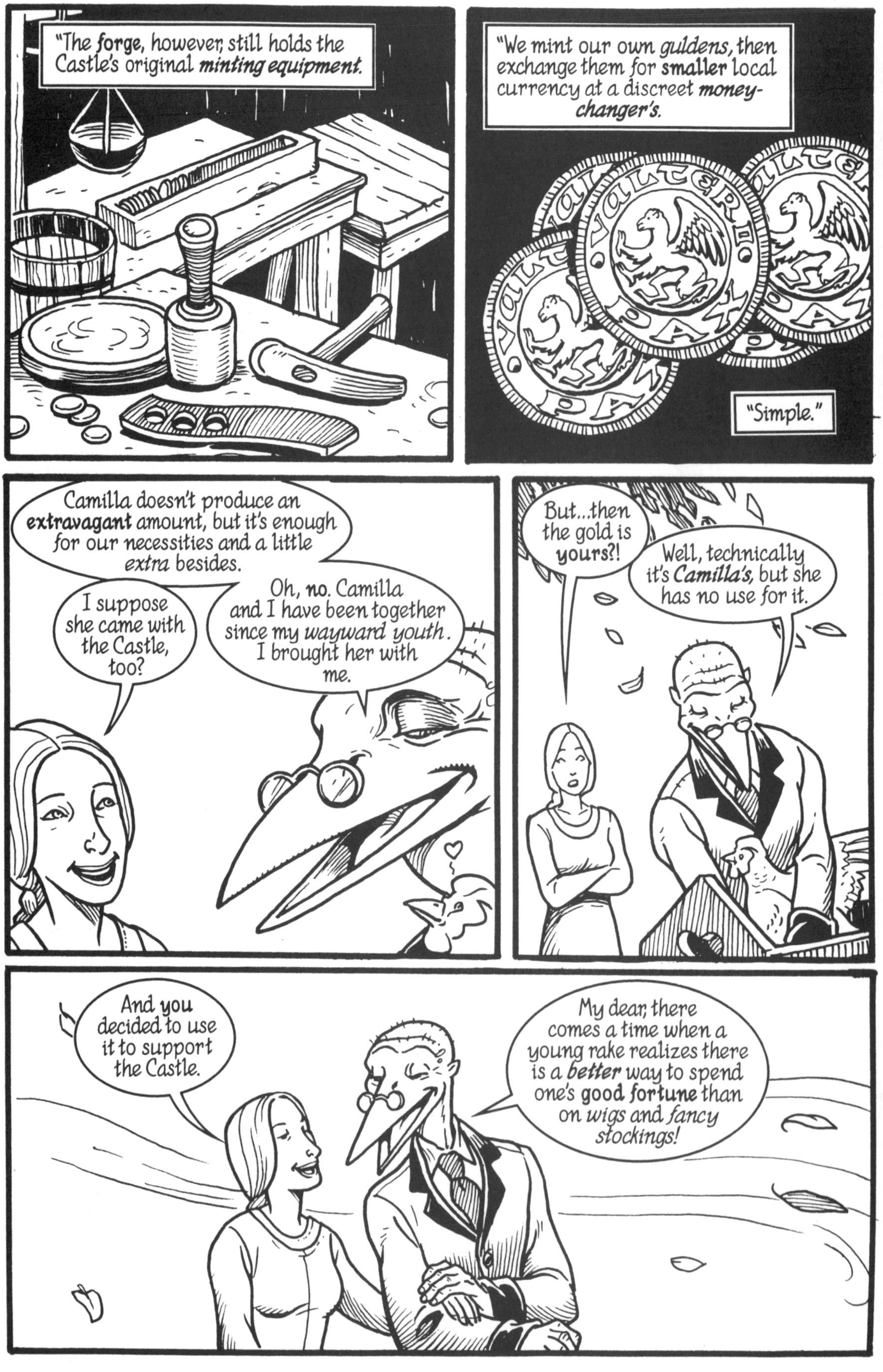
"The forge, however, still holds the Castle's original minting equipment.
"We mint our own guldens, then exchange them for smaller local currency at a discreet money-changer's.
"Simple."
Camilla doesn't produce an extravagant amount, but it's enough for our necessities and a little extra besides.
I suppose she came with the Castle, too?
Oh, no. Camilla and I have been together since my wayward youth. I brought her with me.
But...then the gold is yours?!
Well, technically it's Camilla's, but she has no use for it.
And you decided to use it to support the Castle.
My dear, there comes a time when a young rake realizes there is a better way to spend one's good fortune than on wigs and fancy stockings!

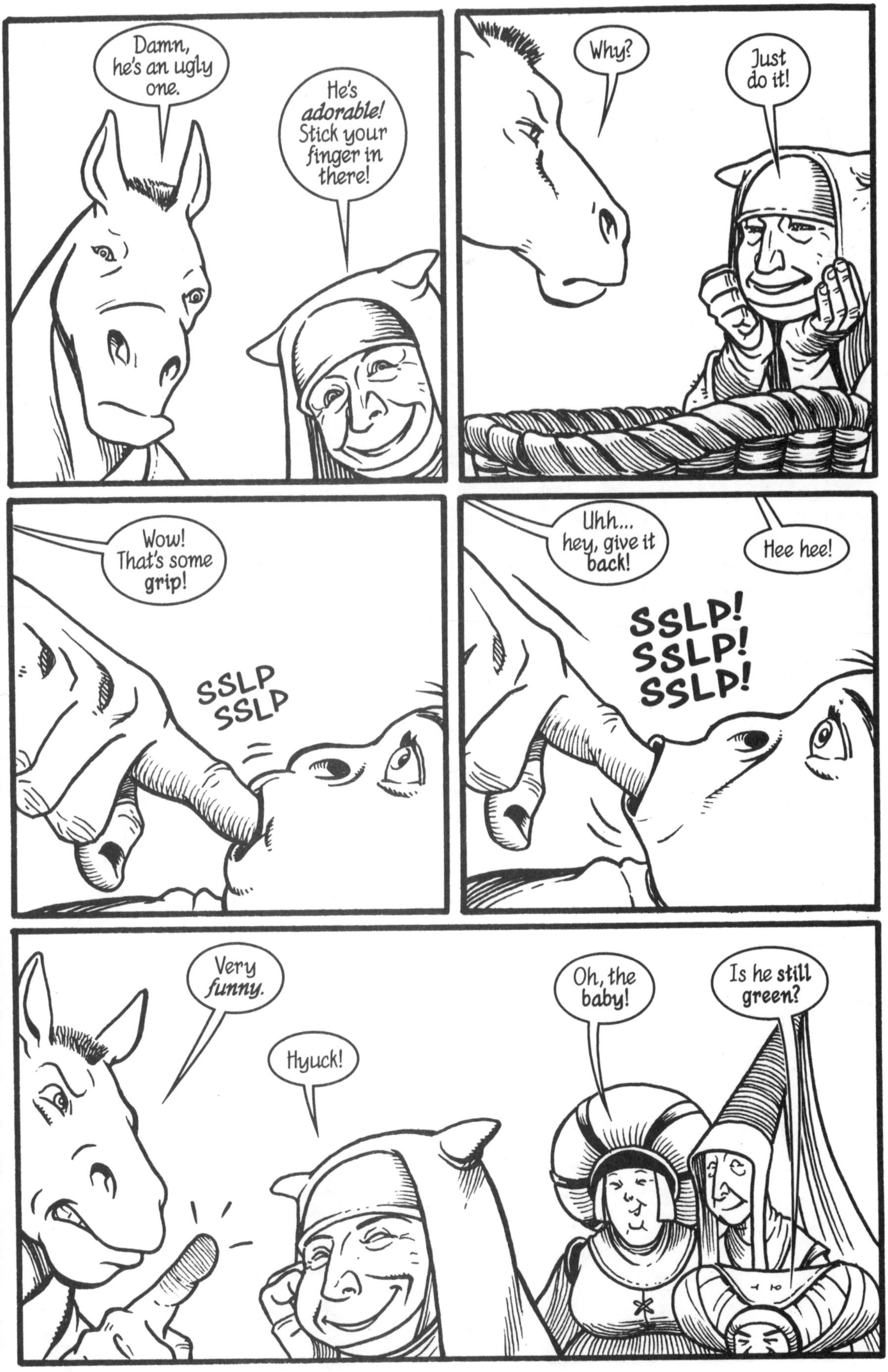
Damn, he's an ugly one.
He's *adorable!* Stick your finger in there!
Why?
Just do it!
Wow! That's some **grip!**
SSLP SSLP
Uhh... hey, give it back!
Hee hee!
SSLP! SSLP! SSLP!
Very *funny.*
Hyuck!
Oh, the baby!
Is he **still green?**

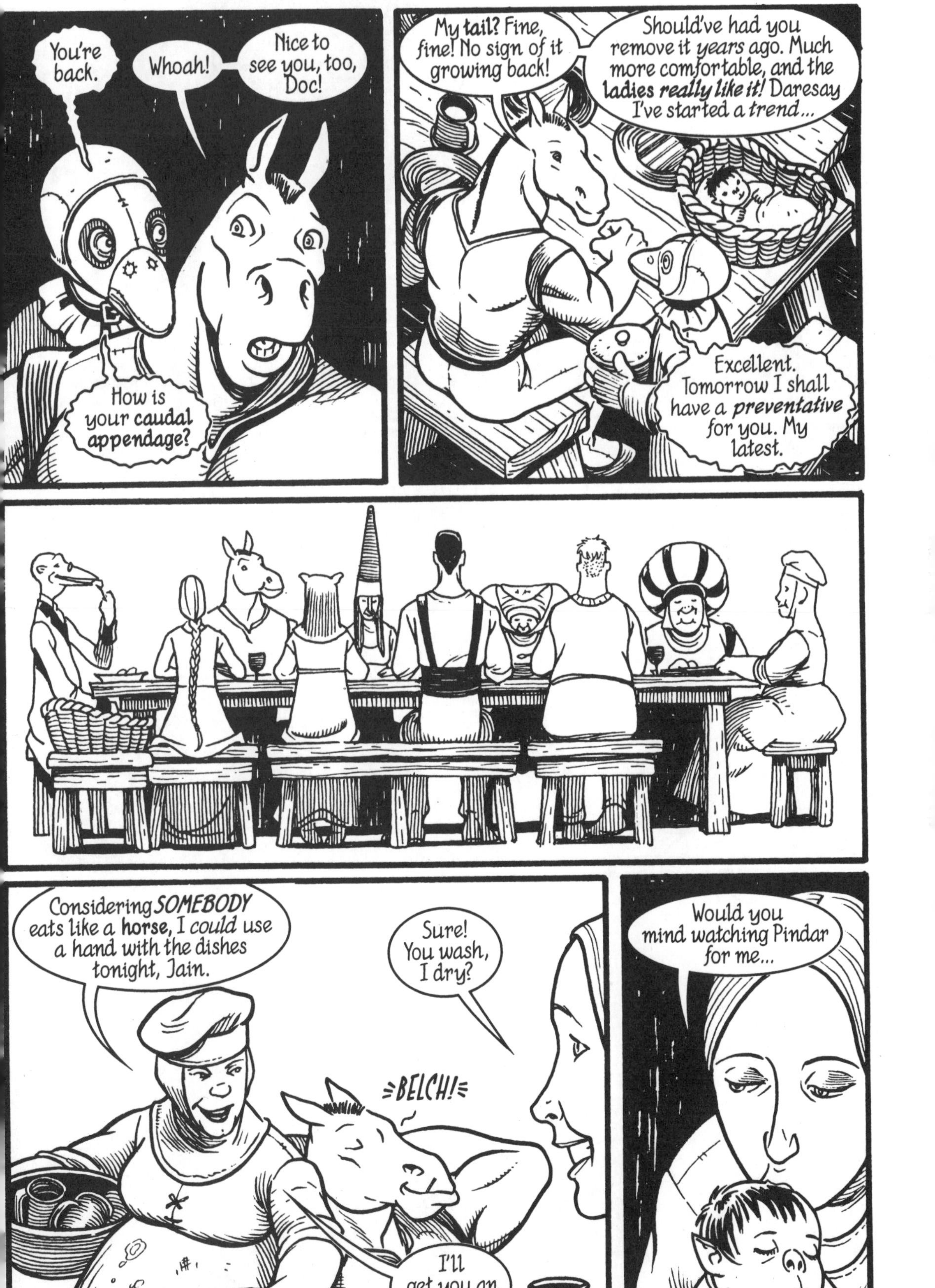
You're back.
Whoah!
Nice to see you, too, Doc!
How is your caudal appendage?
My tail? Fine, fine! No sign of it growing back!
Should've had you remove it years ago. Much more comfortable, and the ladies really like it! Daresay I've started a trend...
Excellent. Tomorrow I shall have a preventative for you. My latest.
Considering SOMEBODY eats like a horse, I could use a hand with the dishes tonight, Jain.
Sure! You wash, I dry?
BELCH!
I'll get you an apron.
Would you mind watching Pindar for me...

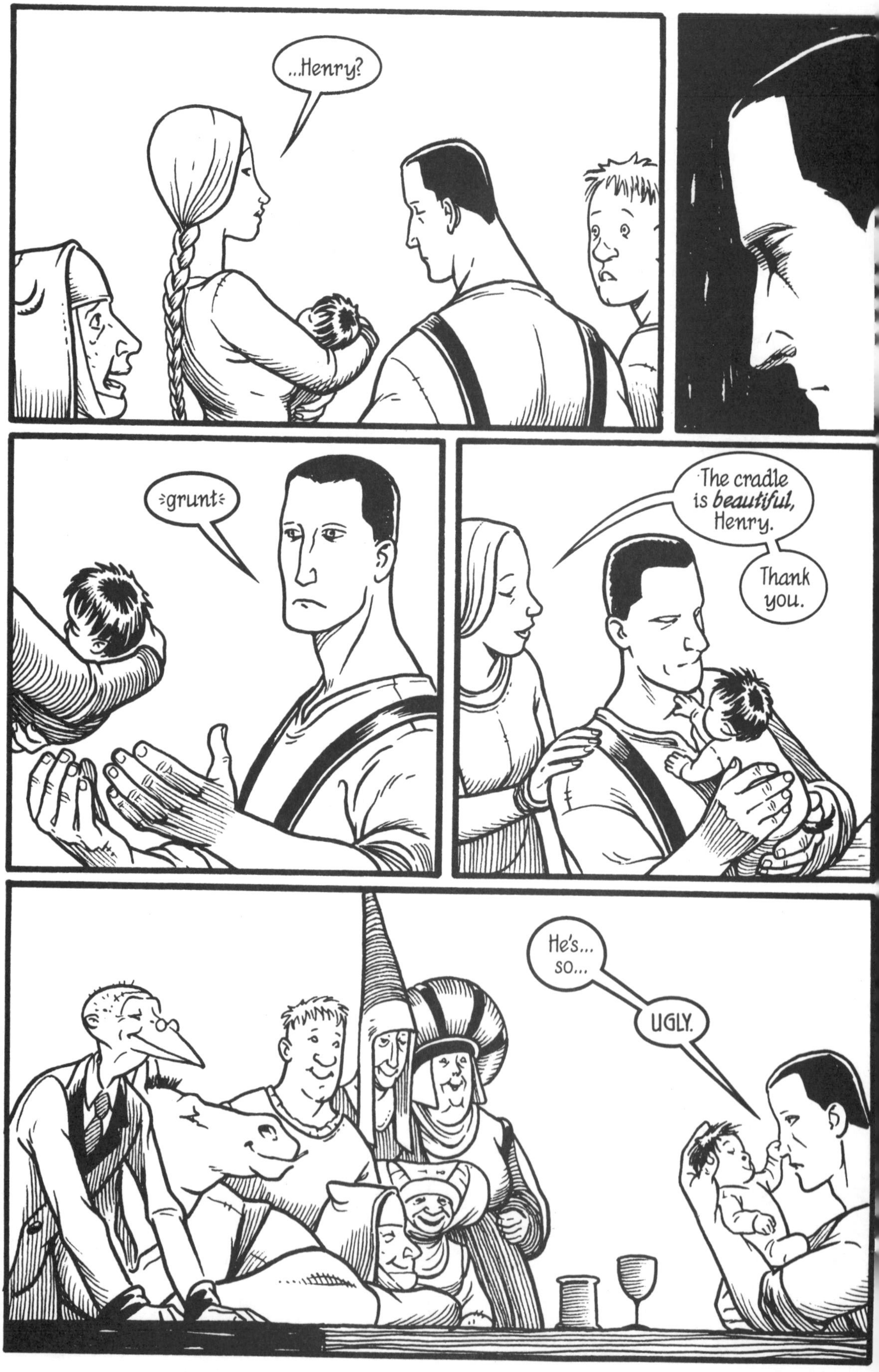
...Henry?
grunt
The cradle is *beautiful*, Henry.
Thank you.
He's... so...
UGLY.

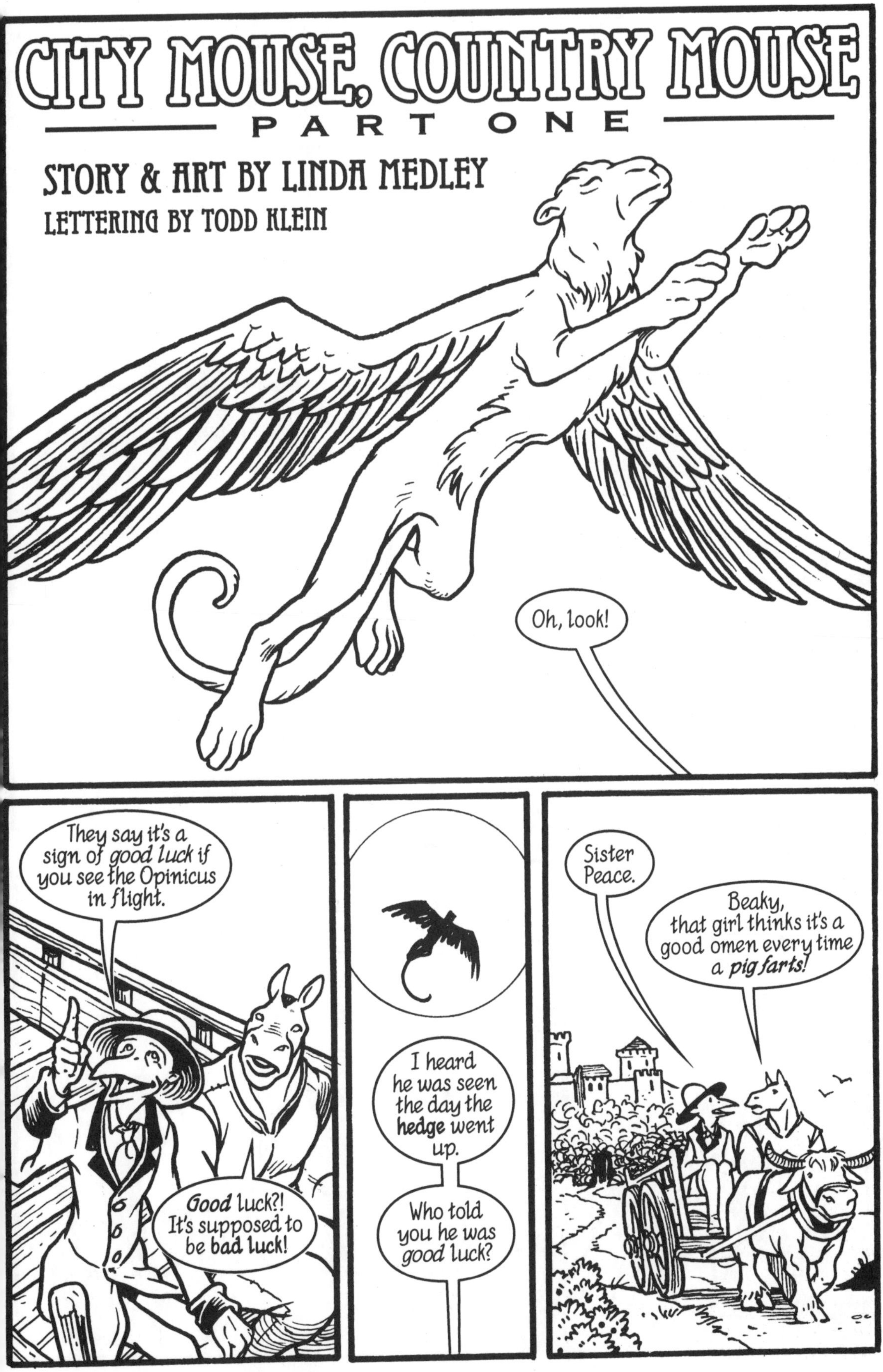
CITY MOUSE, COUNTRY MOUSE
PART ONE
STORY & ART BY LINDA MEDLEY
LETTERING BY TODD KLEIN
Oh, look!
They say it's a sign of *good luck* if you see the Opinicus in flight.
Good luck?! It's supposed to be **bad luck!**
I heard he was seen the day the **hedge** went up.
Who told you he was *good* luck?
Sister Peace.
Beaky, that girl thinks it's a good omen every time a ***pig farts!***

I woke up sad and it just won't go *away*. I don't know what it is...

I do. It's *normal*.

Everyone makes a fuss over the new baby but forgets about the new *mama*. You need a little something *special* to cheer you up, that's all. Some excitement, maybe?

Hmmm...

≥sigh≤

I've got something *special* I've been saving for almost a year now. I never had the guts to use it by *myself*...but I bet it's just the thing to make you *feel* better...!

Come on into the kitchen!

?!

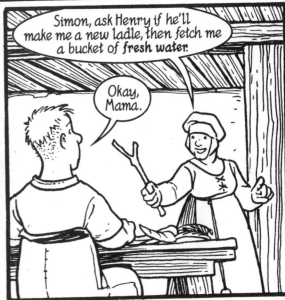

Simon, ask Henry if he'll make me a new ladle, then fetch me a bucket of *fresh water*.

Okay, Mama.

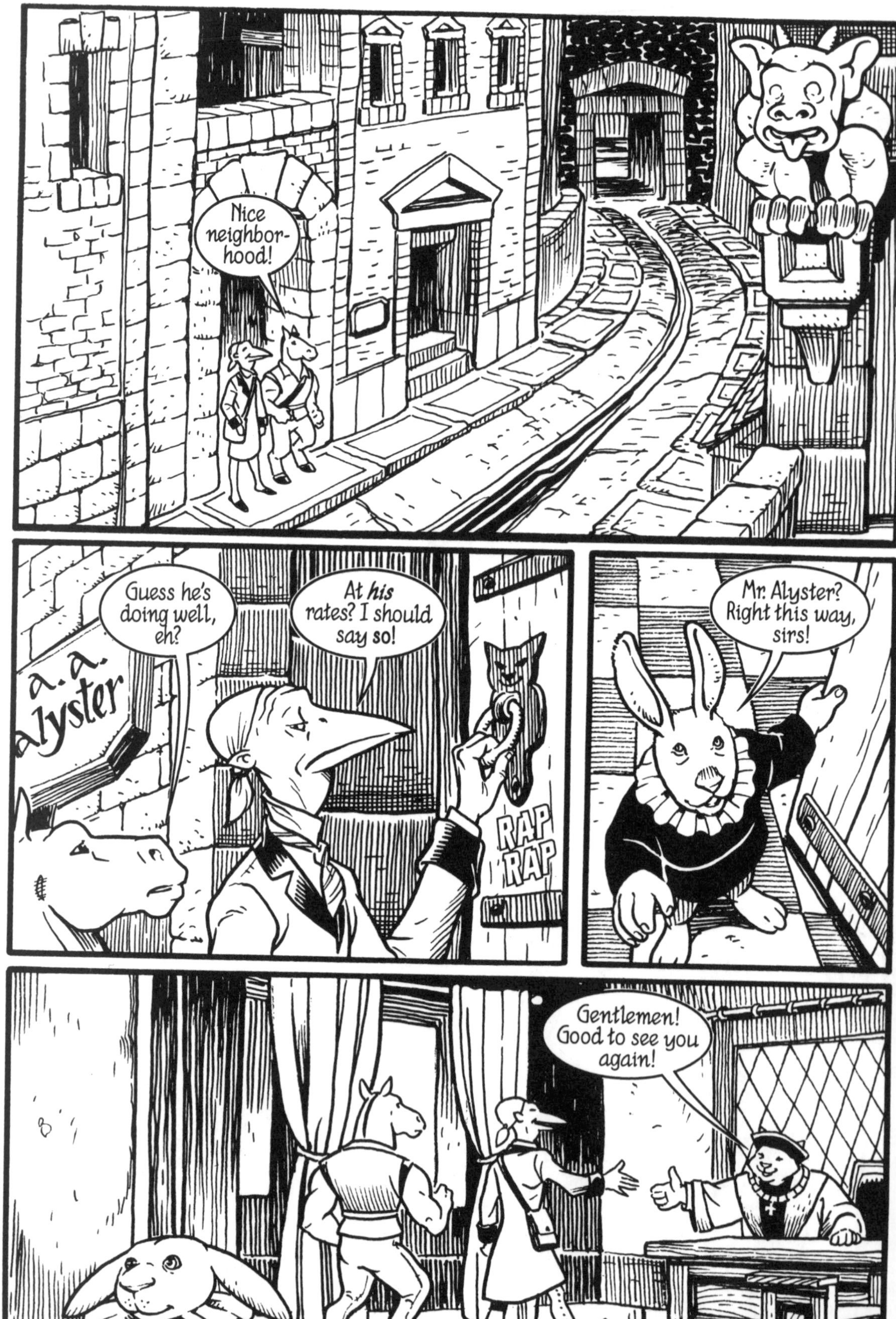

Nice neighbor-hood!
Guess he's doing well, eh?
At *his* rates? I should say so!
a. a. alyster
RAP RAP
Mr. Alyster? Right this way, sirs!
Gentlemen! Good to see you again!

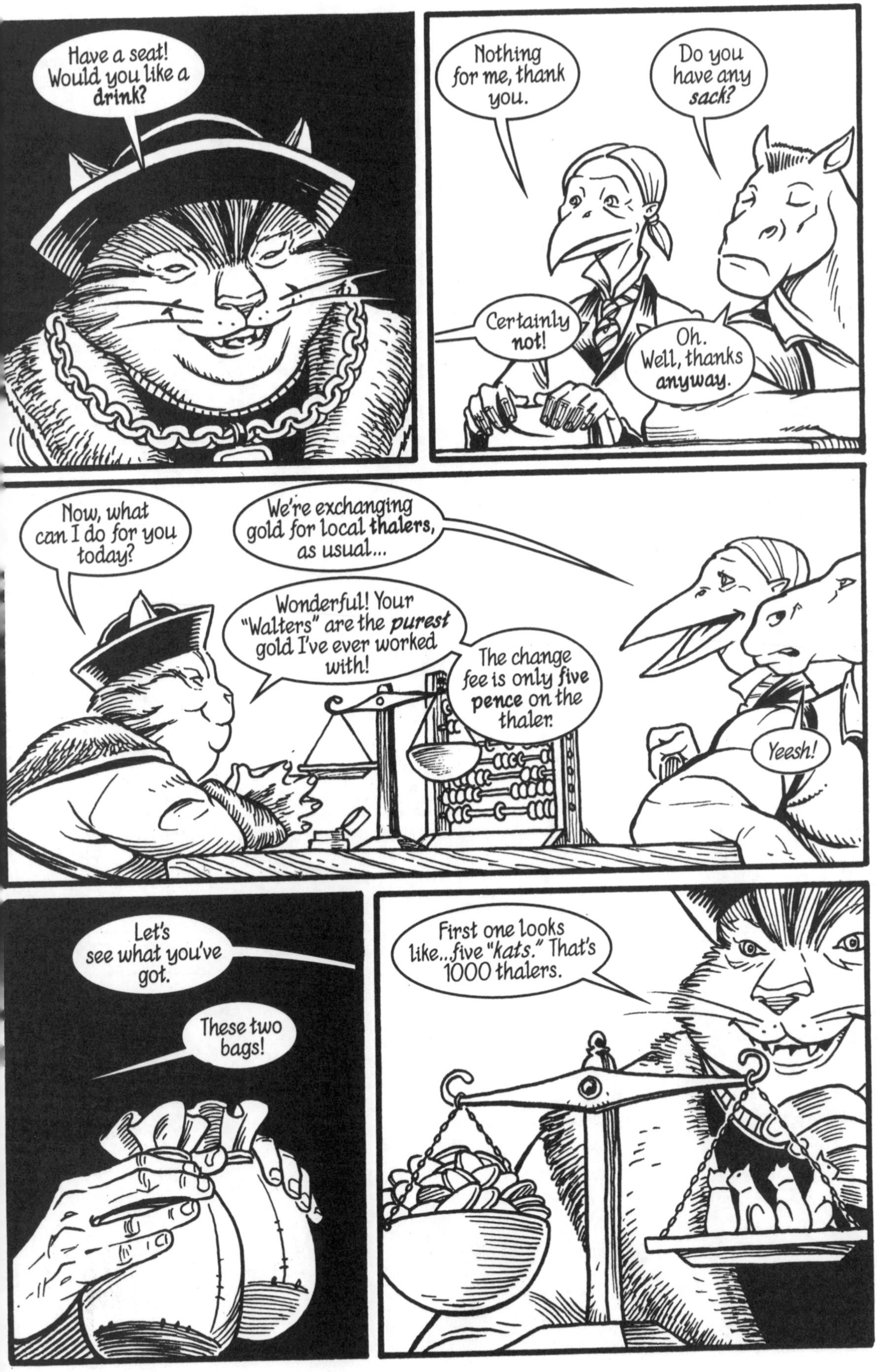
Have a seat! Would you like a **drink?**
Nothing for me, thank you.
Do you have any *sack?*
Certainly **not!**
Oh. Well, thanks **anyway.**
Now, what can I do for you today?
We're exchanging gold for local **thalers**, as usual...
Wonderful! Your "Walters" are the ***purest*** gold I've ever worked with!
The change fee is only **five pence** on the thaler.
Yeesh!
Let's see what you've got.
These two bags!
First one looks like...five "*kats.*" That's 1000 thalers.

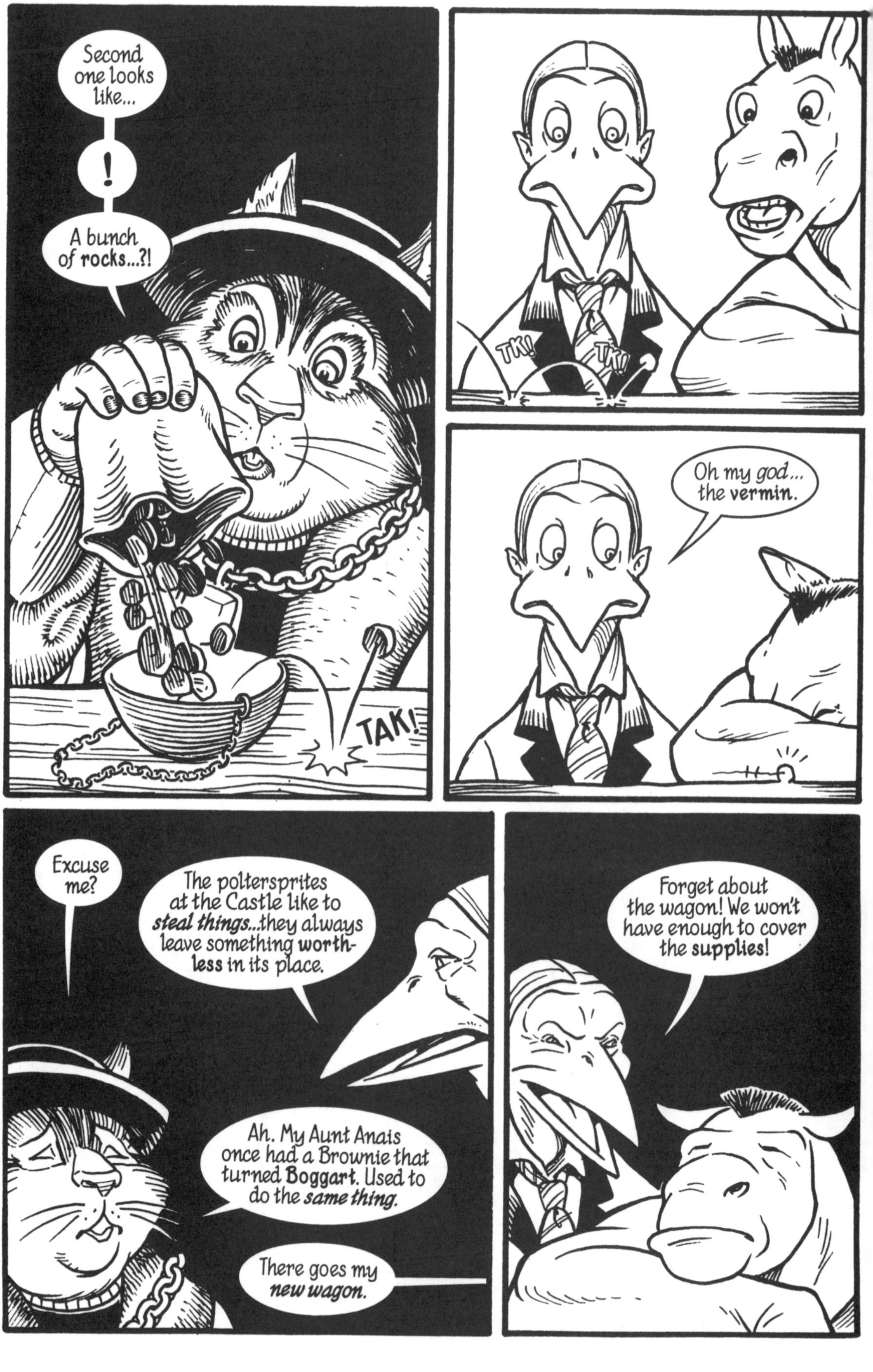

Second one looks like...
!
A bunch of rocks...?!
TAK!
TK!
TK!
Oh my god... the vermin.
Excuse me?
The poltersprites at the Castle like to steal things...they always leave something worthless in its place.
Ah. My Aunt Anais once had a Brownie that turned Boggart. Used to do the same thing.
There goes my new wagon.
Forget about the wagon! We won't have enough to cover the supplies!

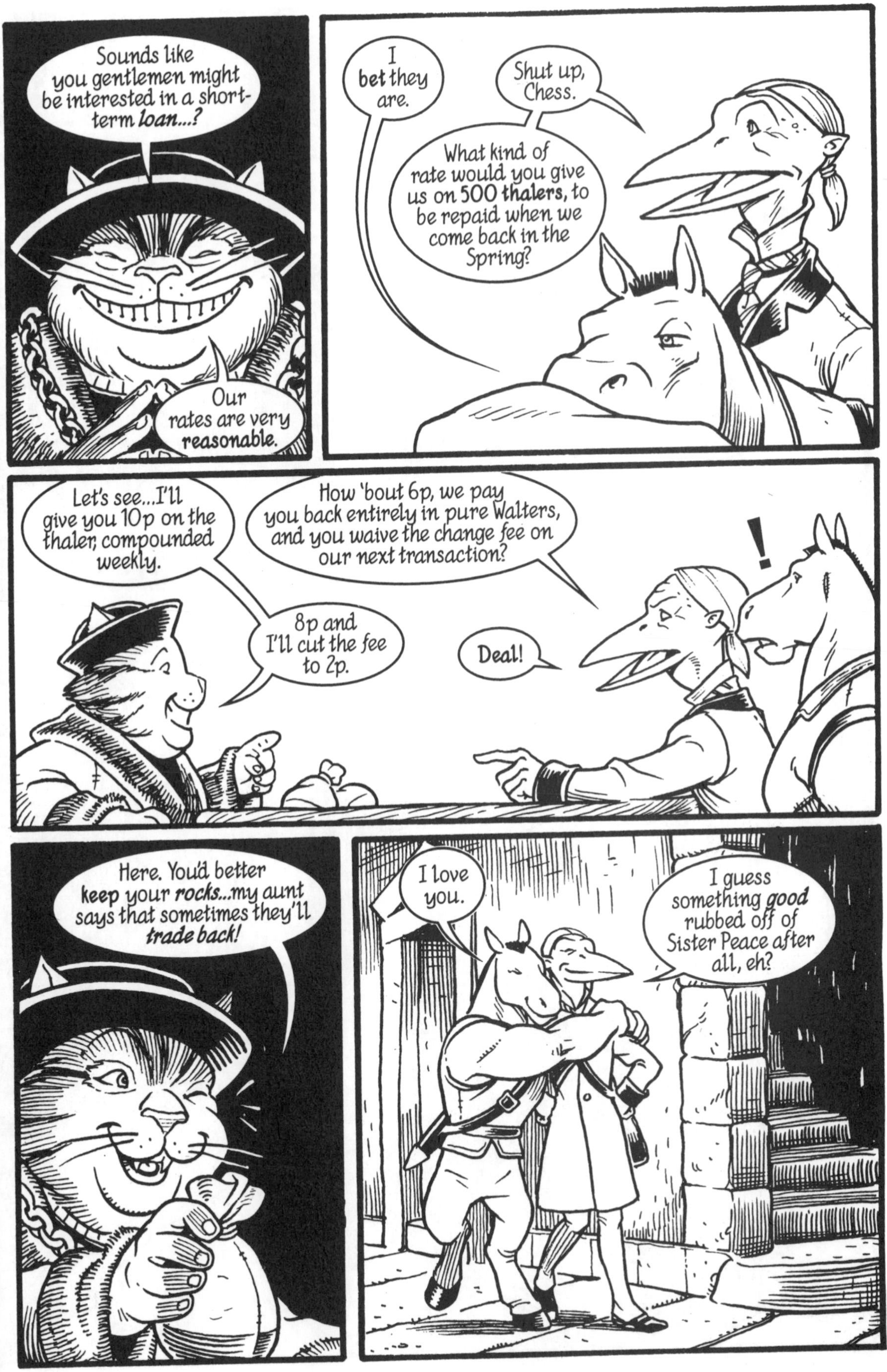
Sounds like you gentlemen might be interested in a short-term loan...?
Our rates are very reasonable.
I bet they are.
Shut up, Chess.
What kind of rate would you give us on 500 thalers, to be repaid when we come back in the Spring?
Let's see...I'll give you 10p on the thaler, compounded weekly.
How 'bout 6p, we pay you back entirely in pure Walters, and you waive the change fee on our next transaction?
8p and I'll cut the fee to 2p.
Deal!
!
Here. You'd better keep your rocks...my aunt says that sometimes they'll trade back!
I love you.
I guess something good rubbed off of Sister Peace after all, eh?

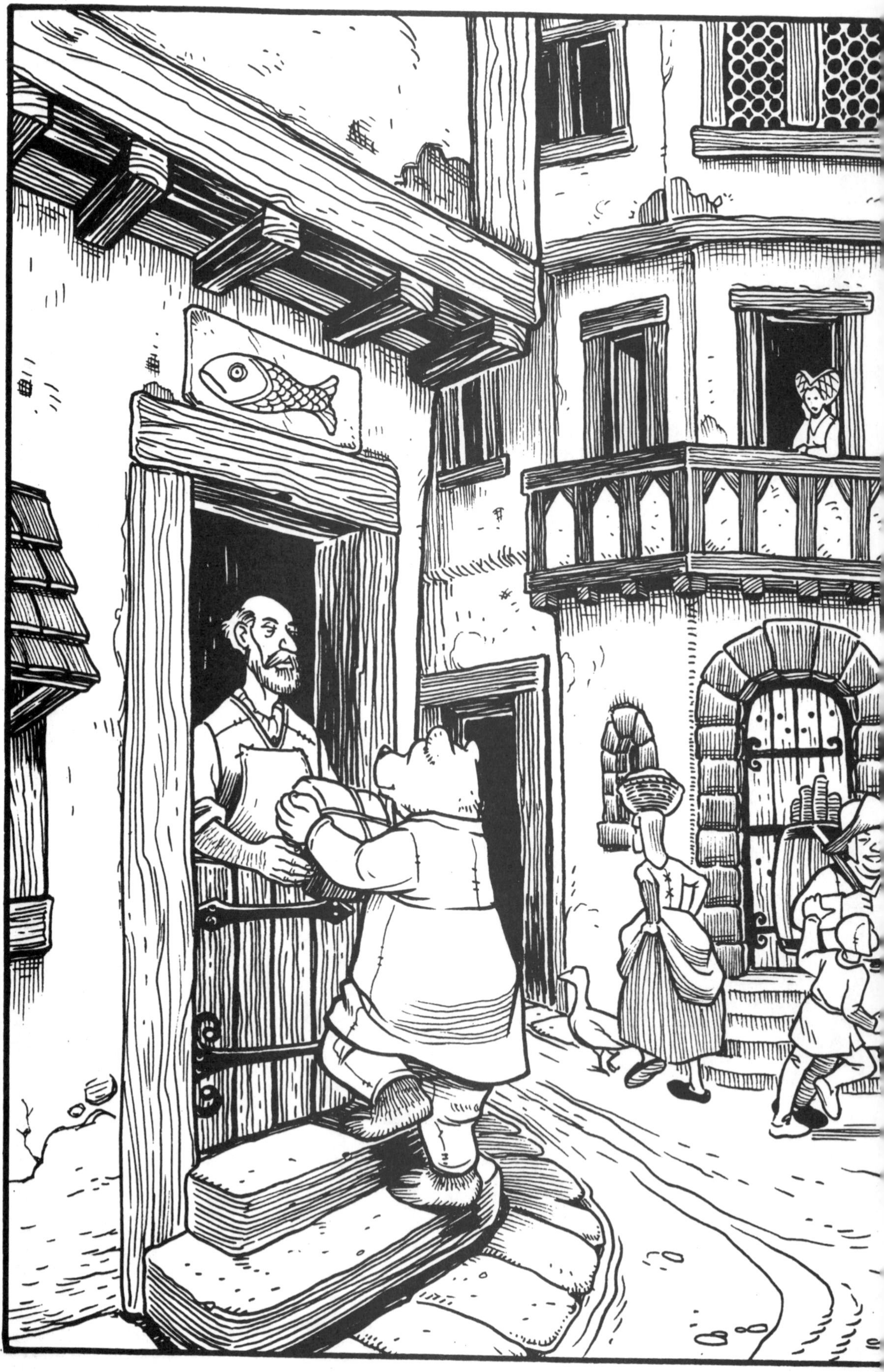

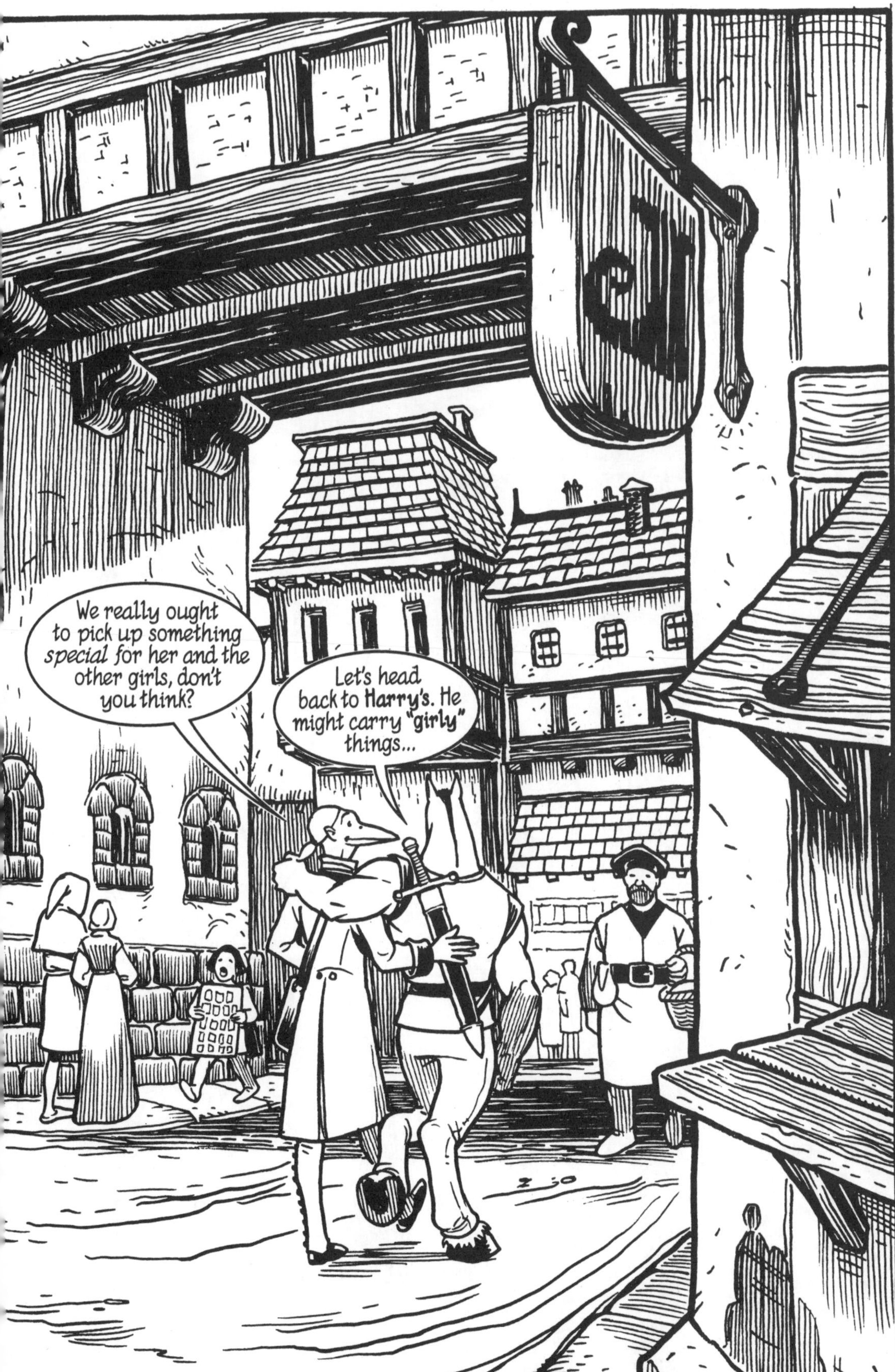
We really ought to pick up something *special* for her and the other girls, don't you think?
Let's head back to **Harry's**. He might carry **"girly"** things...

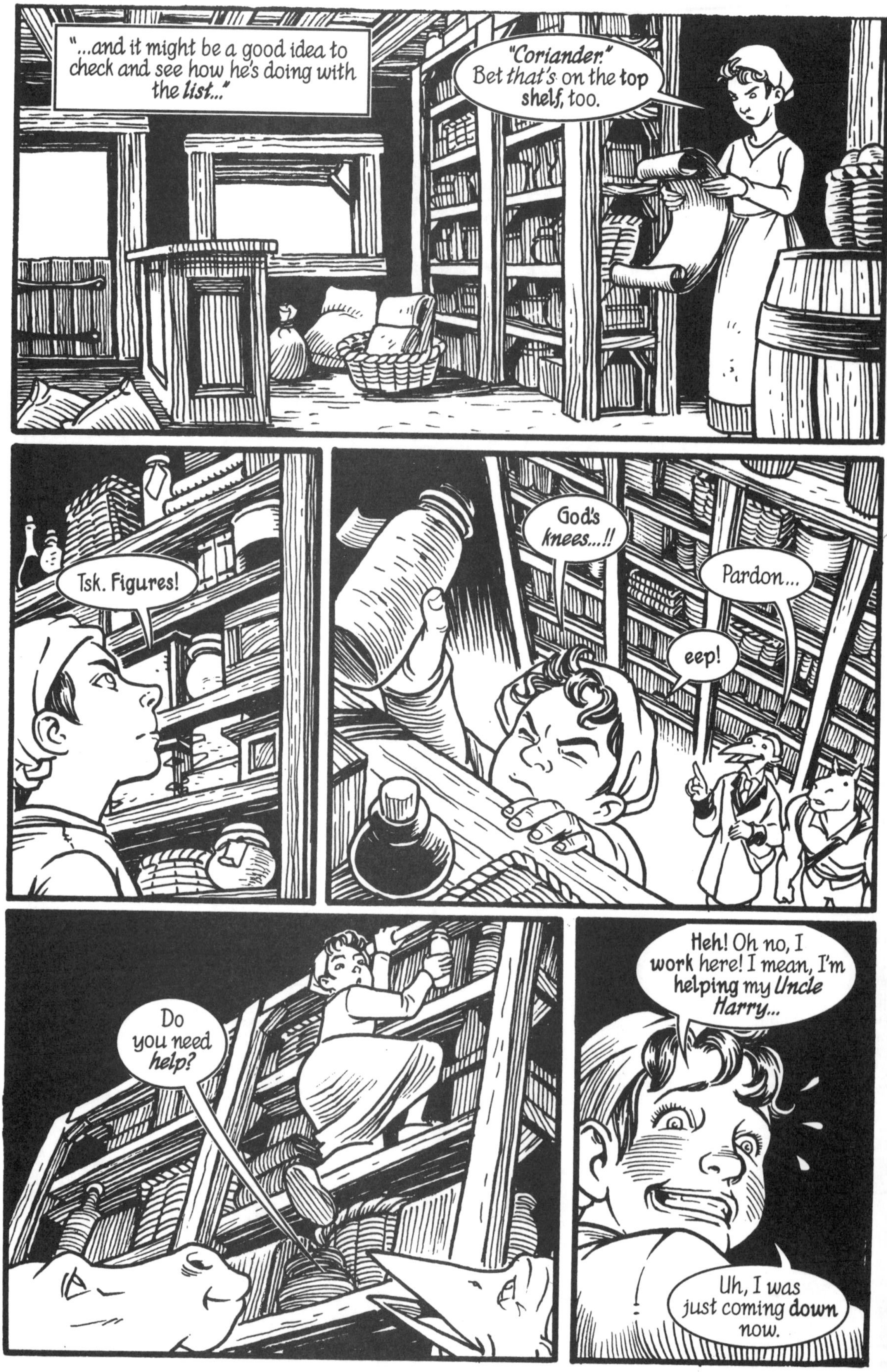

"...and it might be a good idea to check and see how he's doing with the *list*..."
"*Coriander.*" Bet *that's* on the **top shelf**, too.
Tsk. Figures!
God's *knees*...!!
Pardon...
eep!
Do you need *help?*
Heh! Oh no, I **work** here! I mean, I'm helping my *Uncle Harry*...
Uh, I was just coming **down** now.

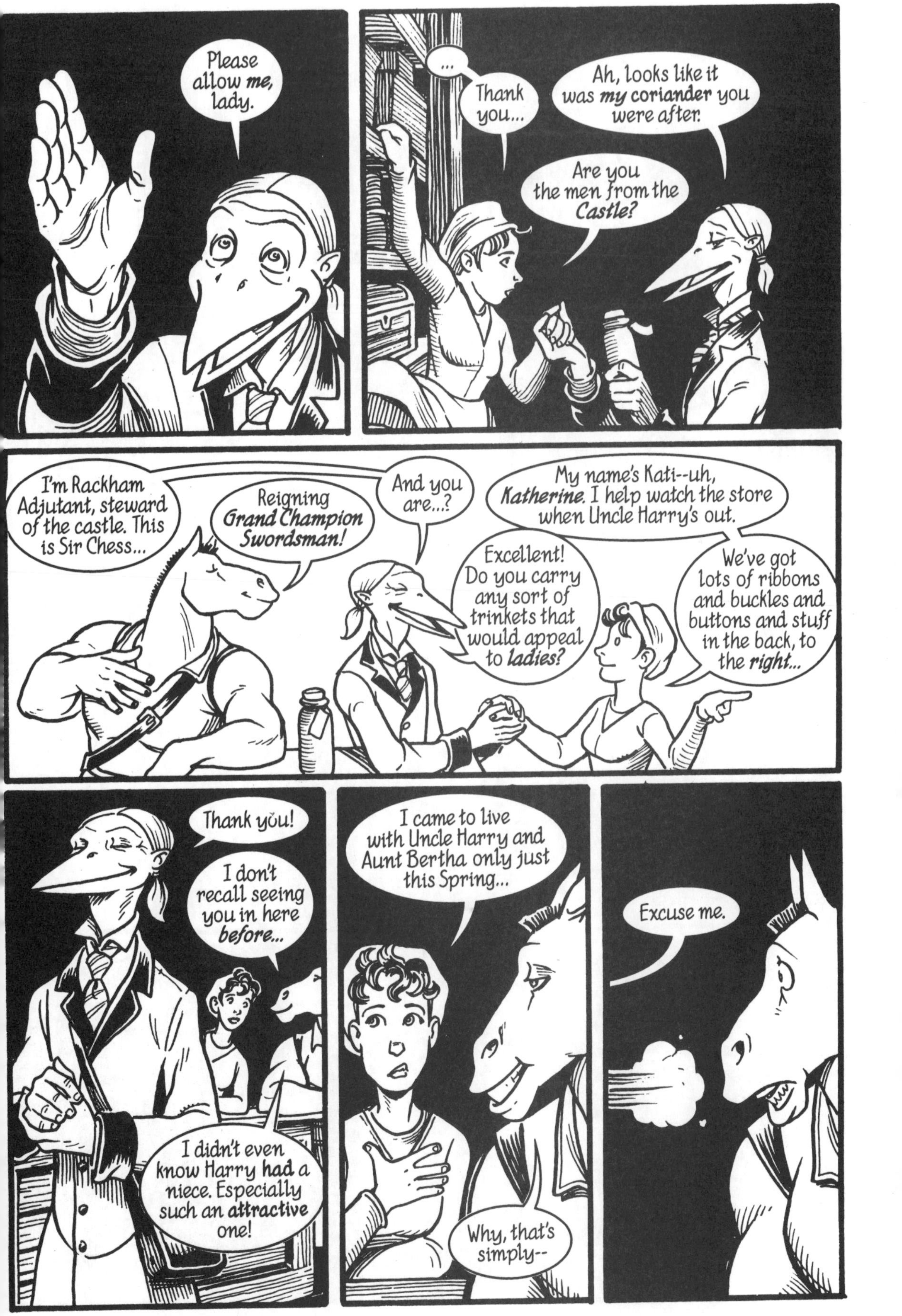
Please allow me, lady.
...
Thank you...
Ah, looks like it was my coriander you were after.
Are you the men from the Castle?
I'm Rackham Adjutant, steward of the castle. This is Sir Chess...
Reigning Grand Champion Swordsman!
And you are...?
My name's Kati--uh, Katherine. I help watch the store when Uncle Harry's out.
Excellent! Do you carry any sort of trinkets that would appeal to ladies?
We've got lots of ribbons and buckles and buttons and stuff in the back, to the right...
Thank you!
I don't recall seeing you in here before...
I didn't even know Harry had a niece. Especially such an attractive one!
I came to live with Uncle Harry and Aunt Bertha only just this Spring...
Why, that's simply--
Excuse me.

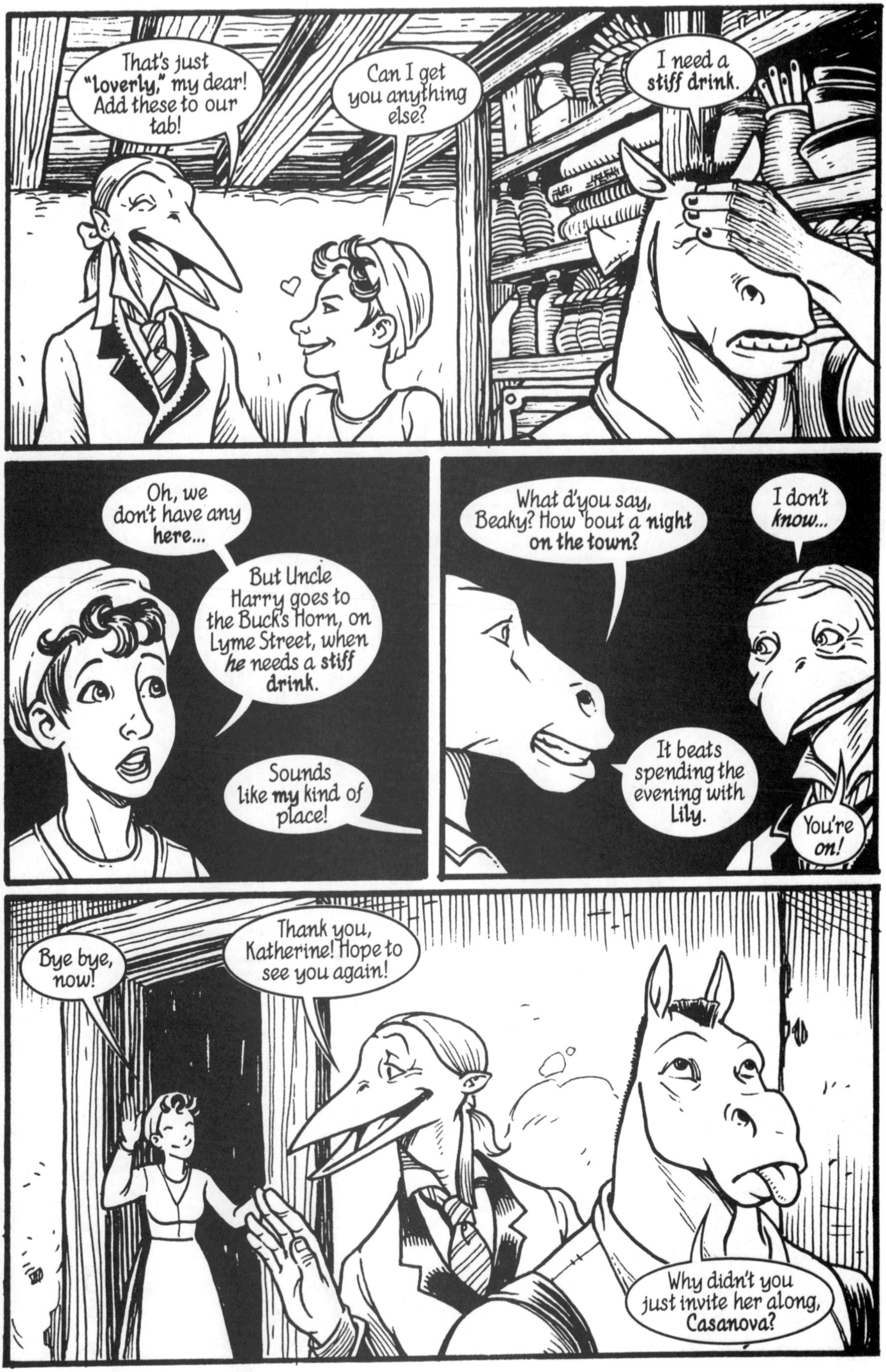
That's just "loverly," my dear! Add these to our tab!
Can I get you anything else?
I need a stiff drink.
Oh, we don't have any here...
But Uncle Harry goes to the Buck's Horn, on Lyme Street, when he needs a stiff drink.
Sounds like my kind of place!
What d'you say, Beaky? How 'bout a night on the town?
I don't know...
It beats spending the evening with Lily.
You're on!
Bye bye, now!
Thank you, Katherine! Hope to see you again!
Why didn't you just invite her along, Casanova?

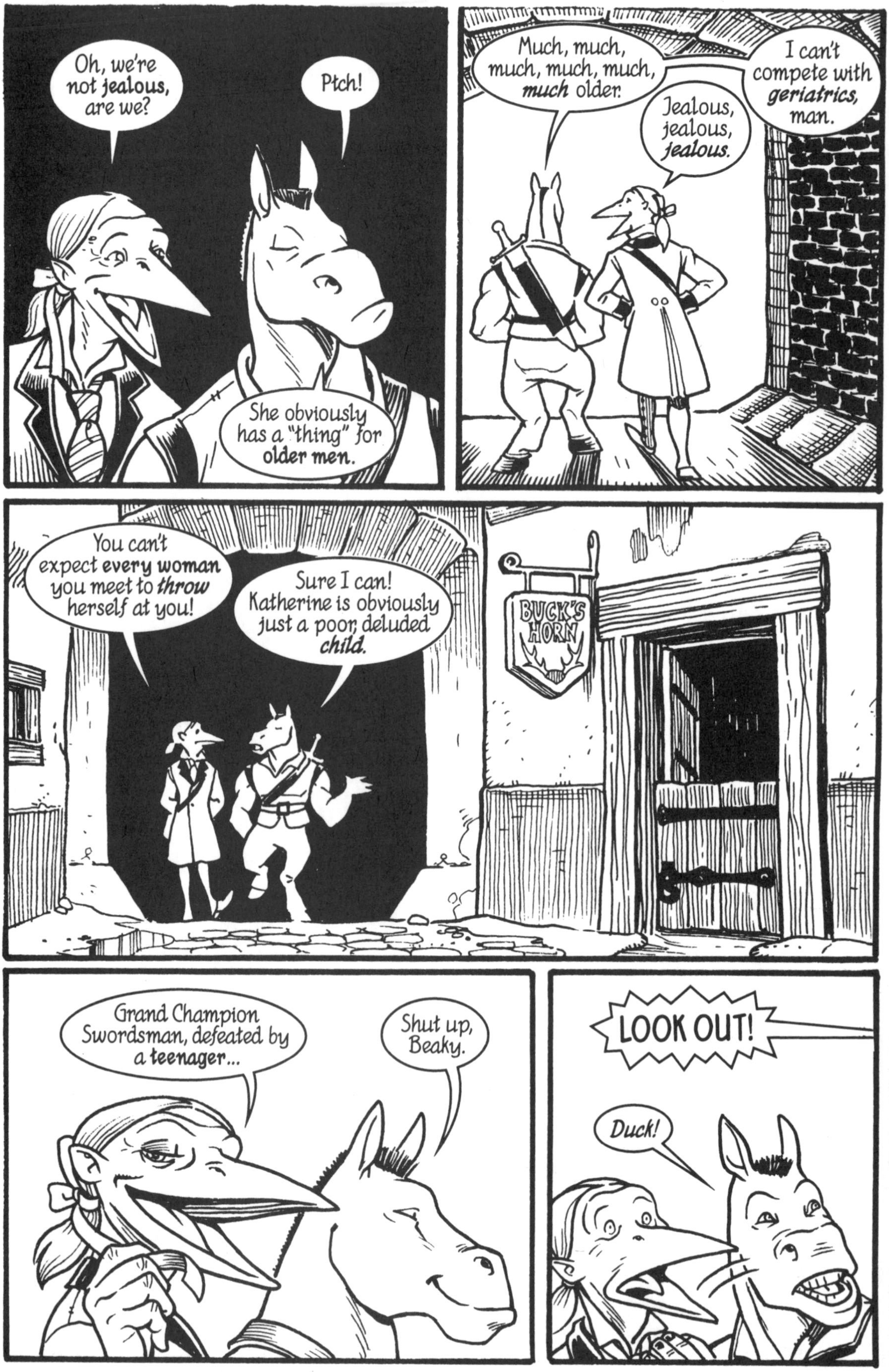
Oh, we're not **jealous**, are we?
Ptch!
She obviously has a "thing" for **older men**.
Much, much, much, much, much, ***much*** older.
Jealous, jealous, ***jealous***.
I can't compete with ***geriatrics***, man.
You can't expect **every woman** you meet to ***throw*** herself at you!
Sure I can! Katherine is obviously just a poor, deluded ***child***.
BUCK'S HORN
Grand Champion Swordsman, defeated by a **teenager**...
Shut up, Beaky.
LOOK OUT!
Duck!

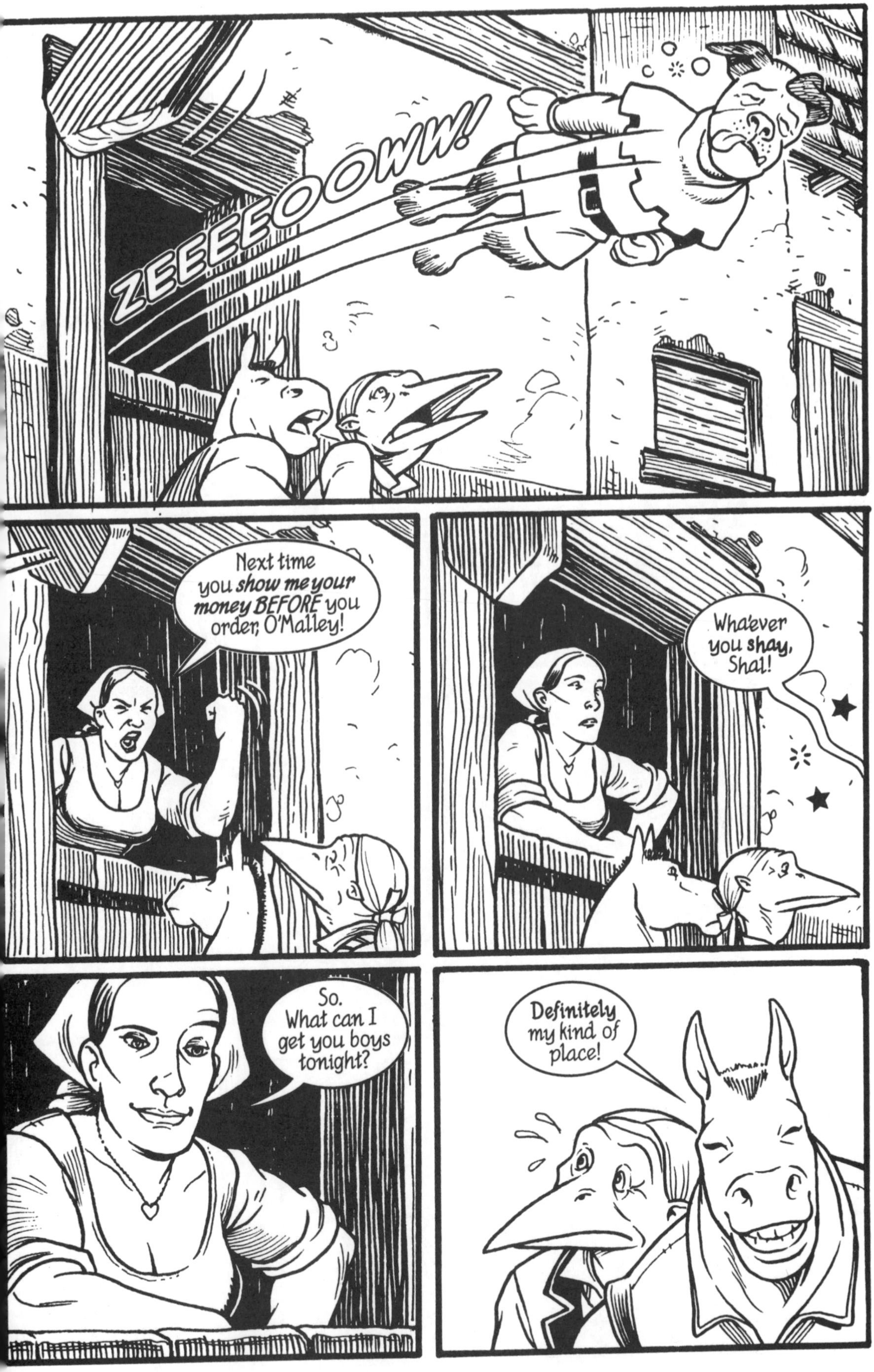
ZEEEEOOWW!
Next time you show me your money BEFORE you order, O'Malley!
Wha'ever you shay, Shal!
So. What can I get you boys tonight?
Definitely my kind of place!

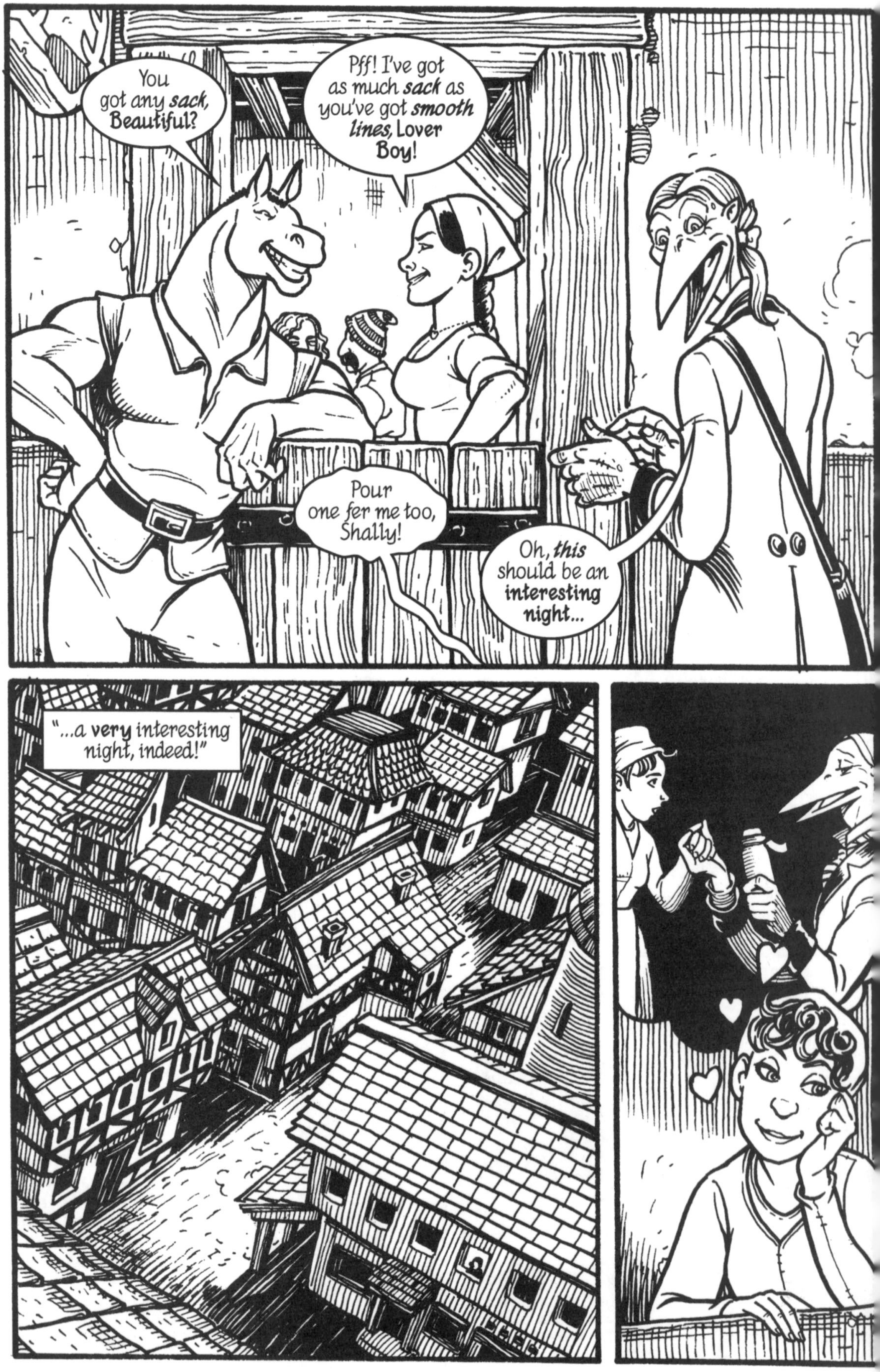
You got any *sack*, Beautiful?
Pff! I've got as much *sack* as you've got *smooth lines*, Lover Boy!
Pour one fer me too, Shally!
Oh, *this* should be an **interesting night...**
"...a **very** interesting night, indeed!"

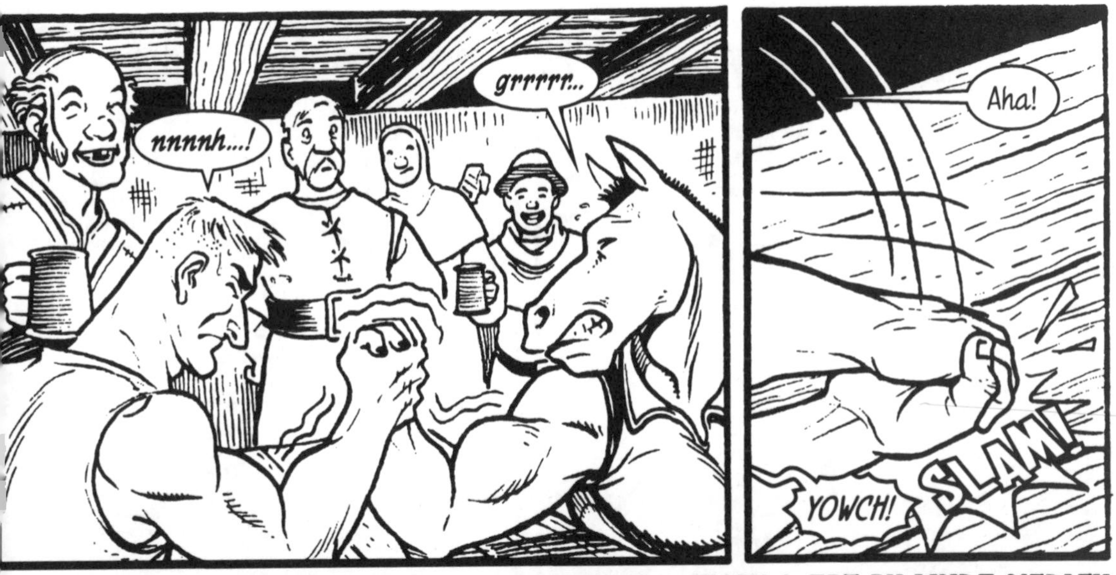
nnnnh...!
grrrrr..
Aha!
YOWCH!
SLAM!

CITY MOUSE, COUNTRY MOUSE

STORY & ART BY LINDA MEDLEY

PART TWO LETTERING BY TODD KLEIN

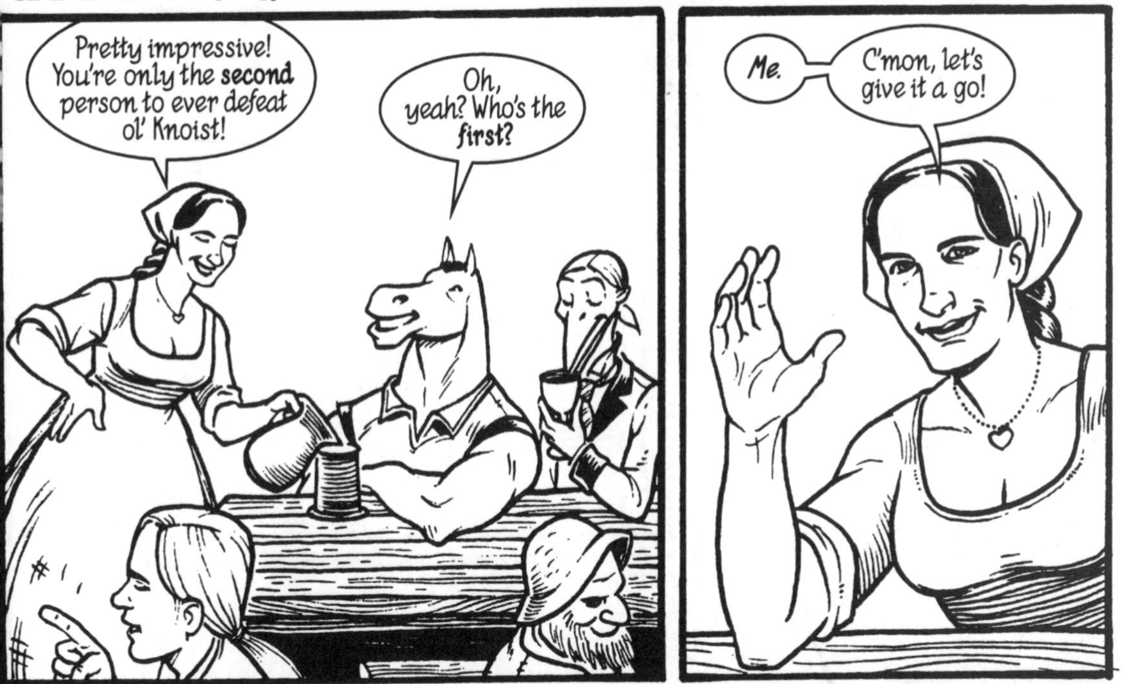
Pretty impressive! You're only the **second** person to ever defeat ol' Knoist!
Oh, yeah? Who's the *first*?
Me.
C'mon, let's give it a go!

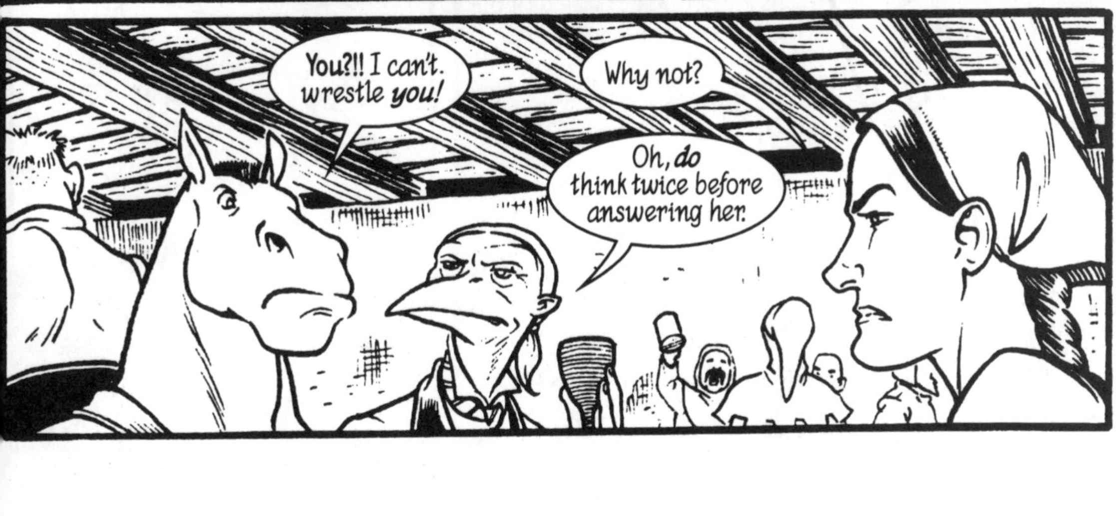
You?!! I can't. wrestle *you!*
Why not?
Oh, *do* think twice before answering her.

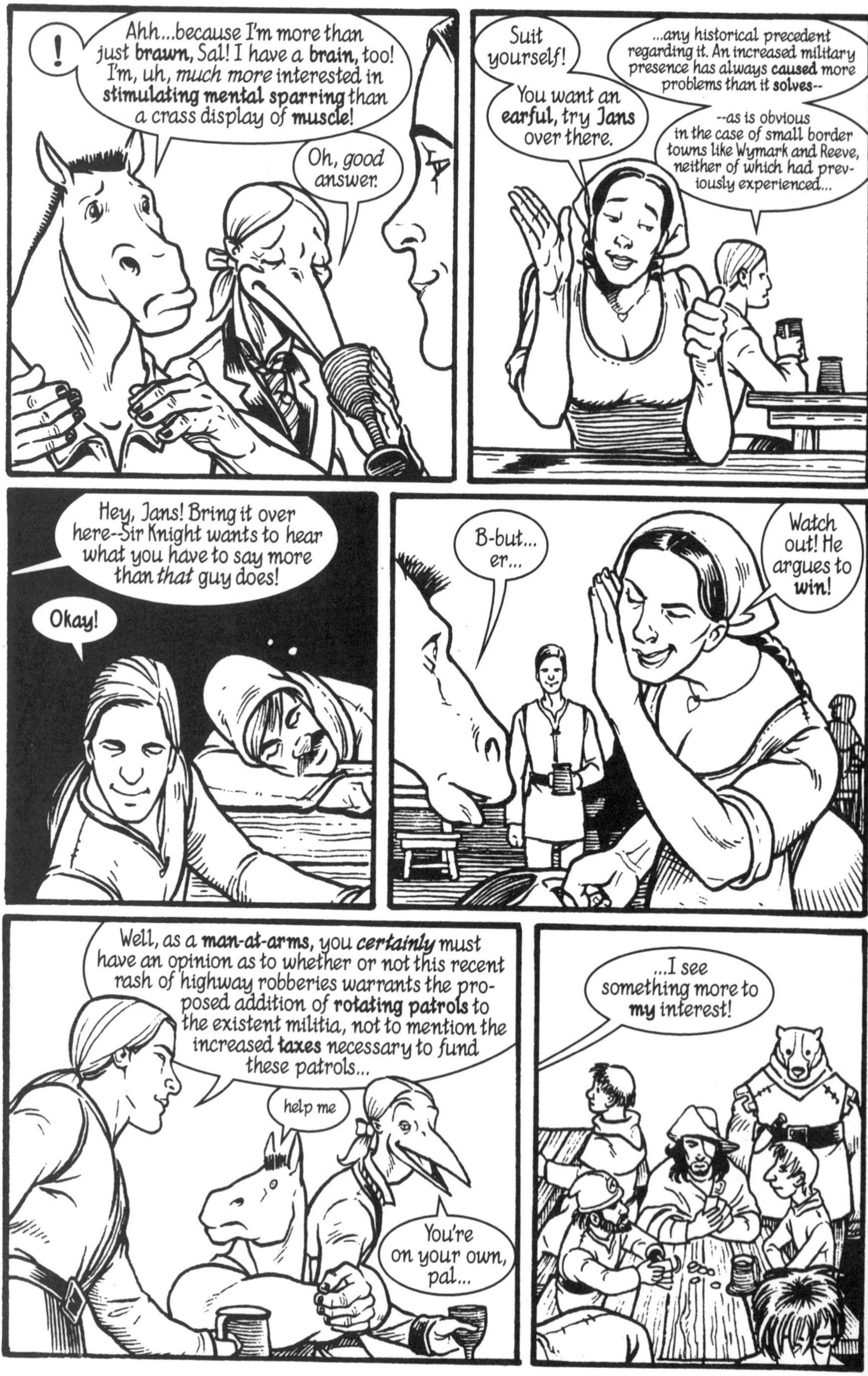
!
Ahh...because I'm more than just **brawn**, Sal! I have a **brain**, too! I'm, uh, *much more* interested in **stimulating mental sparring** than a crass display of **muscle**!
Oh, *good* answer.
Suit yourself!
You want an **earful**, try **Jans** over there.
...any historical precedent regarding it. An increased military presence has always **caused** more problems than it **solves**--
--as is obvious in the case of small border towns like Wymark and Reeve, neither of which had previously experienced...
Hey, Jans! Bring it over here--Sir Knight wants to hear what you have to say more than *that* guy does!
Okay!
B-but... er...
Watch out! He argues to **win**!
Well, as a **man-at-arms**, you ***certainly*** must have an opinion as to whether or not this recent rash of highway robberies warrants the proposed addition of **rotating patrols** to the existent militia, not to mention the increased **taxes** necessary to fund these patrols...
help me
You're on your own, pal...
...I see something more to **my** interest!

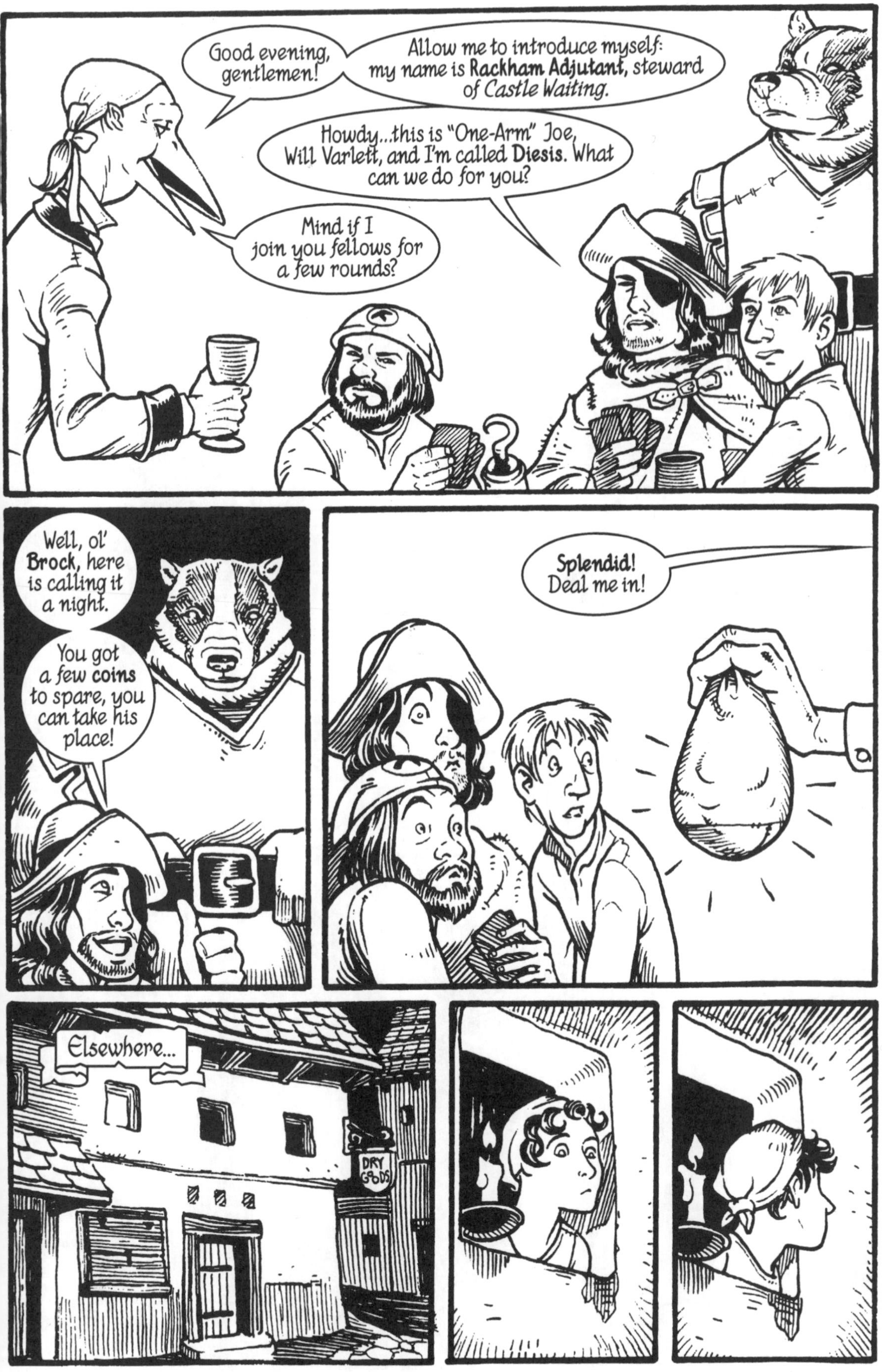
Good evening, gentlemen!
Allow me to introduce myself: my name is Rackham Adjutant, steward of Castle Waiting.
Mind if I join you fellows for a few rounds?
Howdy...this is "One-Arm" Joe, Will Varlett, and I'm called Diesis. What can we do for you?
Well, ol' Brock, here is calling it a night.
You got a few coins to spare, you can take his place!
Splendid! Deal me in!
Elsewhere...
DRY GOODS

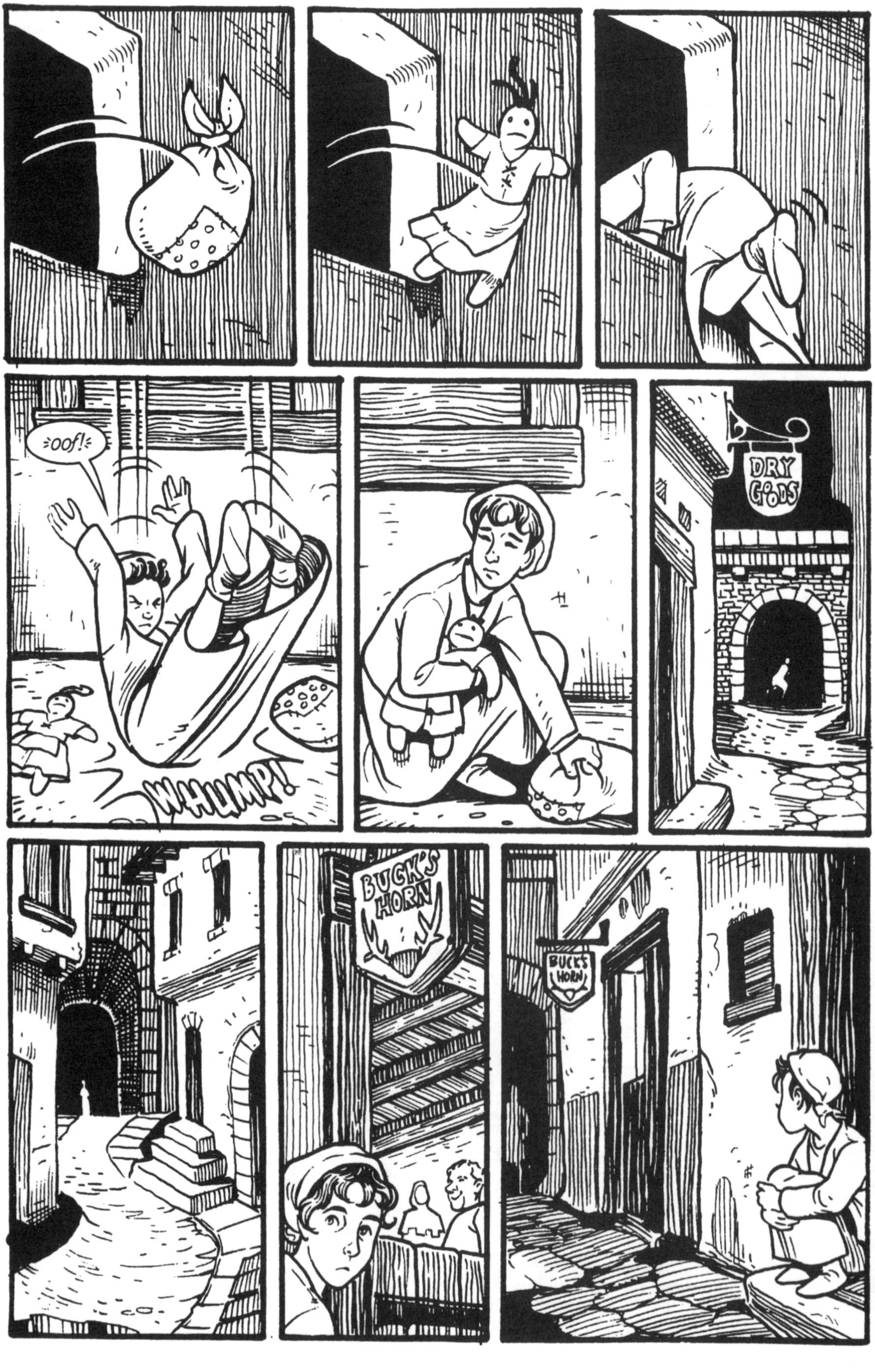

oof!
WHUMP!
DRY GOODS
BUCK'S HORN
BUCK'S HORN

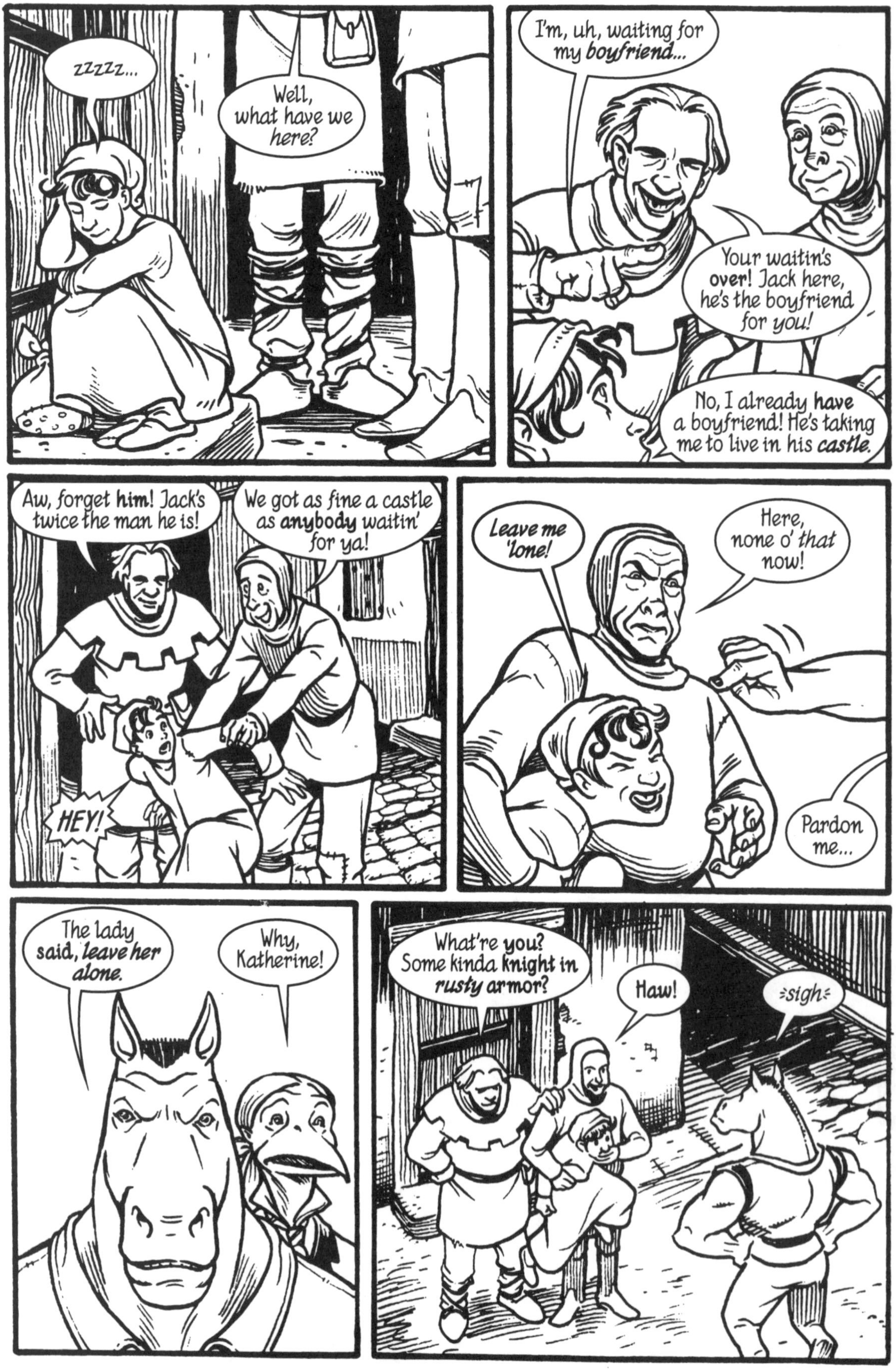
zzzzz...
Well, what have we here?
I'm, uh, waiting for my *boyfriend...*
Your waitin's **over**! Jack here, he's the boyfriend for *you!*
No, I already **have** a boyfriend! He's taking me to live in his ***castle.***
Aw, forget **him**! Jack's twice the man he is!
We got as fine a castle as **anybody** waitin' for ya!
HEY!
Leave me 'lone!
Here, none o' *that* now!
Pardon me...
The lady **said**, ***leave her alone.***
Why, Katherine!
What're **you**? Some kinda **knight in *rusty* armor?**
Haw!
sigh

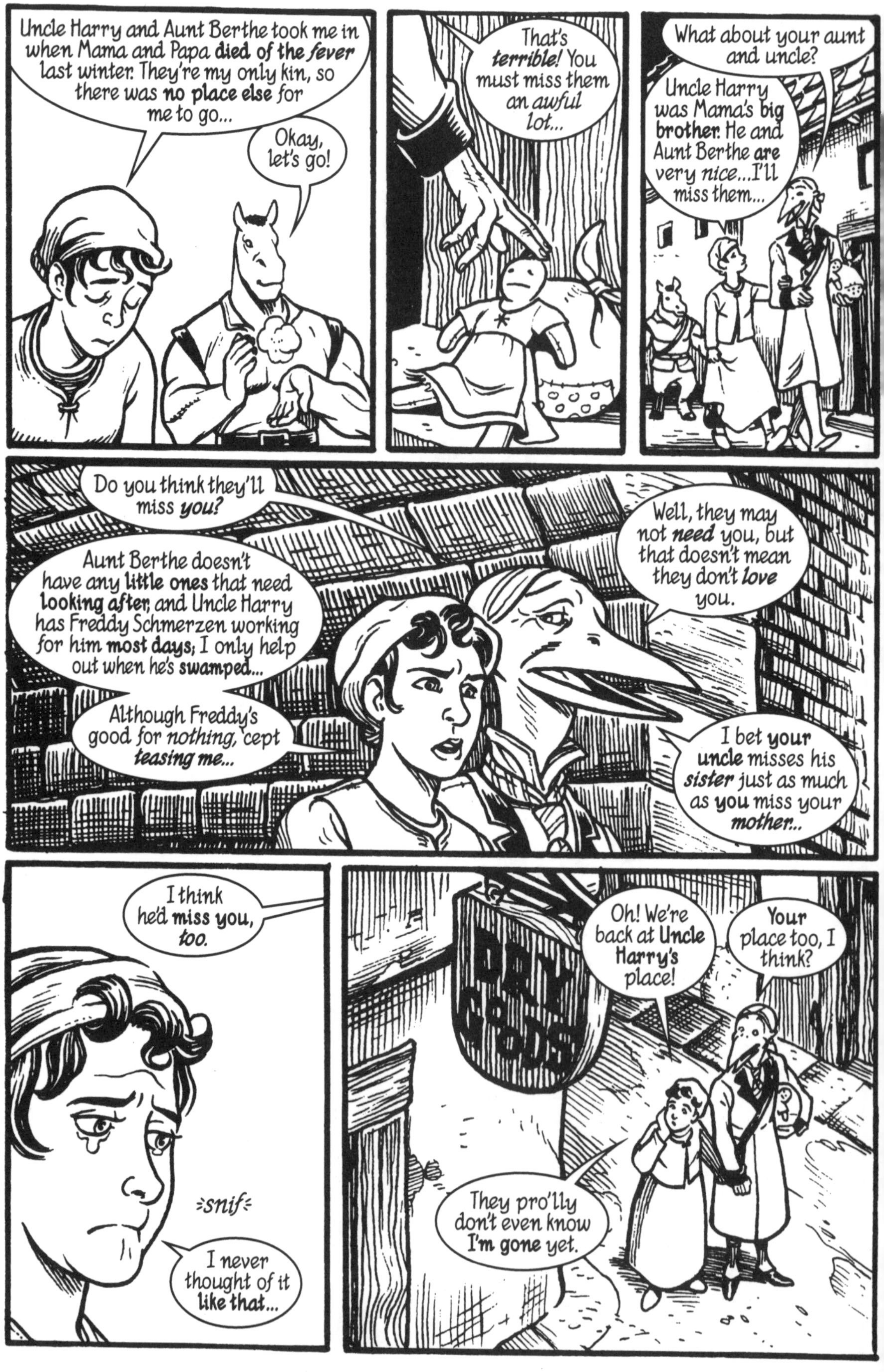
Uncle Harry and Aunt Berthe took me in when Mama and Papa died of the fever last winter. They're my only kin, so there was no place else for me to go...
Okay, let's go!
That's terrible! You must miss them an awful lot...
What about your aunt and uncle?
Uncle Harry was Mama's big brother. He and Aunt Berthe are very nice...I'll miss them...
Do you think they'll miss you?
Aunt Berthe doesn't have any little ones that need looking after, and Uncle Harry has Freddy Schmerzen working for him most days; I only help out when he's swamped...
Although Freddy's good for nothing, 'cept teasing me...
Well, they may not need you, but that doesn't mean they don't love you.
I bet your uncle misses his sister just as much as you miss your mother...
I think he'd miss you, too.
snif
I never thought of it like that...
DRY GOODS
Oh! We're back at Uncle Harry's place!
Your place too, I think?
They pro'lly don't even know I'm gone yet.

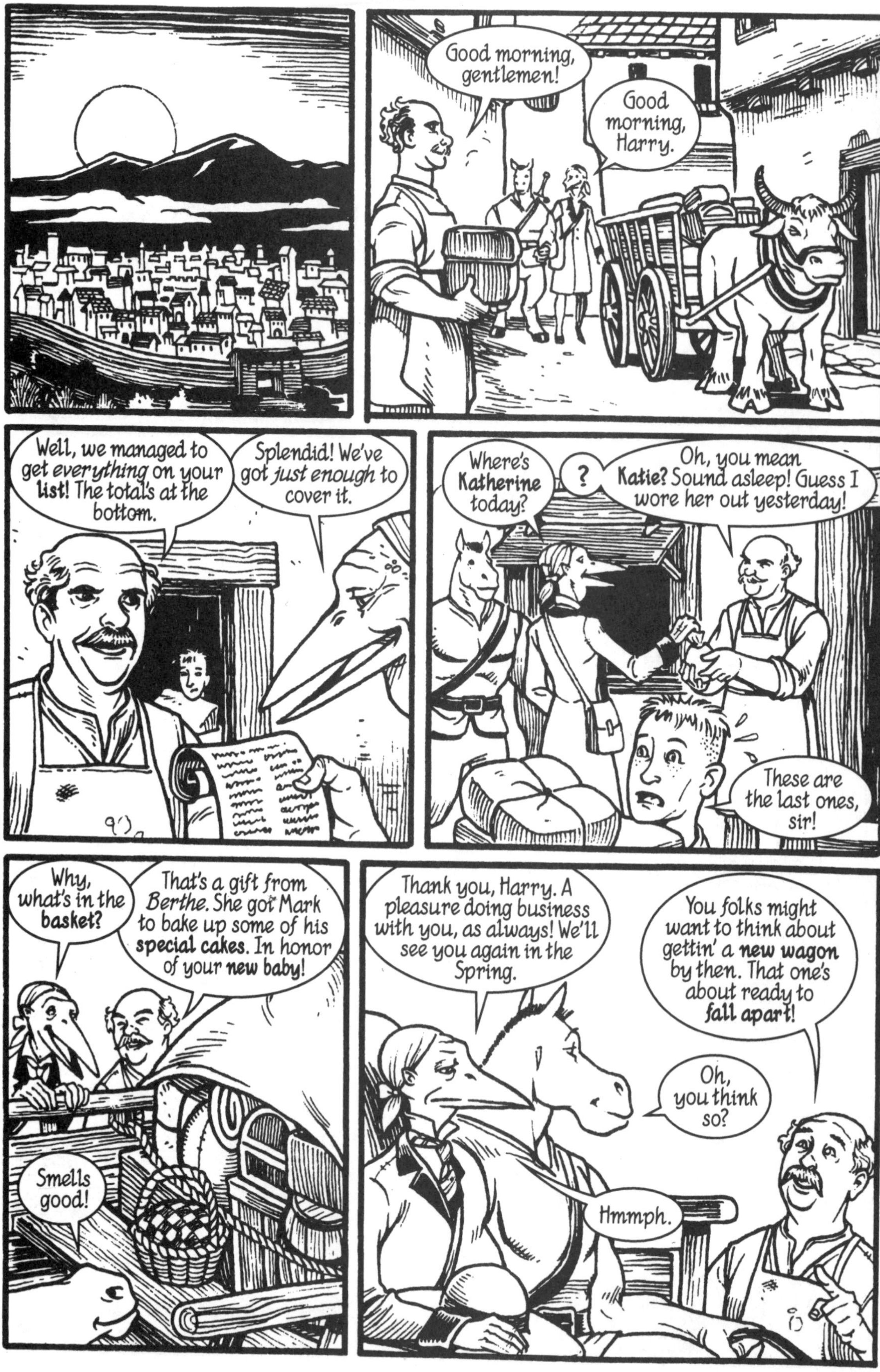
Good morning, gentlemen!
Good morning, Harry.
Well, we managed to get everything on your list! The total's at the bottom.
Splendid! We've got just enough to cover it.
Where's Katherine today?
?
Oh, you mean Katie? Sound asleep! Guess I wore her out yesterday!
These are the last ones, sir!
Why, what's in the basket?
That's a gift from Berthe. She got Mark to bake up some of his special cakes. In honor of your new baby!
Smells good!
Thank you, Harry. A pleasure doing business with you, as always! We'll see you again in the Spring.
You folks might want to think about gettin' a new wagon by then. That one's about ready to fall apart!
Oh, you think so?
Hmmph.

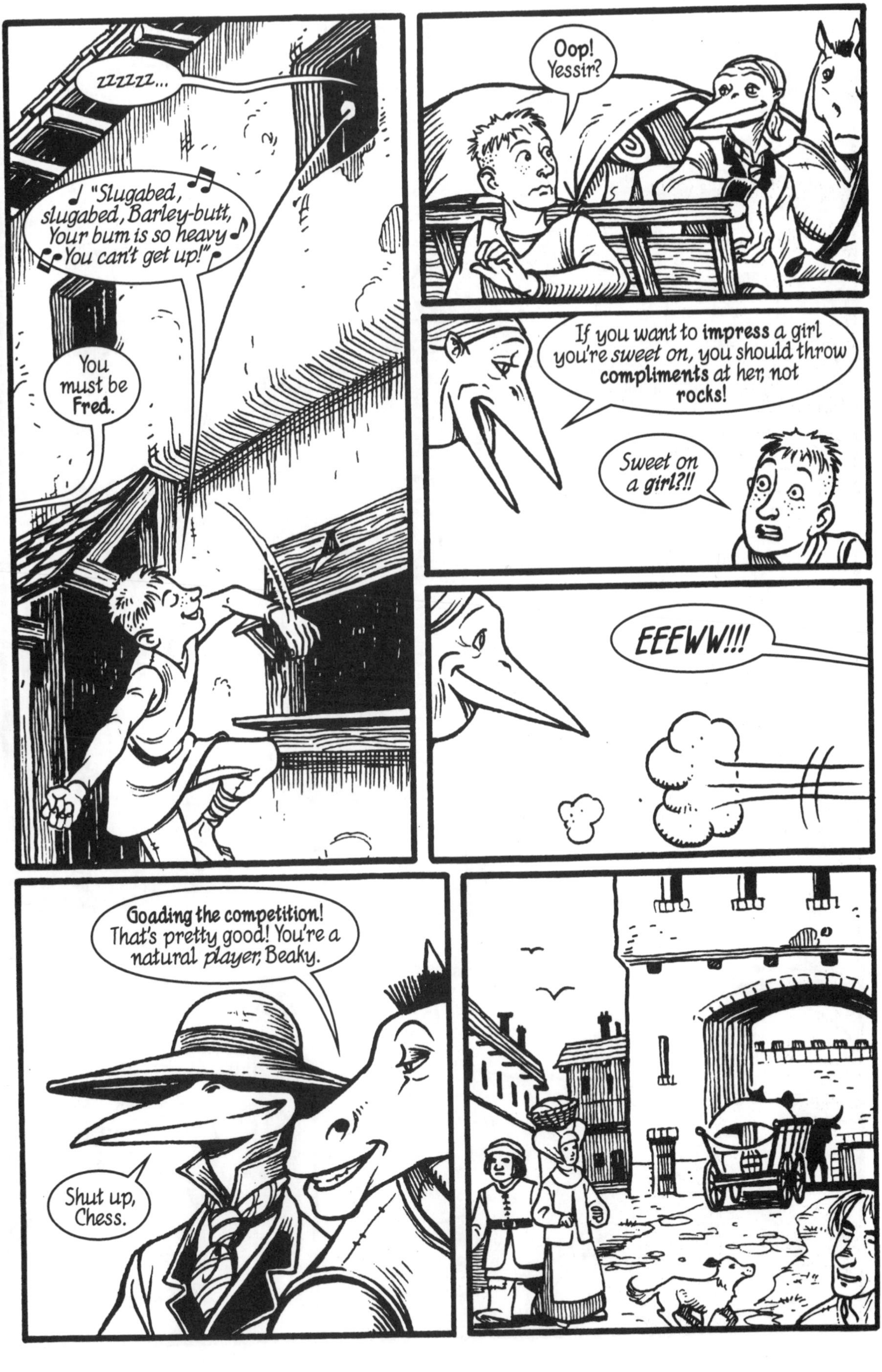
zzzzzz...
♩ "Slugabed, slugabed, Barley-butt, Your bum is so heavy ♪ You can't get up!"
You must be Fred.
Oop! Yessir?
If you want to impress a girl you're sweet on, you should throw compliments at her, not rocks!
Sweet on a girl?!!
EEEWW!!!
Goading the competition! That's pretty good! You're a natural player, Beaky.
Shut up, Chess.

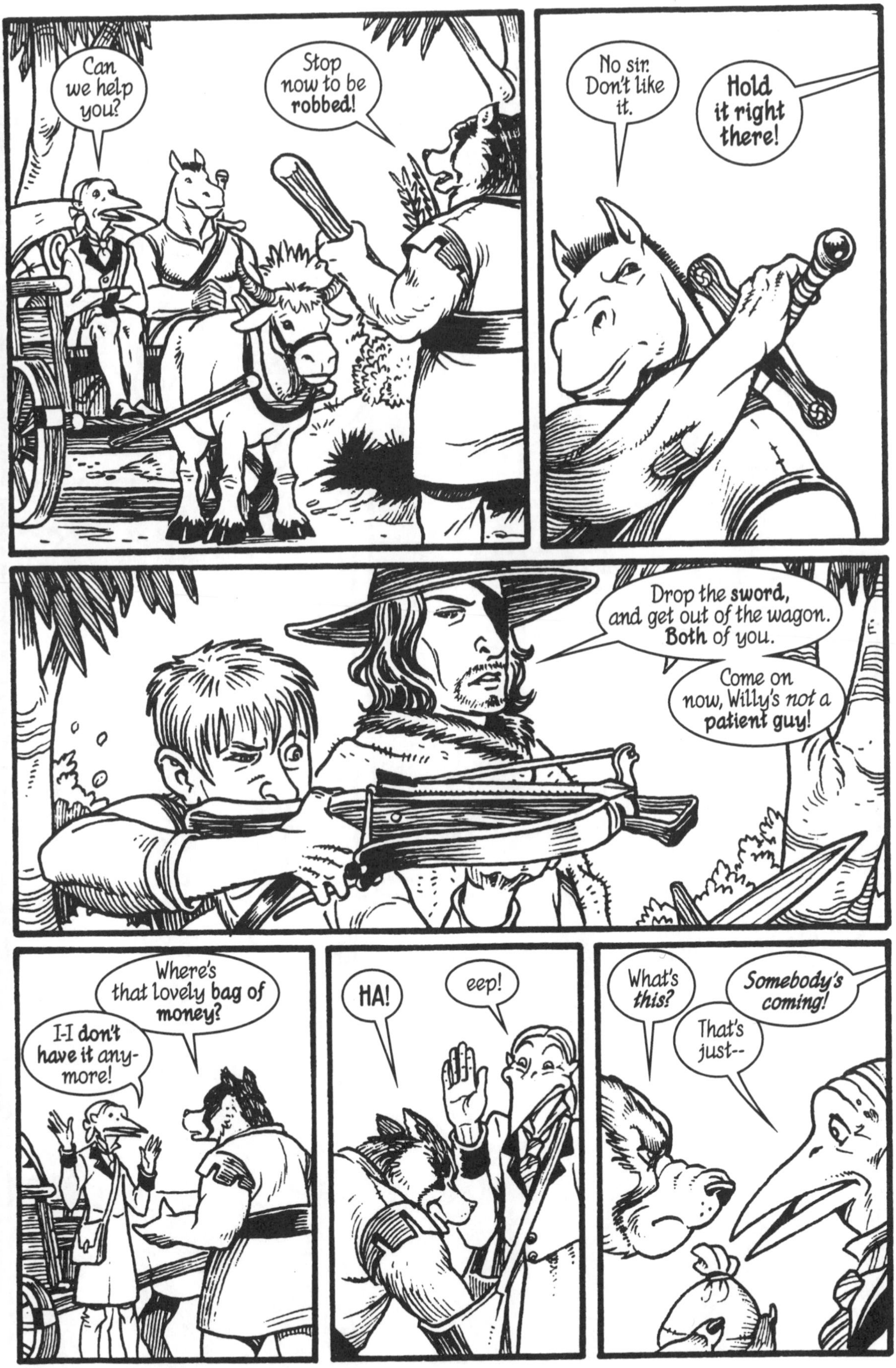
Can we help you?
Stop now to be robbed!
No sir. Don't like it.
Hold it right there!
Drop the sword, and get out of the wagon. Both of you.
Come on now, Willy's not a patient guy!
Where's that lovely bag of money?
I-I don't have it any-more!
HA!
eep!
What's this?
Somebody's coming!
That's just--

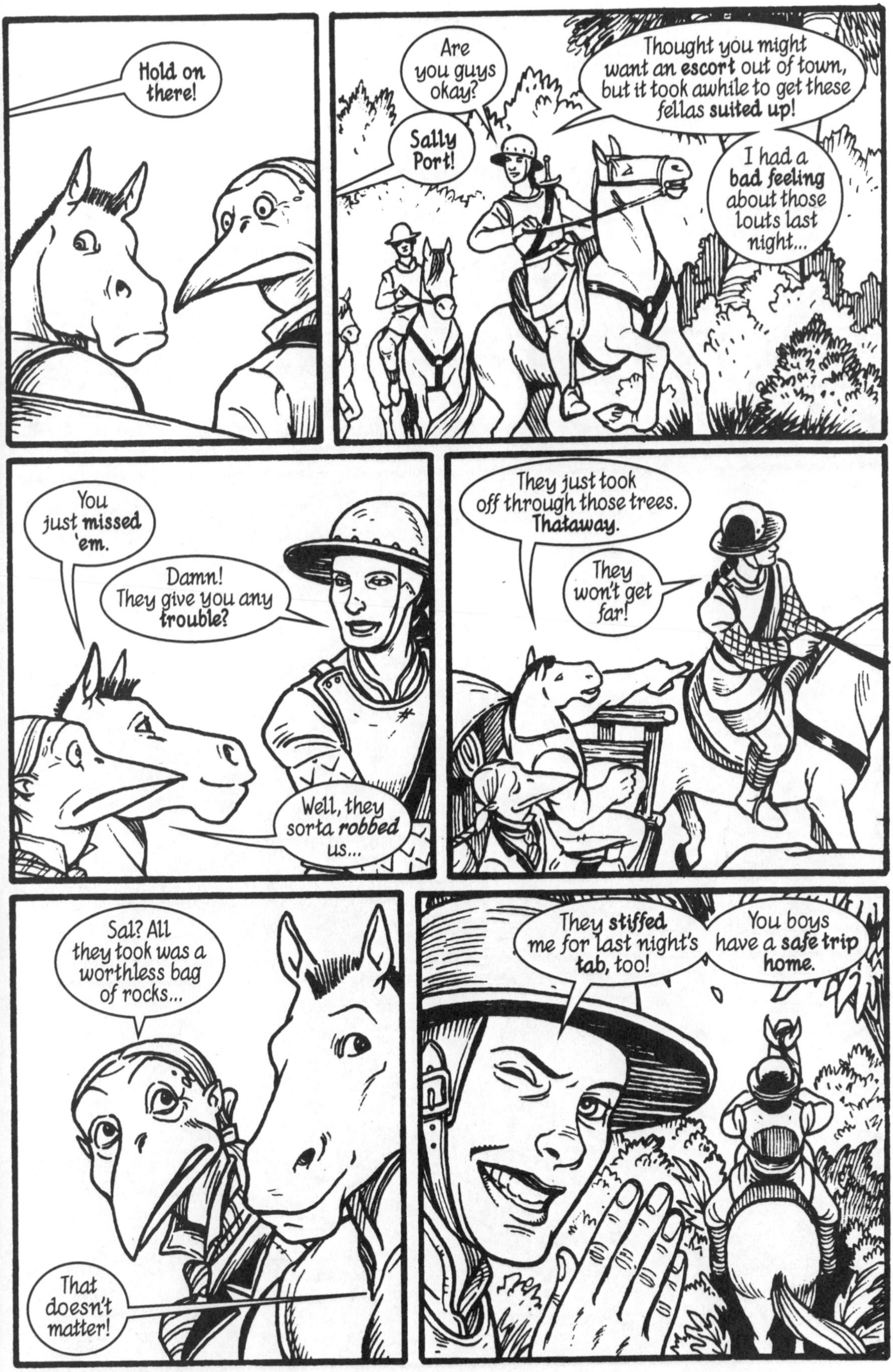
Hold on there!
Are you guys okay?
Sally Port!
Thought you might want an **escort** out of town, but it took awhile to get these fellas **suited up**!
I had a **bad feeling** about those louts last night...
You just **missed 'em**.
Damn! They give you any **trouble?**
Well, they sorta ***robbed*** us...
They just took off through those trees. **Thataway.**
They won't get far!
Sal? All they took was a worthless bag of rocks...
That doesn't matter!
They **stiffed** me for last night's **tab**, too!
You boys have a **safe trip home.**

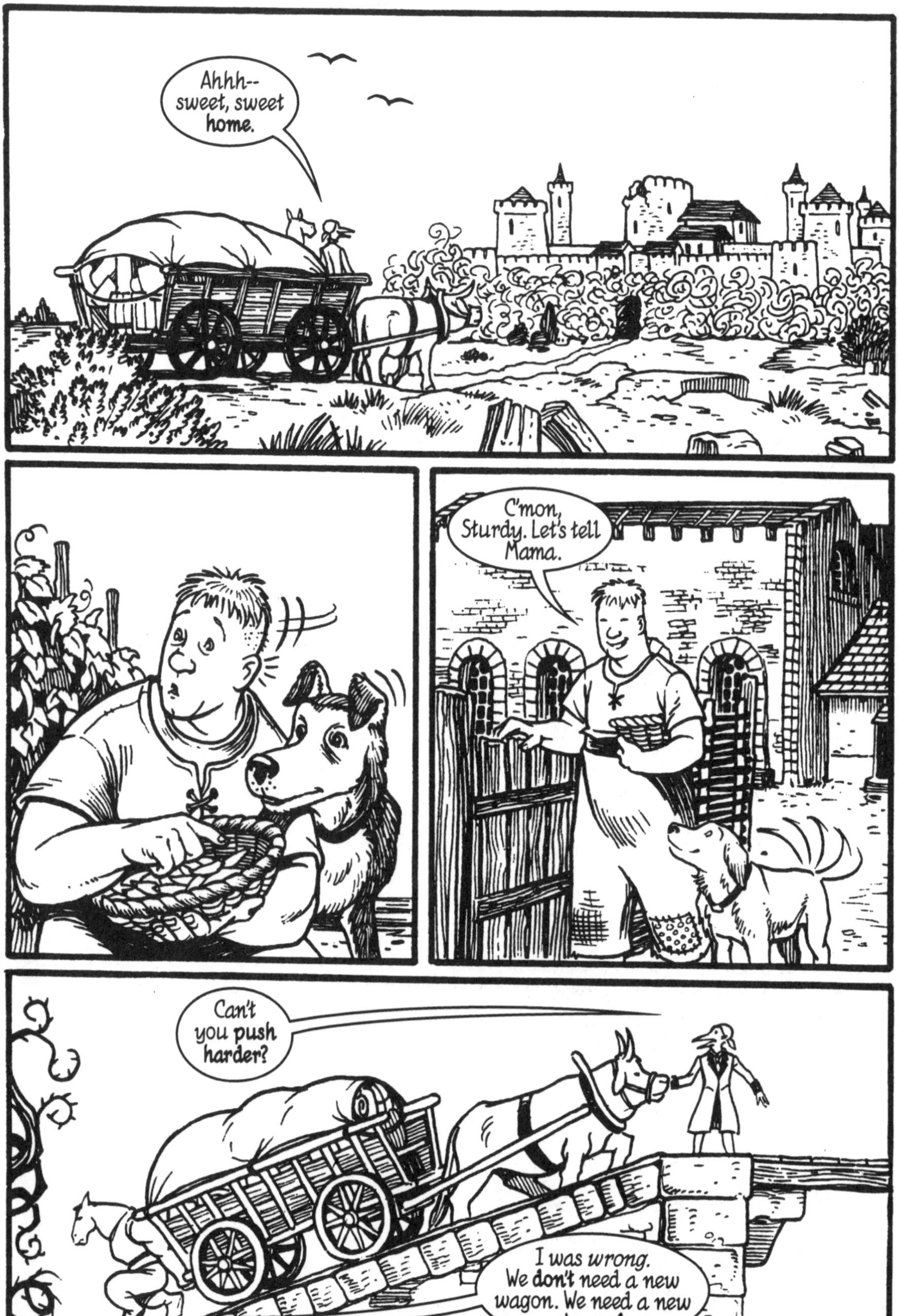
Ahhh-- sweet, sweet home.
C'mon, Sturdy. Let's tell Mama.
Can't you push harder?
I was wrong. We don't need a new wagon. We need a new steward.

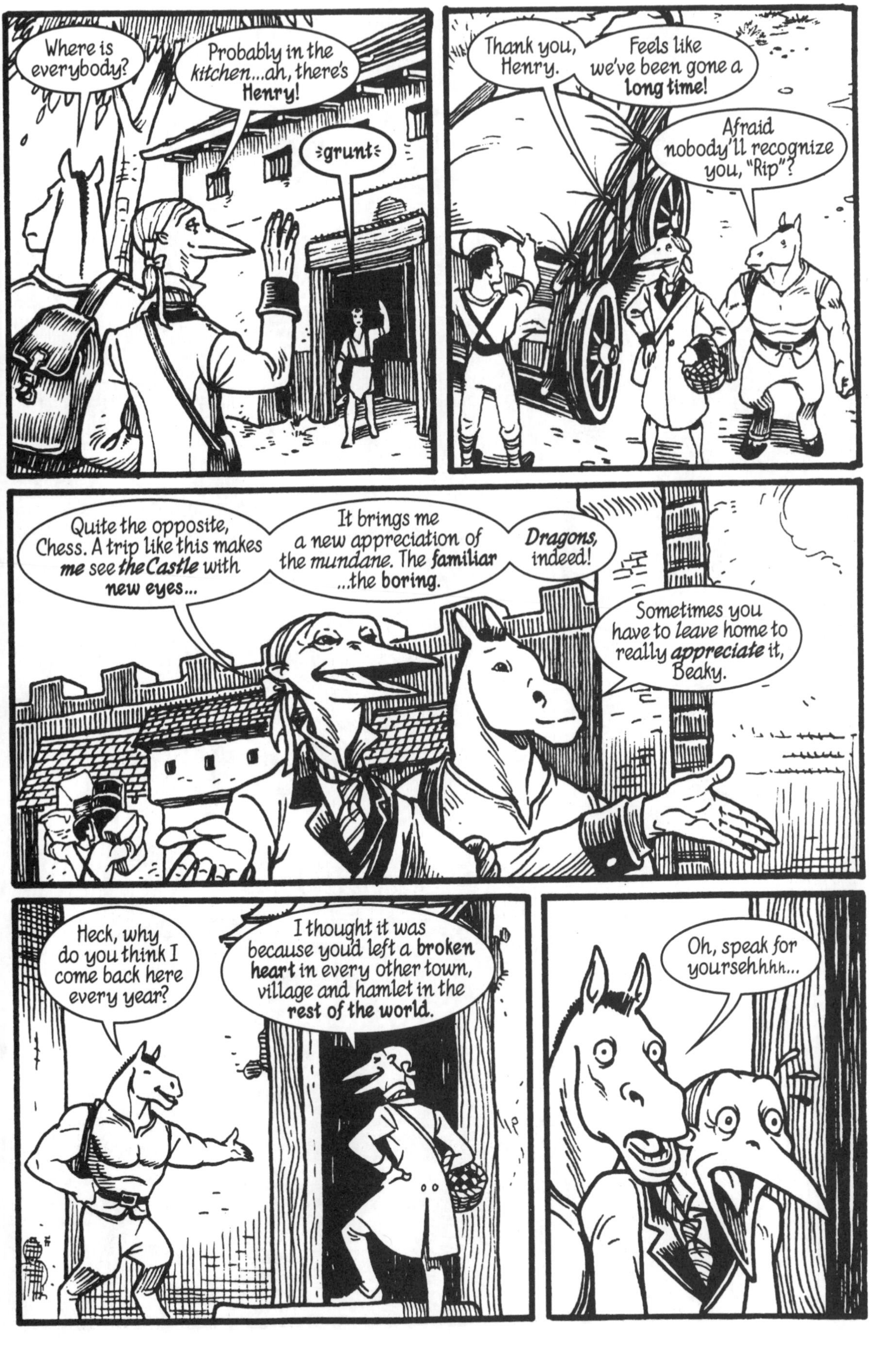
Where is everybody?
Probably in the kitchen...ah, there's Henry!
:grunt:
Thank you, Henry.
Feels like we've been gone a long time!
Afraid nobody'll recognize you, "Rip"?
Quite the opposite, Chess. A trip like this makes me see the Castle with new eyes...
It brings me a new appreciation of the mundane. The familiar ...the boring.
Dragons, indeed!
Sometimes you have to leave home to really appreciate it, Beaky.
Heck, why do you think I come back here every year?
I thought it was because you'd left a broken heart in every other town, village and hamlet in the rest of the world.
Oh, speak for yoursehhhh...

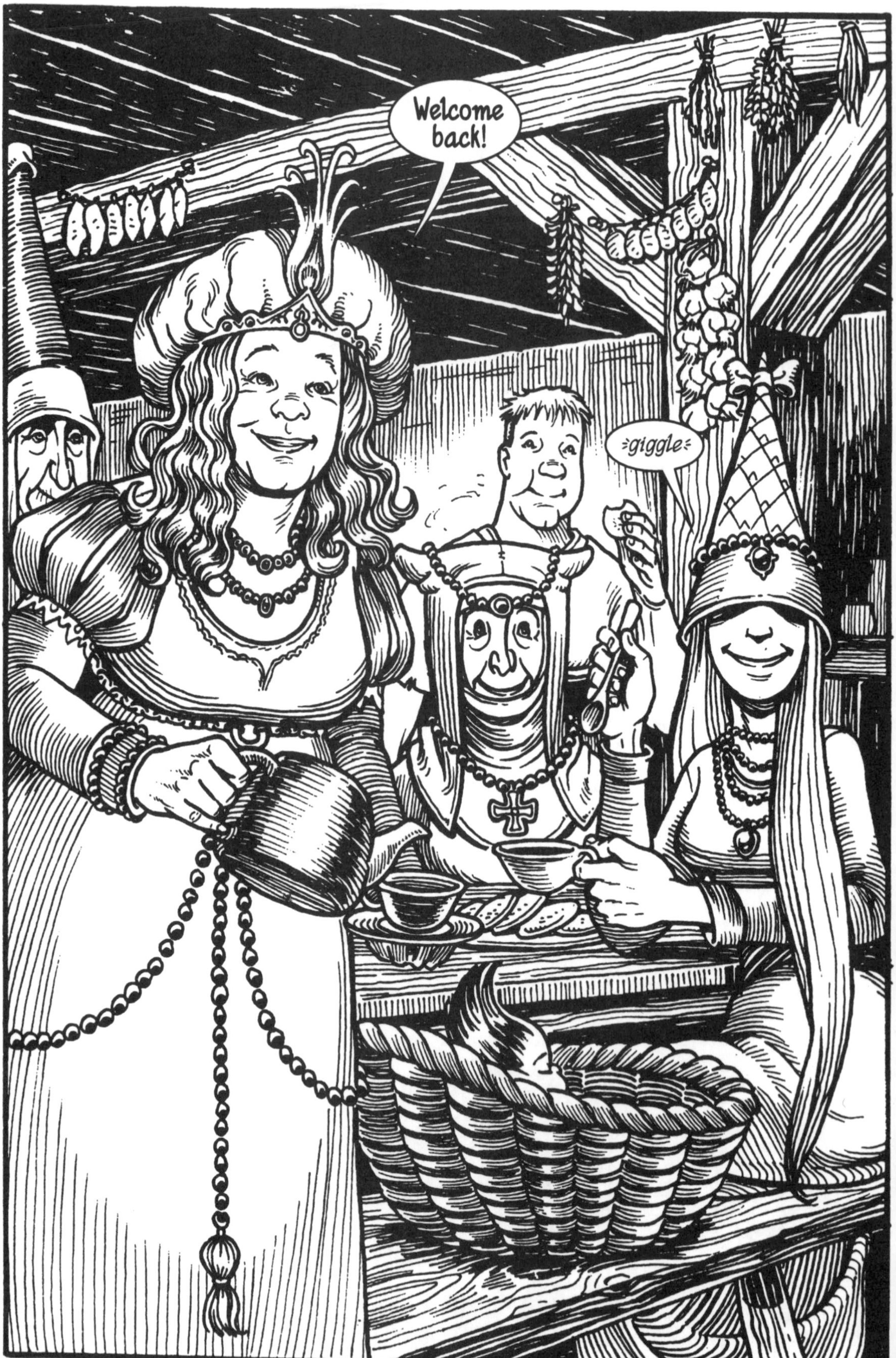
Welcome back!
giggle

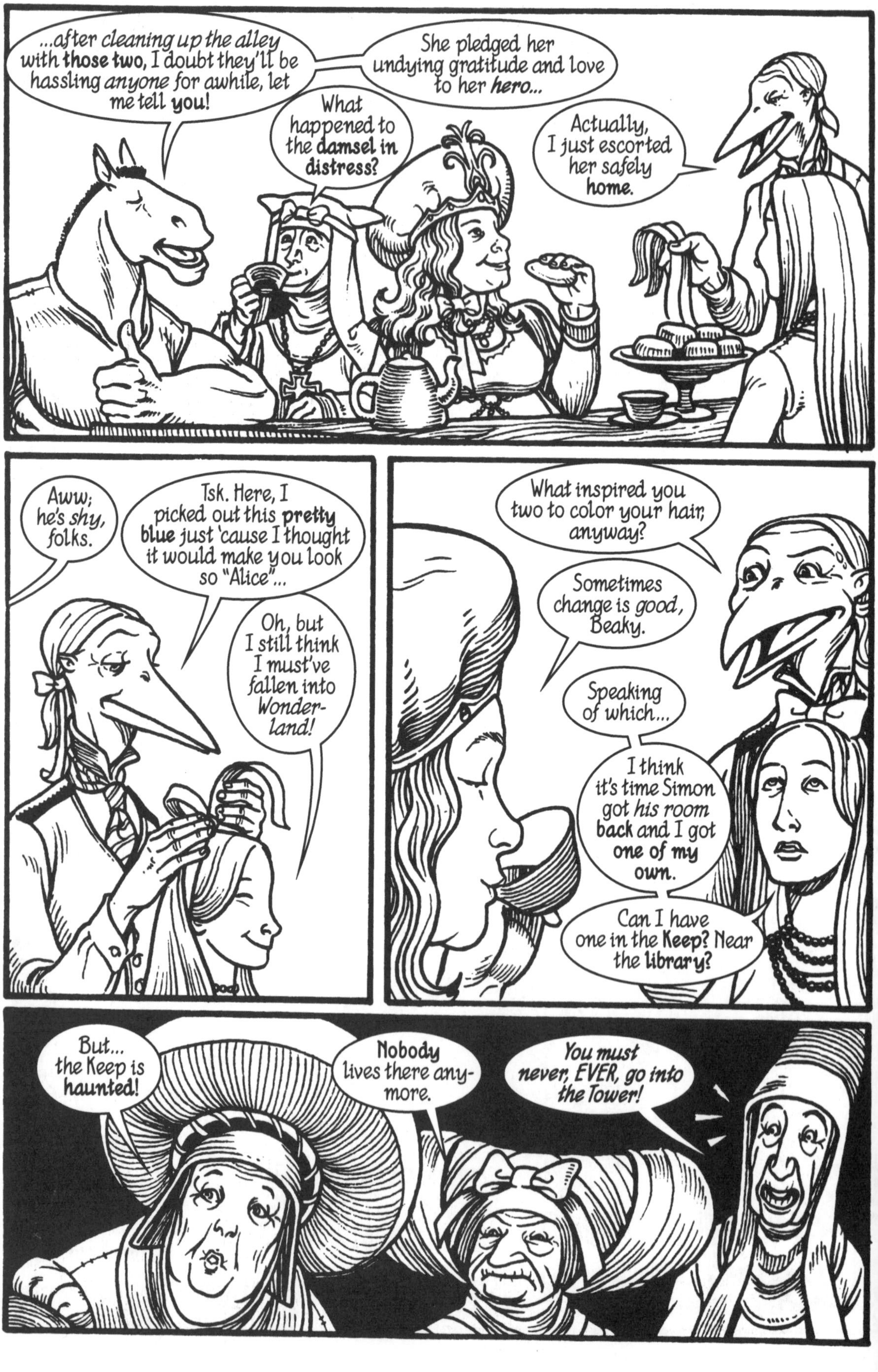
...after cleaning up the alley with those two, I doubt they'll be hassling anyone for awhile, let me tell you!
She pledged her undying gratitude and love to her hero...
What happened to the damsel in distress?
Actually, I just escorted her safely home.
Aww; he's shy, folks.
Tsk. Here, I picked out this pretty blue just 'cause I thought it would make you look so "Alice"...
Oh, but I still think I must've fallen into Wonder-land!
What inspired you two to color your hair, anyway?
Sometimes change is good, Beaky.
Speaking of which...
I think it's time Simon got his room back and I got one of my own.
Can I have one in the Keep? Near the library?
But... the Keep is haunted!
Nobody lives there any-more.
You must never, EVER, go into the Tower!

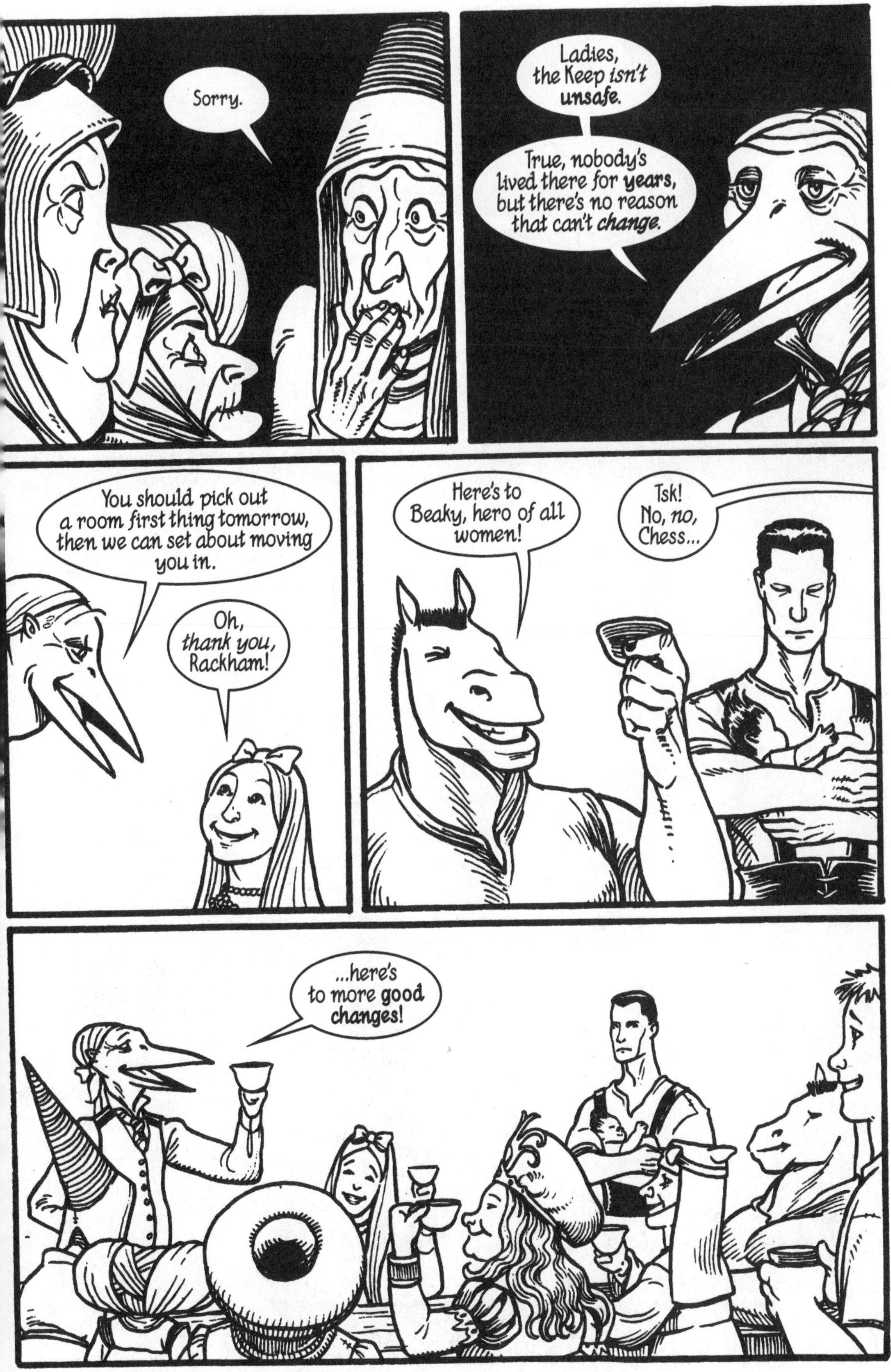
Sorry.
Ladies, the Keep isn't unsafe.
True, nobody's lived there for years, but there's no reason that can't change.
You should pick out a room first thing tomorrow, then we can set about moving you in.
Oh, thank you, Rackham!
Here's to Beaky, hero of all women!
Tsk! No, no, Chess...
...here's to more good changes!

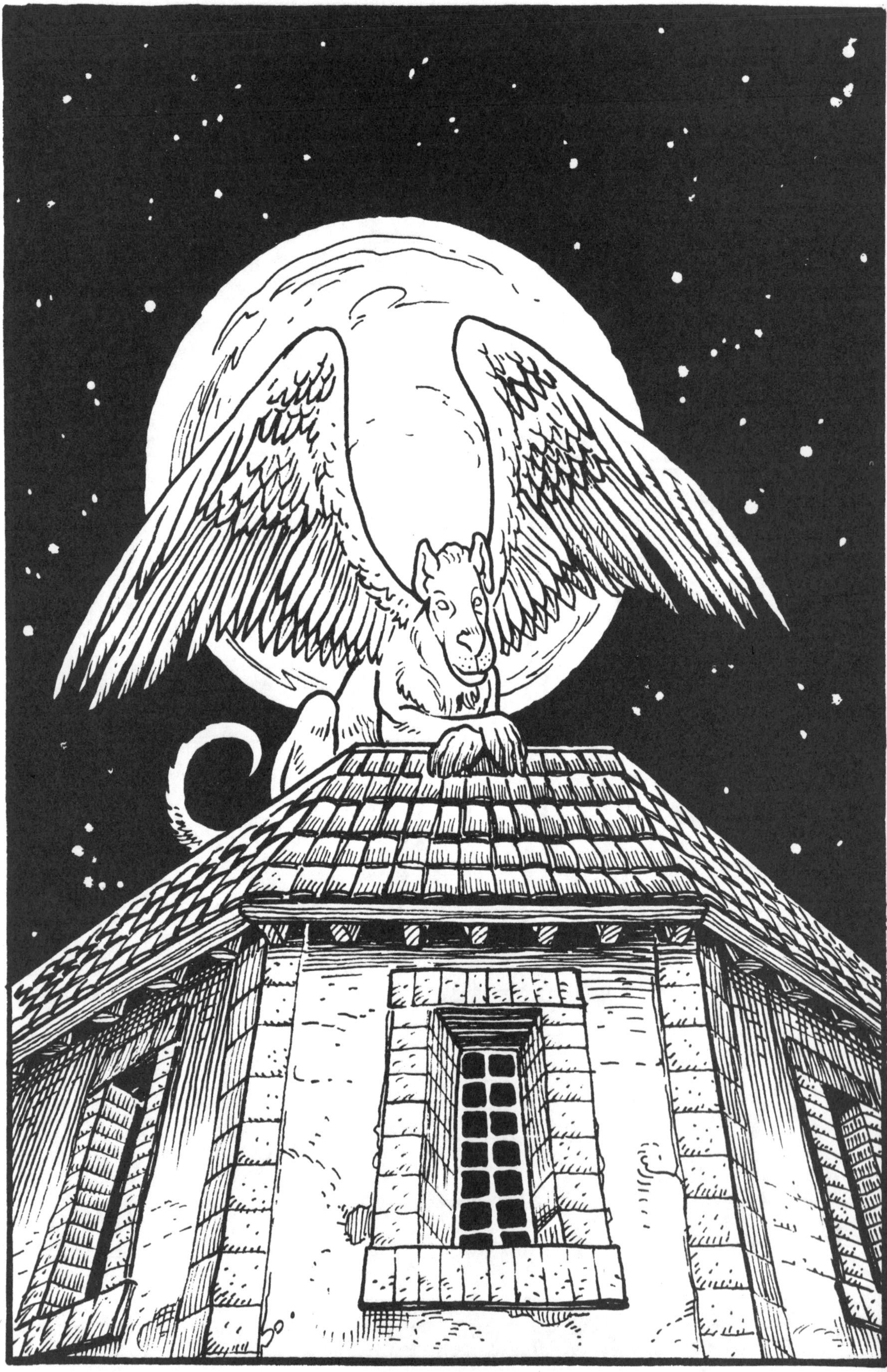